Challenges of Education

Technology • Trends • Globalisation

Challenges of Education

Technology • Trends • Globalisation

Hemlata Talesra

Maneesha Shukul

Uma Shanker Sharma

AUTHORSPRESS

Under the auspices of

Rajasthan Council of Educational Administration and Management

(Affiliated to Commonwealth Council of Educational Administration and Management)

Worldwide Circulation through Authorspress Global Network
First Published 2003
Reprinted 2005, 2006
Reprinted 2007
by Authorspress

E-35/103, Jawahar Park
Laxmi Nagar, Delhi-110092

e-mail: authorspress@yahoo.com

Typeset in NewCenturySchlbk by Chitra Computers

Challenges of Education: Technology, Trends, Globalisation
ISBN 81-7273-134-5

Printed in India at Tarun Offset, Delhi.

Preface

The world has entered into new millennium with a bundle of challenges to meet. The Global Challenges encompass various fields—economic, political, educational, environmental, physical, social technological—to identify a few. The strides of development in these fields witnessed by the world in the twentieth century has also experienced associated problems. It has become imperative to view the challenges and issues posed in various fields and to identify and implement suitable strategies to meet the problems. This calls for cumulative deliberations of experts, in each field. The present book *"Challenges of Education: Technology, Trends, Globalisation"* is an effort in this direction. It is a compendium of thirty seven selected papers contributed by eminent national and international scholars. The papers highlight various issues and challenges faced by the world having direct concern with education in the present millennium and suggest suitable strategies to meet them. Which will prove to be highly beneficial at not only at local and national level but also at global level.

The attention of the world has recently been drawn towards Human Rights. Many rights have been recognised such as those of consumers, Women's and the Fundamental Rights whereas those of children have been recognised very recently. Protection of human rights is one of the important challenges that the world of 21st century would face. Part one of the present book addresses the issue of human rights, its concepts policies significance, awareness amongst people, the need for sensitisation and the role of education for this purpose.

Part two highlights on the *Challenges of Teacher Education in Globalisation Era,* one of the important aspects of 21st Century. The role of teachers in shaping the society of world order cannot be underestimated. It is essential that their education and training are given special attention and importance because they, inturn, would pass on their knowledge to the new generation—the citizens of future. The eminent contributors of papers on this theme have highlighted the critical challenges of teachers' education for 21st century and emphasised on performance appraisal and teacher accountability as the need of the hour.

Part three of the book discusses various dimensions of *Empowerment of Women and Education* in 21st century. The world has recognised the significance of women's education. It is highly essential in the developing countries, India being one of them, to concentrate all the efforts for educating women. One women influences two families—the family of origin and the family of matrimony. She influences not only the present generation but also the generation of the future. She passes on her values, perceptions, attitudes, behaviour and ethics to her children. Moreover she influences the people around her in the workplace if she is gainfully employed. Women have been considered as better managers and leaders than men, though society does not accept the gender equality in various fields. Women managers do face various barriers. The need is to empower the women with education in the 21st century.

There can be no better person than women for the protection of environment. One of the important challenge of the 21st century, the deteriorating quality of environment and depletion of resources can effectively be handled by women. They are in close contact with the environment when they collect food, fodder, wood and water for family and the cattle. They use various resources of the mother earth in daily consumption. Their individual efforts towards conservation of precious resources can have significant effect cumulatively. Hence it is important to educate women for environment protection as well. Such important aspects have been discussed in part three of this publication.

Part four of this edition discusses one of the important issue for 21st century *Education For All in Infoage* recognising the role of education in development of human resources of the world. It is all the more important for the weaker section especially the backward class and tribals, that they are educated to be empowered and to enter into the mainstream of development in the 21st century.

The book will prove to be rich source of relevant literature for students, and teachers. It would provide strategies to the policy makers to frame suitable policies for the 21st century.

The editors express their sincere gratitude towards the contributors of papers.

Editors

Contents

PART II

Challenges of Teacher Education in Globalisation Era

PART III

Empowerment of Women and Education

PART IV

Education For All in Infoage

PART I

Governance of Education and Human Rights

1

Concept and Reality of Human Rights and Duties

*U. Guha**

The ancient *Vedas* have pronounced in *Atharva Veda* that, "Man is not an individual".

He is a social organism. His glory lies in being a member of a big family. On the one hand, man is bound by blood-kinship; on the other, he is linked with every individual of society. Man thus lives, works and dies for society possessed of certain alienable rights. Man is expected to develop his craft, sciences and technology and lead society from poverty to prosperity, with a happy today and a happier tomorrow.

Therefore, it is clear that in India, right from ancient times, there is a mandate for a man to observe duties from taking society from poverty to prosperity.

Again our Hindu texts say, 'Manur Bhava' in Sanskrit, meaning, become a human being.

Islamic texts refer to the greatness a man can achieve by becoming a Momin. Momin is a person who loves other persons. The texts go on to say that no one can be given a higher place by virtue of his wealth or power. All are equal.

Thus the very concept of 'Man' implies no disparity between two men about dignity. All are created equal, hence all are entitled to justice, democracy and peaceful co-existence.

**Ex-Principal, Radhika TT College, Gandhi Nagar, Nagpur.*

Now, the question is whether the children or youth in our society are "Man". Whether those who are waging wars, fighting or are committing crimes are not "man". Today terrorism has become a culture on this planet earth. There is a global threat to everybody's life. We are inhaling the air of violence. In this situation every mind is raked with the million dollar question—What is the root cause of all this violence? How can this fear of terrorism be cleared? How long would this state continue?

The simple answer is, as a volcano will only yield fire, so a violent mind can only think of war. The remedy to war is only a change of mass mind. Minds of the masses can only be changed in schools and playgrounds. Teachers can play the role of a friend, philosopher and guide. They can be a catalytic agent in running the process through which the concept of rights and duties can be implanted in the minds of children.

The teacher should also know, understand and practise protecting human rights and discharge duties.

The teacher should make it second nature to protect and abide by the principles of human rights.

PRESENT SITUATION

The general educated mass thinks that human rights is a matter of law, police or terrorism. We have still not understood the root or source of all the trouble. The trouble lies at the root of the mind which is stuffed with matters that are quickly inflammable. Thus training of mind is necessary and it is only the teachers who can do it successfully.

Today, we mix up the matters of human rights education with rights of tribal, rights of prisoners and rights of thousand other areas. In fact, human rights education is a subject in itself. It is the education of moral values and education for living and leading a human life. If you do not learn to live together with your fellow beings then why do you call yourself a social creature? Why do you pine to become cultured and civilised? These are the questions which remain to be answered. The fact is the root of all the above process lies in a peaceful mind. The mind wants to be nurtured with the concept of dignity. Even human beings need to be ultimately happy and peaceful. Man is yet to attain this stage. We, in India, are yet to realise the need of awareness and practice of human rights and duties.

RAZZMATAZZ OF POTO, HR & DE

The Prevention of Terrorism Ordinance (POTO) is the new anti-terrorism ordinance. They say that POTO is the legal instrument of fight to global and escalating threat of terrorism. In Maharashtra and Karnataka TADA existed from 1985. But, ever since 1985 when the TADA statute was passed, terrorism has not decreased, it has increased in volume and in the extent of the operations. This shows there is something along with the remedies.

The simple argument is that you let the seeds of violence, hatret, religionism, fanaticism, fundamentalism grow in the mind and hearts of people, old and young. After the above characters become diehard characters in the form of virus, you medicate or devise the preventive inoculation of POTO. The question is, why do you not nip the seed or virus at the bud? Why do you water the plant of violence and fanaticism to grow with the fountain of blood? Wars are waged not in the battlefield but in the minds of men.

We do not need legal sanction, we need a healthy educated mind with education. Human rights and duties education (DE) lead to a subtle and sombre state of mind which does not fall prey to the glamour of violence and power. One educated personality of a child will form a sociogram of many educated children.

Let us see that the chain of such wise children grow exponentially so that youngsters, children, school, society and state would be peaceful, HR & D education is the only ethical route to peaceful co-existance of human life and prevent terrorism. We promise that we would not need POTO after 10 years since there will be no terrorism in all our youth's cognitive domain after being thoroughly trained in HR & Duties, principle and ethics.

Indicators

Annual reports on the progress of nations by UNICEF, Amnesty International, etc., have made us aware of the current status of human rights in India.

The NGO's have found that out of all the HR activities, human rights education is yielding positive result in the form of attitude formation which is only 10 per cent (approx.) The indicators (UNICEF, NGO's, etc.) have evaluated that human rights is a concept understood and followed only by and for the organs of the Home Department. Human rights is considered to be a legal subject.

Reality

The reality is stark. In India, only 50 per cent of the education faculty believe that HR & D is a subject of education. Leave apart thinking and implementation, the top class of educationists do not feel it necessary to be a subject. Educationists have greater things to think of and act upon. The proposal of NEERI and the NCTE document on HR & National Valuer in the year 1999 is yet in a corner of the reference section of the library shelf. The disturbing part of the reality is why the universities do not unanimously think it fit to be introduced in B.Ed. and as a special paper in M.Ed. Though there are universities who have already introduced it, yet there are many who have vehemently kept HR & D at bay and have conveniently handed over the subject to law and sociology.

reason and conscience. The concept of human rights has emerged out of mankind's reasoning and conscience.

Everyone has the right to life, liberty and security of person. This means that everyone has the right to live and to live in freedom and safety. The societies are governed by political systems which exercise control over the actions of its members, institutions, and organisations, both formal and informal. Chosen members of society constitute a government. A government functions according to the laws passed by the society. A law is a general rule of external human action enforced by an authority/government, and human rights are no exception to it.

The responsibility of every government is to ensure and protect the human rights of its citizens. Since the rights to life, liberty and security of a person are the fundamental rights of human beings, a government must ensure these rights for all citizens irrespective of their religion, caste, creed, colour, sex, race, and place of birth. Hence, all persons have the right to legal help and protection. No one can be imprisoned or punished without the due process of law.

Human beings differ amongst themselves, but the concept of human rights implies that all human beings are equal and have to be treated alike irrespective of their religion, caste, creed, colour, sex, race, place of birth and so on.

Society defines roles to its members, institutions and organisations. In the performance of these roles, tangible decisions affecting the lives of individuals, on the basis of individual difference are taken.

A reputed school is making admissions. The seats are limited and the applicants are numerous. All the children seeking admission vary amongst themselves on various attributes, like intelligence, achievements and motivations. The concept of right to equality implies that school authorities should consider the applications of all children irrespective of their religion, caste, creed, colour, sex, place of birth and may make proper selection on the basis of other specified attributes like intelligence, achievements and motivation.

The right to equality emphasises that everyone can claim human rights despite:

a) a different sex
b) a different skin colour
c) speaking a different language
d) thinking different things
e) believing in different religions
f) owning more or less
g) being born in another social group
h) coming from another country.

The cardinal aim of all societies and their governments is to ensure the fullest development of human personality. The right to live is the natural right of human beings but the human right to live with dignity is very fundamental. And the constant growth in the number and scope of human rights is the outcome of the concern of national and international organisations to secure to all human beings the right to live with dignity on this earth.

A child has the right to life, liberty and security of person, but he has the right to education, health and other rights which contribute towards his leading a more dignified life.

Everyone has the right to education. Hence every child has the right to go to school. Moreover, education shall be free, at least in the elementary stages. Everyone has the right to health. In particular, every child has the right to grow, obtain love and care from family or from government. His health has to be protected and cared for at all costs. In fact, the rights such as right to education and right to health and other rights have been instituted to secure to all human beings not only the right to live but the right to live with more dignity.

The cardinal principles of human rights are thus equality and dignity. It is the duty of all governments and members of society to ensure equal opportunities to all children to get education and health services and other rights, and these rights will be granted assuring the dignity of the individual. There should be no compromise on this count because all these rights have been enshrined in the Constitution of India (discussed later). A child's right to life, education, health, etc., with dignity are absolute and unfettered. While it is for the government to perform its constitutional obligations, we, as members of the society, are morally bound to create a conducive atmosphere and an ideal situation wherein all children and other weaker sections of society would be able to develop themselves physically, mentally, socially, and would lead a happy life. This would be the first step for creating understanding and awareness of our rights and respect for the rights of others.

FUNDAMENTAL DUTIES

Human rights and fundamental freedoms offer all men, women and children to develop and use their qualities, their talents and their conscience, and to satisfy their spiritual and material needs. Nevertheless, respect for human rights and human dignity is the foundation of freedom, justice and peace in the world. Furthermore, rights and duties go side by side. Therefore, it is the primary duty of every teacher or educator in communicating the message of fundamental duties. It is the teacher/educator who can create awareness and understanding among the children and young people to perform their fundamental duties which have been entrusted to them by the Constitution (Forty-Second Amendment) Act, 1976. These duties have been reproduced below:

Article 51.A: Fundamental Duties

It shall be the duty of every citizen of India:

a) to abide by the Constitution and respect its ideals and institutions, the National Flag and the National Anthem;

b) to cherish and follow the noble ideals which inspired our national struggle for freedom;
c) to uphold and protect the sovereignty, unity and integrity of India;
d) to defend the country and render national service when called upon to do so;
e) to promote harmony and the spirit of common brotherhood amongst all the people of India transcending religious, linguistic and regional or sectional diversities; to renounce practices derogatory to the dignity of women;
f) to value and preserve the rich heritage of our composite culture;
g) to protect and improve the natural environment including forests, lakes, rivers and wildlife and to have compassion for living creatures;
h) to develop the scientific temper, humanism and the spirit of inquiry and reform;
i) to safeguard public property and to abjure violence;
j) to strive towards excellence in all spheres of individual and collective activity, so that the nation constantly rises to higher levels of endeavour and achievement.

Needless to say, fundamental duties are sacred commandments. They infuse a feeling of patriotism in all men, women and children of this great country to dedicate themselves to the cause of the nation. Respect for the national institutions, of unity and integrity of the nation, preservation of cultural heritage, protection of natural environment, development of scientific temper and safeguarding of public property are some of the cardinal duties which every citizen of the country must perform towards the accomplishment of national goals and objectives.

TEACHER TRAINING

In the present-day world, human rights have assumed great significance. Former UN Secretary General U. Thant had said, "the establishment of human rights provided the foundation upon which rests the political structure of human freedom; the achievement of human freedom generates the will as the capacity for economic and social progress; the attainment of economic and social progress provides the basis for true international peace."

Article 26 of the Universal Declaration of Human Rights, 1948, states:

1. Everyone has the right to education. Education shall be free, at least in the elementary and fundamental stages. Elementary education shall be compulsory. Technical and professional education shall be made generally available, and higher education shall be equally accessible to all on the basis of merit.
2. Education shall be directed to the full development of the human personality and to the strengthening of respect for human rights and fundamental freedoms. It shall promote understanding, tolerance and friendship among all nations, racial and religious groups and shall further the activities of the United Nations for the maintenance of peace.
3. Parents have a prior right to choose the kind of education that shall be given to their children.

Para I and Para III above enunciate the concern of the United Nations towards "education as human rights" and Para II elucidates its concern in respect of "education about human rights". Thus, this Article offers a dual perspective of education as a human right and education about human rights.

This means that national educational systems all over the world may be designed, developed and implemented in such a manner that the students not only acquire knowledge about human rights but should be able to practise and imbibe them in their daily lives. The Indian Educational System has already been reconstructed towards this end. The National Policy on

Education (1986) (revised in 1992) is particularly crucial in this regard. The policy laid down for the first time in the history of Indian education, a National Curriculum Framework with a common core as a basis for building the Nation System of Education. Most of the 'common core' elements identified in the Policy are related to one or another dimension of human rights education. The 'common core' elements identified are 'the history of India's freedom movement, the constitutional obligations and other content essential to nurture national identity'. It has been laid down that these elements will cut across subject areas and will be designed to promote values such as India's common cultural heritage, egalitarianism, democracy, secularism, equality of sexes, protection of the environment, removal of social barriers, observance of the small family norms and inculcation of the scientific temper. All educational programmes will be carried on in strict conformity with secular values. Sufficient stress has been laid on promoting equality.

The Policy lays down, "It will be necessary to provide for equal opportunity, not only in access, but also in the conditions for success. Besides, an awareness of inherent equality of all will be created through the core curriculum. The purpose is to remove prejudices and complexes transmitted through the social environment and the accident of birth". One of the main tasks of the Indian Education System is to enable the teachers to teach core curricular areas by improving upon existing methods and materials, keeping in mind the elements of human rights education as an important component. The educational goal of human rights education is that the students should be able to perceive (according to their developmental stage) that they live with dignity. Each one of us is a human being first and a boy, girl, member of a community and/or religion, etc., only later. Each one of us has rights, privileges which are universal and is based upon the principles of equality and dignity.

The teacher training programme should enable the teachers to set their own teaching goals in human rights for each class.

The teachers of classes I-V should concentrate on nurturing the sense that the students have of their own worth and that of others. They can organise activities like singing, dancing, painting, clay modelling and dramas to make children perceive the worth of human beings. The teachers of classes VI-VIII should foster awareness and knowledge of human rights and the sense of reciprocity and universality upon which it is based. They can do this by teaching appropriate subject matter in social studies, science, mathematics and languages. The students of classes IX-XII should be explained in detail as to how the present century has witnessed two world wars and many events involving massive violations of human rights. The thrust should be on inculcating and strengthening the value of human rights so that they work towards peace and harmony in the world. For this purpose the subject matter related to the concept and principles and practice of human rights has to be incorporated and transacted through all the curricular areas of secondary and higher secondary classes.

All teachers should be trained to identify curriculum elements in the syllabi of their classes where human rights education can be brought in. They should then be trained to develop practical activities, teaching aids and materials.

The teacher trainer should design, develop, implement and evaluate teacher training in human rights to enable teachers to develop and use methods and materials in this area. One of the major tasks of the teacher trainer is to sensitise the teachers in human rights education. Hence it will be useful to organise practical work on observation and analysis of social situations in schools and to engage trainees in participative discussions to resolve conflicting situations. Strategies like role play and buzz session will also be useful. The training of teachers should be supplemented by further research in teaching of human rights. These issues have been dealt with in detail in subsequent units.

3

Human Rights—A Necessity for National Development

*K.S Khichi**

We live in a society. Interdependence of one another makes a society. No man can provide himself with everything he needs. He has to depend on others for fulfilment of his requirements. Society is based on interdependence. This interdependence enforces some kind of adjustments or systematic behaviours among the members of the society. One cannot get merely one's own requirements and neglect the requirements of others. Again, the fulfilment of one's requirements should be done in a systematic manner whatsoever it may be, but in accordance with the norms laid down by the members of the society. Thus a society means some kind of orderly living. It requires some kind of rules which are to be followed strictly by all the members in order to provide smooth living. If one individual obstructs what another wishes to do, society cannot simply go on. The interdependence, therefore, means that there should be some rules by which everybody will behave well towards each other.

Usually, the government provides these rules and so society and the government are very closely linked to each other.

India is a democratic country. Our ideal is a democratic government. In democracy, people choose their rulers. Rulers

**Co-ordinator, Extension Services, Regional Institute of Education, AJMER.*

can remain in power as long as they remain in the confidence of people. Thus the state power resides in the people.

At the start of the Indian Constitution the amended 'Preamble' has been inscribed in the following words:

"We, the People of India having solemnly resolved to constitute India into a Sovereign Socialistic Secular Democratic Republic and to secure to all its citizens;

"Justice, social, economic and political

"Liberty of thought, expression, belief, faith and worship

"Equality of status and/or opportunity; and to promote among them all;

"Fraternity" assuring the dignity of the individual and the unity and Integrity of the Nation."

Here, the resolution is made by the people of India. It clearly indicates the supremacy of the people. The people desire to make the country reach a particular goal or goals, and not the government. The people are above the government. The people of India are Indian citizens.

A citizen is not merely a person residing in a country. The true sense of citizenship lies in a democratic government A citizen is a person who enjoys rights and exercises his duties in a country. A citizen is one who participates in the process of the government. A democratic government has citizens. In the governments which are not democratic, there are only rulers and subjects. The people living under such governments have only obligations towards the state and no rights. They are required to do certain things but the government is not bound to do certain things towards them. The government tells the people what to do and what not to, but does not listen to them in return. This type of government is not required. In the present age, there is a demand for democratic government and this lays more responsibility on the people of the country, i.e., the citizens.

As mentioned earlier, a citizen is a person who enjoys rights that the Constitution provides; and enjoyment of rights also imposes some duties on him. A good citizen is one who is conscious of his rights and duties. The right to vote and elect a government is a political right and if one does not exercise his power he cannot be considered as a good citizen. He may be a very good person but not a good citizen. So one should be conscious of one's own rights and simultaneously perform one's duties. The government makes certain rules so as to provide smooth living for the countryman, and a citizen should obey the laws that are made by the legislatures. The law formed by the government or any other administrative machinery, at times, creates a situation in which the rights of individuals are likely to be violated. There may be a situation in which people's exploitation is possible. It is therefore essential that the people must be aware of their rights so as to check the exploitation.

While enjoying one's own rights, it happens that the rights of others are ignored by the individuals. This becomes a sad state of affairs and a good citizen is one who has concern for the rights of others and does not act in a way so as to violate the rights of others. Thus the qualities of a good citizen must include a consciousness of his own rights, tolerance for others and respect for laws. Rights and duties are always linked. Right and duties together take a society up to its goals.

A democratic state depends on the quality of its citizens. Democracy can be strengthened if the citizens have a clear view of their own rights, if they demand what they can claim from the government, if they know what the government can claim from them. Social evils cannot be eliminated by merely passing the laws. It can be done by creating a sense of social responsibility. There has been instances of exploitation of men by men or organised institutes including the government. In order to provide a dignified living to all human beings, the awareness about human rights is essential. Human rights are generally defined as the rights which every human being, irrespective of religion, nationality or sex, is entitled to enjoy. It is with this spirit that the General Assembly of United Nations on Tenth December 1948 adopted the Universal

Declaration of Human Rights. This is based on the recognition that freedom of speech and belief and freedom from fear and want are the highest aspirations of the common people and the human rights need to be protected by the rule of law. The declaration was proclaimed as a common standard of achievement for all people and all nations. The Universal Declaration of Human Rights (1948) consists of 30 Articles which emphasis equality of all human beings without distinction of any kind like race, colour, sex, language, religion, political or other opinion, national or social origin, property, birth or other status. Every person's right to life, liberty, security, equality before law and entitlement without any discrimination to equal protection of law is emphasized. Every person's right to freedom of thought, conscience, religion, opinion and expression has also been recognised.

The United Nations on 23 March, 1976 brought into force an international covenant on civil and political rights of the people and another on social, economical and cultural rights. The framers of the Indian Constitution have made provisions under the Fundamental Rights and Directive Principles of state policy which are related to human rights. The rights which are inherent in the man's social nature are called human rights. Rights are those conditions of social life without which no one can develop one's personality. But provision of these rights is fruitful if the human beings are not only aware about their rights but also enjoy them. For this purpose they need to be properly educated.

A person needs to be prepared as a good citizen. The educational system should provide a opportunity to the children to promote the understanding of human rights and duties so as to make them responsible citizens who can contribute towards mankind and human dignity. The present system of education with emphasis on teaching of various subjects, leading to acquisition of merely knowledge is incomplete if the children are not made aware about how to live in a society. Students spend a long time in school. What they learn there should not merely help them in getting degrees, but they should also learn how to live in a society, contribute gainfully to the national goals. The education should promote the characteristics of a good citizen among the students. Schools form our habits and attitudes. It tells us what to accept and what not, and this capability should be developed during the course of studies. The evils of the society can be overcome by making people conscious that they have rights too, enabling them to fight for their rights.

Awareness about human rights is essential. This can be done more effectively through the educational system. But it should not be included in the form of separate text materials. The teaching of human rights in any form in the curriculum may not serve the purpose. Mere memorisation of these rights for passing a particular examination is not sufficient. The essence of these rights has to be felt and accordingly reflected in the behaviour of a child. Since the duty of one ensures the rights of others, if one is constrained to behave in a manner that necessary duties are performed, it will automatically protect the rights of others. It is essential that an environment in schools is created so that the students feel that this is how a particular right is enjoyed by the individuals and the group. Right of freedom of movement can be observed under the circumstances when each one of them move freely and not just a few individuals. The school should be designed and organised to provide a social environment in which various situations can be created to enable children to become aware of their rights. Activities like games, debates celebrations, etc., can be recommended for these purposes, making them aware about their rights and then asking them to undertake some project on violation of rights in the immediate surroundings.

The teacher must be aware about the rights of the children, adopted by the General Assembly of the United Nations on 20 November 1989, and the classroom environment should be accordingly created. Debates on burning issues on violation of human rights and the circumstances leading to them can help in better understanding of the situations.

4

Right of Education and Inculcating of Awareness

—Jyoti Christian*

INTRODUCTION

The dawn of the twenty-first century has made all of us conscious and aware of implementation and protection of human rights. Human rights are basically required by all human beings born as a citizen of any country at national and international levels. The knowledge of human rights is the prime concern for today's educationists to educate our next millennium generation. Therefore, it is very important for any individual citizen to know and become aware of his fundamental rights for the very basic foundation for a healthy, peaceful and happy living life in a country. Over and above, it affects in every area of human activity ensuring justice and equality. That is why protection and promotion of human rights is necessary for the development of individuals, raising their standard of living, maintaining stability and equality for their advancement, progress and prosperity of the country at large. It is here the duty of every citizen and its countrymen to care and save the rights of the people.

In India, a new millennium movement will make the youth develop concern, sensitivity and awareness as their fundamental rights enshrined in the Constitution, building

**Retd. Reader in Education, MSU, Baroda.*

foundations to develop understanding and meaning among them which requires hardwork and forwa.d looking faith "to do small things and gain big results." Once a theologian, Franas Schaefter, wrote in his book, *No little people*: "In God's right there and no little people and no little place."

HISTORICAL BASES OF HUMAN RIGHTS

The human rights movement got an impetus after the adoption of the United Nations Charter in 1945, and the Universal Declaration of Human Rights on 10 December, 1948, adopted by the United Nations General Assembly known as "Human Rights Day".

The United Nations Charter vide Articles 55 and 56 promote universal respect for observance of human rights and fundamental freedom of speech and equality before law for all without distinction as to race, sex, language or religion.

A thrust to the Universal Declaration of Human Rights was further provided with the adoption of three famous covenants by the United Nations General Assembly in 1966, viz., The Convention:

i) The Civil and Political Rights.
ii) The Economic and Political Rights
iii) Against all kinds of racial discrimination.

The General Assembly of the United Nations adopted and proclaimed the Universal Declaration of Human Rights and called upon all member countries to publicise the text of the Declaration and 'to cause it' to be disseminated, displayed, read and expounded principally in schools, other educational Institutions and to community agencies, without distinction based on the political status of countries or territories. The major events listed here are:

1. *24 October, 1945:* United Nations Established for World Peace, Brotherhood and International Understanding.
2. *20 December, 1948:* United Nations Declaration of Human Rights.
3. *June 1993 at Austria*: Hena International Conference for Human Rights
4. *1 January, 1995:* All India Human Rights Educators Forum (AIHRE) was established for the diffusion of Human Rights.

The human rights was the result of the Second World War which changed man's thinking. It was further evolved with the signing of Paris Peace Treaties with Italy, Rumania, Bulgaria, Hungary and Finland in 1947, wherein each state undertook to take all measures necessary to secure to all persons under its jurisdiction, without distinction as to race, sex, language or religion, freedom of expression, press, publication, of religious worship, of political opinion and of public meetings.

The Universal Declaration of Human Rights Education (1995-2004) is to complete the task of the United Nations for making the entire human race "Literate" under Human Rights. Therefore, 10 December, 1999 was celebrated all over the world as 'International Human Rights Day'.

EDUCATION AS A RIGHT

The National Policy of Education (1986, 1992) has made particular mention of "Education for equality." It emphasizes the removal of disparities and equalisation of educational opportunity by attending to the spiral needs of those who have been denied equality so far. Now, the question arises, "Can we be the doers of the future actions who decide what they want and accordingly take action to gain it? Each day of our efforts is the foundation for tomorrow to those searching for life's true meaning and purposes as the ultimate realisation. The concern for human rights focuses on reducing constrain and ensuring the "wholeness, i.e., integrity of the individual. Here, "Education is the only powerful instrument for the successful learning of knowledge, skills and attitudes, where development occurs and where what is learned is worthwhile to a learner and in such a way that he can express his own individuality through what he learns and can subsequently apply it, and adapt it, flexibly, to various life and work situations and problems other than those he considered in learning it." Again, according to the New Education Policy (NEP, 1986), "Education develops manpower for different levels of the economy. It is also the fundamental for our all-round development, material and spiritual."

The humanistic view has the strong conviction that each Individual is unique and he brings into this world a unique contribution of qualities in work and life. It is in his social interactions that he grows and learns and becomes what he really potentially is. A unique core of human nature is not bad but each one is born to be a wholesome, productive, and creative individual. Although, affected by the environment, important aspect of the person comes from within. The educationists, efforts should be to free up each individual to find his inner self to let each person become what he truly can be or can become; to be healthy and productive rather than troubled and neurotic.

According to UNESCO (1990), "Around 200 million children under the age of 15 in the Third World are forced to make their own living, exploited, working on the streets, working for their parents and their debts. Therewere 34.59-1 children out of school because of ignorance of education and in A.D. 2000 there will be 40.36-1 millions. Does our educational system and the Declaration of Human Rights movement promote in them the capacity to learn to become lifelong learners? Under all circumstance they are placed, can we help them to find out a specific meaning for their life in a given situation? It they find meaning in life they will continue to grow in spite of all indignities and they will be able to bear much hardship, misfortune and unhappiness faced by them.

RIGHT OF EDUCATION

The United Nations Declaration of Human Rights (1948), Article 26, states: "Every one has the right to education, education shall be free, at least at the elementary and fundamental stages; elementary education shall be compulsory; technical and professional education shall be made generally available and higher education shall be equally accessible to all on the basis of merits." To sum up, "All children have the right to an appropriate free and compulsory school education."

The Preamble of the Indian Constitution states; "And to secure to all its citizens justice, social, economic and political, liberty of thought, expression, belief, forth and worship, equality of status and opportunity and to promote among them all fraternity assuming the dignity of the individual and the unity and the integrity of the nation." Our constitutional commitment to the protection and promotion of human rights finds reflection in the preamble of the Indian Constitution and in various other provisions in relation to the fundamental rights. It resolves to all its citizens Justice, Liberty, Equality and Fraternity."

Under the heading "Directive Principles", Article 37 enjoins upon the state to secure a social order in which justice, social, economic and political shall be ensured in all the institutions of social life. In particular, the state is to direct its policy towards securing adequate means of livelihood, just and humane conditions of work, a living wage, free and compulsory education for all children particularly of the weaker sections of society." The fundamental duties contained in Part IV A of the Constitution are in consonance with Article (29, 1) of the Universal Declaration of Human Rights which says, "Everyone has duties to the community in which alone the free and fully development of his personalty is possible. Therefore, there is a need to make conscious efforts to promote an awareness of the constitutional obligation among the citizens. The Constitution of India visualised development of a pluralist society based on the principles of equality and social justice. The cohesive nature of state wherein 'unity in diversity' is the core value, the citizens should constantly be reminded to preserve this value for growth and advancement of the country.

EDUCATION FOR ALL

The National Policy of Education (1986) formulated a number of strategies for a national system of education which lays the greatest stress on elimination of disparities and promotion of the equality of women, with special attention to the need of minorities and other disadvantaged sections, so that the system could "move towards the ideals enshrined in the Constitution."

The Jomiten World Conference in 1990, emphasised on "Education for All" (EFA), Article One (1) of the World Declaration on "Education for All:" Meeting Basic Needs" states: "Every person—child, youth or adult shall be able to benefit from educational opportunities designed to meet their basic learning needs. These needs comprise both essential learning tools and basic learning content required by human beings to be able to survive, develop their full potential, to live and work in dignity, to participate fully in development, to improve the quality of their lives, to make informed decisions and continue learning.

Again, the World Declaration laid stress on universalising access and promoting equity. It states, "Basic education services of quality should be expanded, and consistent measures must be taken to reduce disparities." Underserved groups, the poor, street and working children, girls and women, rural and remote populations, nomads and migrant workers, indigenous people, ethnic, social and linguistic minorities, and refugees should not suffer any discrimination in access to learning opportunities. More, significantly, "Whether or not expanded educational opportunities will translate into meaningful development for an individual or for society depends ultimately on whether they actually learn as a result of those opportunities, i.e., whether they incorporate useful knowledge, reasoning ability, skills and values. The focus of basic education must therefore be on actual learning acquisition and outcome, rather than exclusively upon enrolment, continued participation in organised programmes and completion of certification requirements. Active and participatory approaches are particularly valuable on assuring learning acquisition and allowing learners to reach their fullest potential" (Articles 3-4; emphasis as in the original). Significantly, the Declaration views education as a means for human development, of the development of the individual first and subsequently of society, and lays stress on the states being responsible to ensure that all human beings are allowed to develop their full capacities and are able to live and work in dignity.

The seaside city in Brazil, the Racife meet of the world's nine high population countries (Bangladesh, Brazil, China, Egypt, India, Indonesia, Nigeria, Mexico and Pakistan) emphasised, "the importance of technological and life skills in education of the future toward the system of internet and satellite." Furthermore, there is need for "linking education" with "workforce", reaching children in remote regions and children with special needs, and above all instilling democratic values of justice, fairness, tolerance, equity and education of quality. "Education is to be our biggest challenge and our biggest hope." That hope is predicted largely on how soon we learn the languages of the twenty-first century and learn it well!

INCULCATING AWARENESS IN THE COMMUNITY: A THEMATIC MODEL

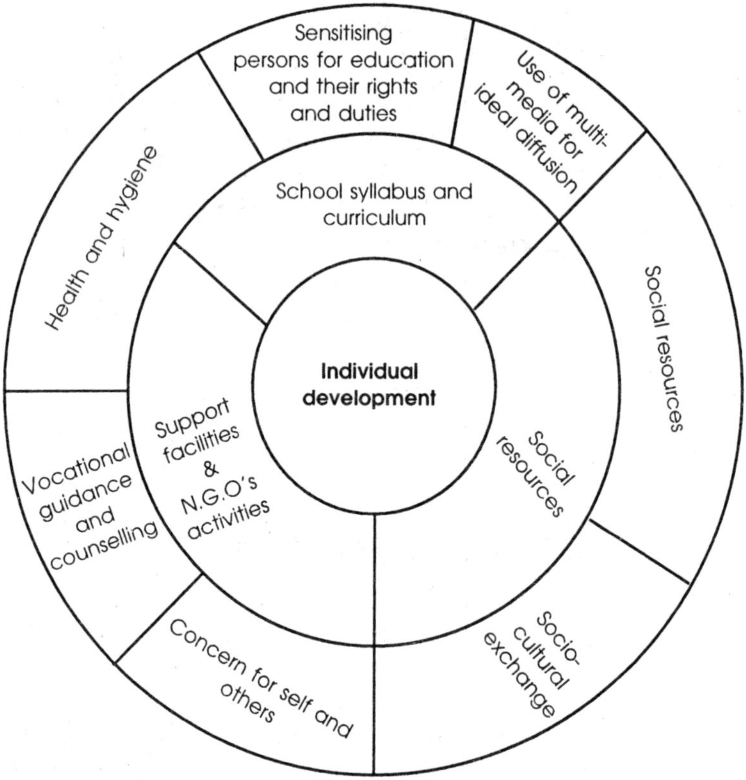

REFERENCES

DPEP special Issue, September, 1996.

Human Rights: A Source Book, NCERT, New Delhi, 1996.

Indian Constitution 1949.

National Policy on Education, 1986, HRD Ministry of Education, New Delhi.

UGC. Report on Thrust Area on "Education of the Disadvantages groups", *CBSE Compiled Report*, M.S.U. Baroda, 1996.

5

Creating Awareness about Human Rights and Duties: Role of Education

—*Gajendra Singh Tomar**

> The right to life and dignity of an individual cannot be assured unless it is accompanied by the right to Education.
>
> *Justice Kuldeep Singh*

INTRODUCTION

Human rights is global phenomenon. Rights are inherent in nature and have come up in our society over the years. Human rights refer to the fundamental freedoms and basic liberties without which men, women and children cannot live with respect and dignity.

We all have ambitions and aspirations in life. Nevertheless, right to life, liberty and security are the basic rights which every man, woman and child must possess. People's rights are regulated by rule of law and it is the duty of the government to enforce and protect these rights and fundamental freedoms irrespective of their caste, creed, colour, race sex, religion and place of birth.

**L.M.T.T. College, Dabok, Udaipur (Rajasthan).*

The Universal Declaration of Human Rights, 1948 was a major step towards the emancipation of rights of human beings. It is a basic 'code of conduct'. It lays emphasis for the protection of human rights of all men, women and children of the world. Besides this the Indian Constitutional provisions have equally played a rightful role for shaping the concept of human rights into a reality. The Preamble, the Fundamental Rights, the Fundamental Duties and the Directive Principles of State Policy are the concrete steps towards the realisation of human rights.

Without awareness there is no linguistically formulated knowledge about things and concepts; without awareness there are no humanly phenomenally expressed experiences of human beings. Awareness is a window. People look to the outside world and get influence by what they see, hear, experience. The way they do it is disrobed and studied in cognitive science.

Human rights education at all levels of education is most relevant to all of us. The students should know that education is an important human rights in their daily lives. Education being concerned with human beings and with their orientation for the future does play a fundamental role. It provides individuals with the capacity and motivation to act. It becomes very important to understand right in the very beginning that the term human rights implies universality.

Teachers do not only negotiate in technical aspects of knowledge gathering but also in the contents of the information, providing learning opportunities by making choices for materials and concepts. At this point the educational and political role of a teacher is crucial.

Concept of Human Rights

S.P. Mallick and C.J. Malhotra note that human rights are those basic rights and fundamental freedoms which are natural and inherent in human nature and without which human survival in this universe is impossible. These rights include right to life, right to liberty and security, right to health, right to education, right to freedom of conscious thought, expression, association, privacy and freedom of movement whereas needs relate to the day-to-day requirements of a person, viz., physiological, social and economic needs. Both human rights and human needs are interrelated.

All persons have the right to legal help and protection. No one can be imprisoned or punished without the due process of law. Thus the concept of human rights has emerged out of mankind's reasoning and consciences. Human beings differ amongst themselves, but the concept of human rights implies that all human beings are equal and have to be treated alike irrespective of their religion, caste, creed, colour, sex, place of birth and so on.

HISTORICAL BACKGROUND OF HUMAN RIGHTS

S.P. Mullick and C.J. Malhotra further write in their paper on human rights and teacher training. Some important events which have affected the human rights movement are as follows:

1. Renaissance

It is a name given to 'Revival of learning' which started in Italy and spread throughout Europe in the fifteenth and sixteenth centuries. It was greatly helped by the invention of the printing press through which precious books were multiplied. As a result, the rights of human beings enunciated in the ancient books of wisdom of polity were renovated. These rights infused a feeling of the right to live with dignity and self-determination among the masses.

2. French Revolution

It was the collapse of an outdated socio-economic order. France was on the verge of financial bankruptcy because of the wars of Louis XVI. The intellectual background of the revolution was prepared by the creative works of Voltaire and Rousseau. The French Revolution of 1789 stood for 'Liberty, Equality and Fraternity'.

3. Bolshevik Revolution in Russia

In 1917, a general strike in Russia was called and the army refused to fire on the strikers. In this way full revolt broke out. Russia came under the rule of Bolsheviks. Lenin emerged as the strong man of Russia and he restored the fundamental rights of the citizens.

4. Industrial Revolution

As a result of industrial progress England was turned into a manufacturing country. However, the condition of workers employed in the factories was very deplorable. Their basic rights were being ignored and in 1930, the government enacted industrial laws and ensured human rights to work and secure proper wages and suitable working conditions.

5. World War II

The axis powers (Germany, Italy and Japan) were defeated by the Allies (England, France, USA & USSR) in 1945. The war ended when two atom bombs were dropped by America on the two Japanese cities of Hiroshima and Nagasaki on civilian targets. This sent shock waves throughout the world because this was an act against humanity as also against the basic rights to live.

All these factors led to the establishment of the United Nations in 1945 and the Universal Declaration of Human Rights in 1948.

6. Universal Declaration of Human Rights, 1948

The preamble to the Universal Declaration of Human Rights,

1948 acts as a mirror through which the essence of this instrument could be visualised. It embodies the expectation of humanity as also the foundation of freedom, justice, peace and oppression. The preamble lays emphasis on equal rights of men, women and children and the need to live with dignity. There are 30 rights given in the Universal Declaration of Human Rights, 1948. These rights embody the basic liberty and fundamental freedom which all men, women and children can enjoy in order to make this world a better place to live in.

Indian Constitutional Provisions

Indian Constitutional provisions have equally played a rightful role in shaping the concept of human rights into a reality. The Preamble, the Fundamental Rights, the Fundamental Duties and the Directive Principles of State Policy are the concrete steps towards the realisation of human rights.

Preamble

The Preamble provides for all citizens justice, liberty, equality and fraternity. It has implications in all walks of life of an Indian. In a school situation, it ensures to every child the right to life, liberty, security and to freedom from any form of cruelty, inhuman or degrading treatment in any way.

Fundamental Rights

Some of the fundamental rights important from the point of view of school education are as follows:

1. Right to equality
2. Right to freedom
3. Right against exploitation
4. Right to freedom of religion
5. Cultural and educational rights
6. Rights to constitutional remedies.

Human rights and fundamental freedoms offer all men, women and children to develop and use their qualities, their talents, their conscience and to satisfy their spiritual and material needs. Nevertheless, respect for human rights and human dignity is the foundation of freedom, justice and peace in the world.

Fundamental Duties

Fundamental duties are sacred commandments. They infuse a feeling of patriotism in all men, women and children of this great country to dedicate themselves to the cause of the nation. Respect for the national institutions, of unity and integrity of the nation, preservation of cultural heritage, protection of natural environments, development of scientific temper and safeguarding of public property are some of the cardinal duties which every citizen of the country must perform towards the accomplishment of national goals and objectives.

Directive Principles of State Policy

Certain Directive Principles of State Policy based on social, political and economic justice have been laid down for the guidance of the legislatures as well as the government authorities. Although these principles are not enforceable by any court yet they are fundamental in the governance of the country and it shall be the duty of the state to apply these principles in making laws for the general welfare of their men, women and children.

Education for Human Rights

Education for human rights is applicable at all levels of education. From the child's early years, education of human rights is both practical and necessary. Pre-school and early primary education can highlight a sense of common humanity among children.

A national educational system all over the world may be designed, developed and implemented in such a manner that the students not only acquire knowledge about human rights but should be able to practise and imbibe them in their daily lives.

National Policy on Education (1986) (revised in 1992)

A national policy on education is particularly crucial in this regard. Most of the 'Common Core' elements identified in the policy are related to one or another dimension of human rights education. The policy lays down, "It will be necessary to provide for equal opportunity not only in access but also in the conditions for success. Besides, an awareness of inherent equality of all will be created through the core curriculum."

The educational goal of human rights education is that the students should be able to perceive that human life is a precious entity and all efforts are needed to ensure that all human beings live with dignity.

Incorporation of Human Rights Education at Secondary Level

Mahesh Chand Sharma and others write in their paper, *Human Rights Education and Secondary Level Curriculum*: "The secondary stage is more advanced that the elementary stage. Knowledge should now be presented more systematically and students should be encouraged to develop the capacity. Individual and social behaviour should be developed in a more analytical and critical way. Students should reflect upon the values underlying behaviour. The teacher should encourage the students to explore major contemporary world problems."

The secondary school teacher should enable students to work in a democratic manner. They should get themselves enrolled with local, national and international committees so as to promote respect for human rights, the establishment of justice and the safeguarding of peace.

The organisation spirit and atmosphere of the school are essential components of education of human rights. The principles of human rights should ideally be reflected in all the daily operations of school life and in the relations between teachers and pupils as well as between members of the two groups. When the teachers in the school join hands to teach human rights the programme becomes successful because the teaching of human rights deals with good conduct and this is the concern of every teacher, whatever his or her subject. Teachers have a greater responsibility on themselves. They will probably have in their care a county's future leaders and administrators, boys and girls who may later be among those who influence progress in industry, science or the arts.

Schools can play an important role in the promotion of human rights by developing individuals who have respect for human rights. This can be ensured by providing a democratic environment enabling children to enjoy their rights and simultaneously learn to respect the rights of others.

Activities for Human Rights Education

Activities which can help to impart a sense of human rights and also cultivate understanding and sympathy for others are done outside the classroom. Some are conducted independently of school courses and programmes, others, like the exchange of correspondence or cultural activities, may be closely related to work in curriculum subjects.

Teachers can motivate students to become involved, to be of service in some capacity to pursue hobbies or to practise artistic skills at leisure. The school may provide a room for club meetings, entertainments and exhibitions with some guidance and encouragement from the teacher. Some activities are suggested by Mahesh Chandra and others in *Human Rights and National Values*, 1999 (N.C.T.E) are as follows:

a) School Clubs

The clubs students organise and are responsible for a variety of activities to promote social welfare in the school and the community to develop understanding of other countries and people, their culture and traditions and to make their own their own country better known abroad. Club members maintain wall newspapers and posters on current events and the work of the United Nations, organise debates and school meetings and celebrations of special days and take part in community welfare schemes.

b) Exhibitions and Displays

Drawing, paintings, photographs and other objects from abroad collected in the course correspondence exchanges may form a permanent exhibition in a school classroom or assembly room. The students take pride in seeing their work displayed and in being able to explain the origin and meaning of exhibit form abroad or the significance of folk songs and dances, while the rest of the school and the community benefit from their work and feel themselves involved in its aims.

c) Project Work

Project work can be equally useful for human rights education. These can be picked up in any discipline and an element of human rights built into it. A project can be thought of in abundance in any subject and can be easily linked up with human rights with some imagination. This can be a very useful method of generating awareness of and understanding human rights.

d) Dramatic & Literary Activities

Co-curricular activities, especially dramatic and literary

activities, play an important role in education for all-round development of children in schools. They can play a constructive role in human rights education. Students should be encouraged to pick up plays or dramas that raise issues of human rights. They can be motivated to created their own literary pieces—prose, poetry, drama or essay—regarding ideas and feelings about the violation of or enhancement of human rights. Debates can be held on similar themes. In fact, these activities can become the backbone of human rights education.

e) Topics of Interest

These are of transport, food, housing and shelter. These topics are frequently studied by the students as centres of interest. Topics of interest can also be developed around themes on international understanding which could also include outlines on the topics of food, water and clothes.

f) Inspiration from Life and Work of Famous Persons

Students can also be encouraged to find inspiration and a sense of pride in human accomplishment in learning about the lives and work of famous persons who are remembered and respected in different parts of the world for their achievement in art, science and culture or for their actions as leaders of social reforms as national freedom fighters.

g) Mechanism in Schools for the Protection of Human Rights

G.L. Arora and others writes in Mechanism for Enforcement of Human Rights, N.C.T.E., (1999). Respect for human rights is the kind of realisation that can be ingrained in the minds of children. The attitudes and values acquired by an individual during childhood generally govern one's behaviour at a later stage. Such an awareness can be created among children in the following ways:

1. *By developing human rights education programmes at all levels of education*—Various issues related to human rights should be integrated with the subjects already being taught in the schools. Ideally, a human rights culture should be built in the whole curriculum yet in practice, it will have to be treated as part of the establishment of disciplines like the social and economic sciences and the humanities.
2. *By providing an environment conducive for the inculcation of faith in human rights*—It is essential that the classroom and school environment should reflect respect for human rights. There should be no discrepancy in the functioning of the school and the principles they cherish. Schools can play an important role in the promotion of human rights by developing individuals who have respect for human rights. This can be ensured by providing a democratic environment enabling children to enjoy their rights and simultaneously learn to respect the rights of others.
3. *Avoiding violation of rights of the child*—A committee comprising teachers, students and parents can be constituted at the school level. The committee can perform various functions such as investigation, evaluation and advising in matters pertaining to violation of a child's rights in the school.

Role of Teacher Education

A student teacher has to be provided an opportunity to develop his effective domain, i.e., essential qualities such as empathy and respect for students, male or female, and a positive attitude towards fellow beings, children and society within and outside formal learning institutions.

It is important for the teacher to develop in the learner through a multipronged approach a sensitivity towards the rights of human beings. As per the Acharya Ramamurti Committee report training programmes for teachers should be competence-based and provision for integration of theory and practice in situational applications should be made, so teachers should be able to develop in the students empathy and perception of the learner profiles of children from different sections of society.

Teacher educators need to be cautious, the manner of addressing the whole co-educational class or certain group.

As a trainer of prospective teachers it becomes their prime duty to ensure that they imbibe the correct attitudes so that the coming generations may not suffer from the violation of basic rights. Some steps can be taken during the course of teaching suggested by R.L. Phutela in his paper *Rights of the Child Human Rights and National Values,* (1999), N.C.T.E.:

a) Orient the student teachers to be aware of the rights of the child and be vigilant against their violation at any point.

b) Orient the student teachers to develop a curriculum which caters to the diversified need of children.

c) Strive for a change in attitudes of the student teachers so that all children irrespective of their class or caste or sex, get equal treatment in class.

d) Ensure that the student teachers appreciate the need of children for adequate rest, play and recreation during a day and that they take measures to ensure it through activities like physical exercise, through plays dramatics, music and dance, etc.

e) Instill in the student teachers the concept that all children are autonomous citizens in their own right and should be treated as such and not as lesser human beings in the process of learning and development.

f) Ensure that the student teacher appreciates activities like pooling of tiffins in the classroom where feasible so that all children share their food and learn to appreciate variety in eating styles, irrespective of caste or class.

g) Encourage the student teachers to undertake community work as a part of their course so that they have an opportunity to build positive social attitudes towards the position of children.

h) Emphasise on the use of teaching aids in classroom teaching and other specific methods so that the slow learner is able to learn easily.

REFERENCES

Arora, G.L., Ashok Arora, Singh, D.V., *Mechanism for Enforcement of Human Rights in N.C.T.E.*, New Delhi 1999, pp. 69-70.

Basic Documents on Human Right, 1992, Clarendon Press, Oxford, pp. 15-18.

Constitution of India: Preamble 2(A), *Universal Declaration of Human Rights*, 1948 Preamble.

Department of Education (1986, 1992) *National Policy on Education 1986* (Revised in 1992), New Delhi, Ministry of Human Resource Development.

Kuldeep Agarwal, *Education and The Secondary Level Curriculum in Human Rights and National Values 1999*, N.C.T.E., New Delhi, pp. 48, 54-56.

Lanson Edward 1991, *Encyclopedia of Human Rights*, Taylor and Francis Inc., London.

Michael Vander Dussen, "The Role of Awareness And Cognitive Science in Educating Teachers" in (ed) Donald K. Sharpes (1988), International Perspective on Teacher Education, Routledge, London and New York. pp. 117-119.

Mallick, S.P., Malhotra, C.J., "Human Rights and Teacher Training" in *Human Rights and National Values*, N.C.T.E., New Delhi, 1999, pp. 4-8.

National Human Rights Commission, *Annual Report (1994-95)*, New Delhi.

N.C.E.R.T., *Fifth All India Educational Survey*, New Delhi, 1986.

______________ , Status of Woman Through Curriculum, *Elementary Teachers Hand Book*, 1982, New Delhi.

________________, Status of Woman Through Curriculum, *Secondary Teachers Hand Book*, 1982, New Delhi.

Phutela R.L., assisted by Ms. Sandhya Kumar, "Rights of The Child", in *Human Rights and National Values*, N.C.T.E., New Delhi, 1999, pp. 107-108.

Sharma, Mahesh Chand, Amita Dev Raj, Human Right.

Walia Dr. K. and Anil Kumar (Production Team), *Human Rights and National Values*—Self Learning Modules for Teacher Educators, N.C.T.E. 1999, New Delhi-16.

6

Position of Management of Human Rights in India: An Evaluation

*—Rakesh Kala**

Today the world over, there is considerable discussion on human rights and various United Nation bodies and non-governmental organisations are concerned about the implementation and protection of human rights. This is because human rights are essential for all the individuals as they are consonant with their freedom and dignity and are conducive to physical, moral, social and spiritual welfare. They are also necessary as they provides suitable conditions for the material and moral uplift of the people.[1] Human rights, which are also sometimes referred to as fundamental rights, birthrights, inherent rights and natural rights, are essential for the maintenance of human dignity.[2] Thus, because of this immense significance to human being, human rights have become an important issue in the modern world.

Today there are several national and international norms of human rights in practice, but in spite of setting the various norms of human rights, the violations are rampant. Everyday, every hour, in each region, flagrant abuses are taking place.[3] Human dignity and human norms are being destroyed and

**Lecturer, Deptt. of Political Science, H.N.B.G.U. Campus, Pauri, Gadhwal, Uttranchal.*

superseded by authoritarian values and systems. Hence, for the protection of human dignity and human norms there is a great need for proper management of human rights. Without the proper management of human rights, there can be neither peace, lasting security, nor sustained economic and social development.

The concept of human rights is very old and the roots of the rights of man may be traced as back as in the Babylonian laws, Assyrian Laws, and in the Dharma of the Vedic period in India. The history of Greek states proves that they were familiar with the modern concept of freedom of speech (Isogoria), equality before the law (lsonomia) and equal respect of all (lsotimia).[4] But it was the British charter known as the Magna Carta of 1215 which for the first time laid down the foundation of the management of human rights by establishing the rule of law. It was the first incident in the history of mankind when the human rights and liberties of the individual were managed in a written and organised manner against the authority of the state. Later, the embodiment of Bill of Rights, 1776, in the Constitution of the United States of America and the French Declaration of Rights of Man of 1789, further brightened the prospects of the protection of human dignity. The French Declaration of the Rights of Man led other European countries to include the provisions in their laws for the human rights. Hence, Sweden in 1809, Spain in 1812, Norway in 1814, Belgium in 1831, Denmark in 1849, Prussia in 1850 and Switzerland in 1874 made special provisions for the management of human rights.

Internationally, some efforts were also made in the dawn of the present century in this direction and thus, numerous treaties and agreements were concluded to contain slave trade, exploitation of human labour and women, children and racial, religious and national minorities. However, by the end of World War II a profound change occurred in the context of human rights and it was realised that the restoration of the freedom and rights to the people is one of the essential conditions for the establishment of international peace and security. Thus, all the sovereigns, politicians, policy makers, educationists and scientists of the globe expressed their anxieties in this context and wanted that a political mechanism of restraints be so formulated nationally and internationally that the existence of humanity could be saved from annihilation. It is in this context that the General Assembly of United Nations approved the 'Declaration of Human Rights' at the end of 1948.

The year of 1948 was a landmark in the history of mankind when for the first time human rights got international recognition under the Charter. It was a historical event of the world and a great achievement of the United Nations in the historical event of the world and in the history of human rights.[5] The Charter of the United Nations was the first international management of human lights which asserted the fundamental freedoms for all without regard to race, colour, sex, language and religion. Thus, for the first time human rights became the concern of international law.

The Charter recognised that international peace and a stable world order could be established only on the foundation of social justice and human rights. Setting out a common standard of achievement for all peoples and nations, the Charter expressed the resolve of the United Nations to promote social progress and better standard of life.[6]

On December 10, 1948 the United Nations General Assembly adopted the famous Universal Declaration of Human Rights which may be said to be almost the first ever international efforts to codify the fundamental human rights. Then the Declaration was followed by a series of covenants and conventions. Since thereafter the United States of America adopted a declaration of the rights and duties in 1948. Similarly, the Western European State in 1950 and in 1961 adopted the Charter and then all the neo-liberated Afro-Asian countries have made provision to manage the human rights for the people of their country.[7] Since then, various national and international instruments have been adopted to protect the human rights. These instruments together set common standards for all peoples and all nations. They set a comprehensive system and detail procedures to look into country situations or categories of abuses that are occurring around the globe.

So far as India's position is concerned it could be said that India's status of human rights is fairly high. India has not only made sufficient provisions for human rights but also provides the proper machinery to enforce these rights. Its Constitution makes provision for human rights and empowers the Supreme Court and High Courts to enforce these rights. As the framers of Indian Constitution were influenced by the concept of human rights and inspired by the Universal Declaration of Human Rights hence, they adopted the Universal Declaration of Human Rights as well as both the covenants, one on economic, social and cultural rights and the other on civil and political rights. The inspiration is evidenced in the Preamble to the Constitution and the protection of basic human rights (called the Fundamental Rights) in the body of the Constitution.

The ideal of the Universal Declaration of Human Rights is reflected in the Preamble of the Indian Constitution with the specific mention of 'dignity of the individual'. The Preamble of the Constitution declares India to be a 'Sovereign, Socialist, Secular, Democratic Republic.' Here the term 'Democratic' clearly denotes that the political sovereignty vests in the people. It also gives a feeling that all are equal irrespective of their race, religion, language, sex and culture.[8] Further, the Preamble of the Constitution secures to all citizens 'Justice, Liberty, Equality and Fraternity,' which are the main objectives of the Charter of the Universal Declaration of Human Rights.

In order to achieve the goal mentioned in the Preamble, the Constitution laid down the implementation procedure in parts III and IV which are known as Fundamental Rights and Directive Principles of the State Policy, respectively. The former guarantees certain political and civil rights to the individuals, the latter gives direction to the state to provide social and economic rights to its peoples in specified matters.

Under part III of the India Constitution, Articles 14 to 30 provide rights to equality, liberty, against exploitation, freedom of religion, cultural and educational rights with certain limitations with the consideration of keeping national integration and an individual's progress, peace and prosperity preserved. Apart from this, judicial remedies for the protection of the rights have also been provided to the citizens vide the provision of Article 32 of the Constitution. The significance of these rights could be understood from the fact that limitation has also been imposed on the central and state governments and all other local institutions not to amend, abridge or contain the use of these rights as per provisions contained in Article 13, chapter III of the Constitution.[9] The contents of the rights as mentioned under Articles 14 to 30 clearly depict that India has taken every care in guaranteeing civil rights to its citizens with adequate protection. It would also be mentioned here that a number of fundamental rights guaranteed to individuals in part III of the Constitution are similar to the provision of Universal Declaration of Human Rights. (see Appendix-I) and many rights enshrined in the covenant on civil and political rights have been recognised specifically in the Indian Constitution as Fundamental Rights.

Besides the civil and political rights, the Indian Constitution provides social and economic rights to its people under Articles 39 to 46 of the Directive Principles of State Policies. The most important of these are the following:[10]

1. Rights to adequate means of livelihood. (Art. 39)
2. Rights against economic exploitation. (Art. 39. b)
3. Equal pay for equal work for both men and women. (Art. 39 d)
4. Right to work, education. (Art. 40)
5. Right to public assistance in case of unemployment, old age, sickness, etc. (Art. 41)
6. Right to human conditions of work and maternity relief. (Art. 42)

7. Right to improvement of public health and the prohibitation of intoxicating drinks and drugs (Art. 47).

It is to be noted that though the provisions of part IV of the Constitution are not justifiable like Fundamental Rights, nevertheless, these are as much part of the Constitution as the Fundamental Rights. The state is duty-bound to give them effect. It may be stated that Fundamental Rights and Directive Principles, together constitute the conscience of the Constitution.

In addition, there are some other rights of individuals which are enacted in some other part of the constitutional limitations on the governmental powers. Article 265 lays down that no tax shall be levied or collected except by authority for laws. This implies that a person has a right not to be taxed except under a law. Similarly Article 301 guarantees freedom of trade and commerce throughout India. The freedom of trade and commerce can be regulated only under certain conditions specified by a law. Article 300-A guarantees that no person shall be deprived of his property save by authority of law.

In spite of the above, mentioned constitutional rights Indian citizens also enjoy the other important rights which, though not mentioned in the Constitution are regarded as fundamental rights. These rights have been evolved by the Indian judiciary by propounding the theory of emanation, following the example of the American Supreme Court. Applying the theory of emanation, the Supreme Court of India has evolved the following enumerated rights as fundamental rights:[11]

1. The right to privacy.
2. The right to human dignity.
3. The right to travel aboard.
4. The right against torture, cruelty or unusual punishment or degrading treatment.
5. The right to speedy trial.

6. The right to free legal aid in a criminal trial.
7. The right against delayed execution.
8. The right against custodial violence.
9. The right to shelter, doctor's assistance, and health.
10. The right to a pollution-free environment.
11. The right to education of a child until he attains the age of 14.
12. The freedom of press.

It is the unique feature of the Indian Constitution that it has not only given the rights but also made some suitable provisions to protect the same rights, as Article 13 (2) of the Constitution which empowered the judiciary with the power of judicial review. Similarly, judicial remedies for the protection of the rights have also been provided to the citizens vide the provision of Article 32 of the Constitution. Article 32 empowers the Supreme Court to issue any writ, order or direction for the enforcement of fundamental rights. Like this, a similar power is conferred on the High Court under Article 226 to issue any writ, order or direction for the enforcement of any of the fundamental rights and only other legal rights or for any other purpose.[12]

The parliament of India is the other key body which has played a vital role in respect of promotion and protection of human rights. It has made full use of the parliamentary process and of the various substantive and procedural devices available for questioning, criticising and influencing the government and even for correcting or modifying policies. Members of parliament have been quick to take note of any instances of arbitrary or high-handed executive interference with individual rights or violations of the liberties of citizens or oppression of weaker sections, and have raised these issues in the house of parliament through the various devices like Calling Attention Notices, Adjournment Motions, Question and Answer, and Short Notice Questions, etc. Parliamentary committees on

Petitions, Empowerment of Women and on the Welfare of Scheduled Castes and Scheduled Tribes also have been apprised of issues of human rights.[13] Besides, the parliament has enacted a large number of laws in the category of social or human rights legislation which prohibit debt bondage, dowries, immoral traffic of women and secure maternity benefits, protection of children, upliftment of the backward classes, free and compulsory education, etc. Apart from this, Employees State Insurance Act, Minimum Wages Act, Maternity Benefits Act, Workmen's Compensation Act, Protection of Civil Rights Act, Environmental Protection Act and Consumer Protection of Civil Rights Act, Environmental Protection Act and Consumer Protection Act, etc., also have been passed by the parliament to protect the right of individuals.

For the promotion and protection of human rights norms under the Constitution of India and fulfilment of commitments under the international human rights law, India has set up various institutions, such as the National Commission for Women, and National Commission for Scheduled Classes and Scheduled Tribes, the National Commission for Backward Classes and the National Commission for Minorities, which are specifically developed for protection and promotion of human rights. The setting up of a national institution is one of the most effective means to perform the various functions relating to the implementation of human rights. Such an institution raises human rights awareness through education, training, research and conducts impartial investigation into alleged violations. It may also assist the victims by providing relief through a court of law. Keeping in view this fact, India set up another most important institution, known as the National Commission of Human Rights (NCHR), on September 27, 1993 through an ordinance which was later replaced by Protection of Human Rights Act, 1993. The purpose of the Act was to provide for the constitution of a National Human Rights Commission, State Human Rights Commission in states and Human Rights Courts for better protection of human rights and for matters connected therewith or incidental thereto.[14] The National Human Rights

Commission and the State Human Rights Commissions have been established while the human rights court are yet to be established. There are only a few states, as Andhra Pradesh, Assam, Sikkim, Tamil Nadu and Utter Pradesh, which have taken the initiative in establishing such courts. By forming National Commission of Human Rights, India has shown to the world community that it has faith in the promotion and protection of human rights.

Suggestions For Effective Implementation

Undoubtedly, India has made a comprehensive system for the promotion and protection of human rights, But despite the various constitutional provisions, laws, and institutions the violation of human rights is increasing day by day. The number of complaints of human rights violations received by the Human Rights Commission indicate that there is a wide gap between the 'provisions and implementation' because of the absence of an effective implementation machinery. The provisions of the rights alone is not enough. They themselves cannot serve any useful purpose unless there is an effective machinery to enforce them. In addition, there are several other drawbacks in the present system which need to be modified. Thus, to make an effective management for the promotion and protection of human rights in India, the following measures should be taken immediately:

1. Today the immediate urgency of the nation is to develop a human rights culture, for which human rights values and education should be propagated in the entire nation, as these can alone create human rights culture and balance between individual and communal rights. Mutual tolerance, through education, can inculcate human rights values and respect among the functionaries and in the entire population.
2. Emphasis should be given to generate human rights awareness among the people. Most of the people are still

not aware about their human rights and fundamental freedoms. It is, therefore, the need of time to make them aware about their human rights. For this, special courses at all levels of education should be started and human rights education cell in schools and colleges should be opened.

3. The government must train and educate their judiciary police, security and armed forces about the human rights and human rights law, because these are the means by which the state seeks to met its obligation to protect the fundamental human rights, i.e., right to life, liberty and security right to fair trial and equal protection of law. For this, the training courses for police officers, judicial officers and army personals should be organised.
4. The rights of SC, ST, women, children, dalits, girl-child and minority communities should be given top priority, as they are the weaker sections of our society. The government should do something more about them in addition to framing rules, regulations and forming commissions. There is a need to evolve such a system under which the rights of these sections could be protected so that they could become self-reliant and lead a life with dignity and individuality.
5. For better implementation of human rights, the review and amendment of the Protection of Human Rights Act 1993 is necessary to ensure more autonomy to the Human Rights Commission, and it should be empowered to grant relief to the victim or to his family members, in fact, the Human Rights Commission should be developed as an autonomous institution, like the Election Commission of India, so that the functioning of the commission could be more effective. The government of India should immediately implement the recommendations made by the commission for its effective functioning.
6. It has been observed that most of the existing investigation agencies of human rights are not functioning

properly and impartially. An agency such as the state police is not expected to investigate impartially the human rights violations committed by their fellow policemen and superiors. It is therefore desirable that an impartial investigating and monitoring agency should be set up for the cases of human rights violation.

7. There can be no protection of human rights unless the existing police and jail system reformed. The Indian police is still employing primitive and barbaric methods of crime investigation. The graph of custodial deaths is increasing by using the third degree methods. Thus, the more human methods of interrogation and scientific methods of investigation should be generated and the human rights education should be made compulsory to all the policemen. Similarly, all necessary action must be taken by the government for reforming the prison system.
8. However, the role of the Indian judiciary has been significant in upfolding the values of human rights. Nevertheless, a trained judiciary could be more fruitful and effective. Efforts should be made to provide proper machinery for the enforcement of the judicial decisions. Reforms in the existing legal system is also required. Without some drastic restructuring of the legal system human rights cannot be protected like they ought to be protected.
9. Economic development is a precondition for proper safeguards of human rights which are dependent on development. Thus, sincere efforts should be taken by governments in this regard. An economic environment should be generated in which every individual can claim equality of opportunity for development. Development in terms of industrialisation and consumerism must be made from the angle of improvements in living conditions and in the quality of life.
10. For speedy trial of offences of violation of human rights, human rights courts should be established rapidly all over the country.

Thus, in India, like many other developing countries, much has to be done for the better promotion and protection of human rights. All sincere efforts are required to be made to make the people aware of their rights. The social, economic and political problems, like poverty, illiteracy, unemployment, population growth, law and order, corruption, misuse of political power have to be dealt with firmly. Hopefully, the strong will and determination of the nation, for the promotion of human dignity and worth, will certainly make the human rights movement a great success.

APPENDIX-I

Similarities in Universal Declaration and Indian Constitution.

Universal Declaration	*Indian Constitution*
Article-7	Article-14
Article-7(2)	Article-15(1)
Article-21(2)	Article-16(1)
Article-19	Article-19(1)
Article-20(1)	Article-19(1)
Article-23(4)	Article-19(1)
Article-13(1)	Article-19(1)
Article-17(1)	Article-19(1)
Article-11(2)	Article-20(1)
Article-9	Article-21
Article-18	Article-25(1)
Article-22	Article-29(1)
Article-26(3)	Article-30(1)
Article-17(2)	Article-31
Article-8	Article-31

Source: Aggarwal, H.O., *Human Rights*, Central Law Publications Allahabad, 1999, p. 18.

REFERENCES

1. Aggarwal, H.O., *Human Rights*, Central Law Publication Allahabad, 1999, p. 1.
2. Ibid.
3. Aggarwal, Mrs. Nomita, "Human Rights: An Overview", *Employment News,* Vol. XXIV, New Delhi, 14-20 August 1999, p. 1.
4. Ibid., p. 14.
5. Lauterpacht, H., *International Law and Human Rights*, 1950, p. 394.
6. Cited in Keynote Address of Dr. Subhash Kashyap, Seminar of Human Rights, organised by Dept. of Political Science, H.N.B. Garwhal University, Sri Nagar, October 3-5, 1999, p. 5.
7. Chaturvedi, S.K., Application of the Universal Declaration of Human Rights in India, paper presented at refresher course in Pol. Sc., Meerut University, Meerut, 1993, p. 6.
8. Basu, D.D., *Introduction to the Constitution of India*, 1954, p. 23.
9. Pylee, M.V., *Constitutional Government in India,* Asia Publication House, Bombay, 1965, p. 200.
10. Ibid., pp. 328-329.
11. Basu, D.D., *Human Rights in Constitutional Law*, Prentice-Hall of India, New Delhi, 1994, p. 96.
12. Diwan Paras and Peeyushi, *Human Rights and the Law*, Deep and Deep Publications, New Delhi, 1998, p. 20.
13. Cited in Keynote address of Dr. Subhash Kashyap, op.cit., p. 15.
14. Babel, B.L., *Human Rights*, Central Law Publication, Allahabad, 1999, p. 111.

7

Children's Rights and Child Labour: A Paradoxical Reality

—*Veena Gandotra**, *Maneesha Shukul*** and *Neerja Jaiswal****

Respect of human rights begins with the way society treats its children. A caring society will give freedom and dignity to young people, creating the conditions in which they can develop their full potential and so look forward to a full and satisfying adult life. The children of today—half of the world's population—will have to carry on into the future the work of creating a just and human social order.

> To look into some aspects of the future, we do not need projections by super computers. Much of the next millennium can be seen in how we care for our children today. Tomorrow's world may be influenced by science and technology; but more than anything it is already taking shape in the bodies and minds of our children.
>
> *Kofi Annan*
> *Secretary General of the United Nations (1998)*

*Prof., Deptt. of Home Management, Faculty of Home Science, M.S. University of Baroda, Vadodara.

**Reader, Deptt. of Home Management, Faculty of Home Science, M.S. University of Baroda, Vadodara.

***Lecturer, Deptt. of Home Management, Faculty of Home Science, M.S. University of Baroda, Vadodara.

Today's child is tomorrow's citizen. Children are vital resources and the most important national asset. Children need special protection and care because of their physique and tender age, as well as mental immaturity and incapacity to look after themselves. Hence, it becomes so essential that they are brought up in an atmosphere of love, affection, care and attention of parents. This will help them to attain full emotional, intellectual, spiritual stability and maturity.

This enables them to acquire self-confidence and self-respect. It is with the guidance of the parents that they develop appreciation and realisation of the role which they have to play in the nation-building process without which the nation cannot develop or attain full prosperity.

Carol Bellamy, Executive Director of the UNICEF, aptly says in *The Progress of the Nations* (1998):

> ...The community of nations is rapidly coming to grips with the fact that each and every child is entitled to whole series of fundamental rights...As we celebrate the 50th Anniversary of the Historic Document (Universal Declaration of the Human Rights, 1948), we must rededicate ourselves to ensuring that the rights set out in the declaration and the galaxy of human rights instruments that have flown from it, including the Convention on the Rights of the Child, are fulfilled for every child.

Children's Rights

Children—their welfare and their rights—have been the central concern of the United Nations since its creation in 1945. The result was the establishment of UNICEF. The Universal Declaration of Human Rights adopted by the General Assembly in 1948 recognised that children must be the subject of special care and attention. Since then, the United Nations has protected children's rights in general international treaties, such as the International Human Rights Covenants and in an instrument specifically addressed to the children's rights in the

1959–'Declaration on the Rights of the Child'. The Convention on the Rights of the Child goes further than the Declaration by making state "legally accountable" for the actions towards children.

The Convention on the Rights of the Child was adopted unanimously by the United Nations General Assembly on 20 November 1989. This event has been hailed as a landmark in international efforts to strengthen justice, peace and freedom in the world through the promotion and protection of human rights. The convention was the most complete statement of children's rights ever made and was the first to give these rights the force of international law. This convention represents "a commitment to the future" of the children.

Emerging from this, on 9th July 2001, the Charter for Children's Rights was framed and was open for suggestions and soon to be accepted by United Nations. It would not be out of place to mention a few rights as listed in the charter. They are the right to:

1) Survival
2) Health
3) Nutrition
4) Standard of Living
5) Play and leisure
6) Early childhood care
7) Education
8) Protection
9) Protection of the girl child
10) Equality
11) Of adolescents to education and skill development
12) Life, liberty, name and nationality
13) Freedom of expression
14) Freedom to seek and receive information

15) To a family and
16) To be protected from economic exploitation.
(19/08/2001, http:/www.weca.nic.in/cnar on no.ntm)

The proposed "right of children to be protected from economic exploitation" specifies that the state shall provide protection to children from economic exploitation and from performing tasks that are hazardous to their well-being. It also specifies that the state shall ensure that there is appropriate regulation of conditions of work in occupations and processes where children perform work of a non-hazardous nature and the rights of the child are protected. The most important part of it says that the state shall move towards a total ban of all forms of child labour.

Child Labour: A Paradox to Child's Rights

Child labour constitutes a violation of children's rights. Despite constitutional and legal provisions made by various countries, children continue to be employed and occupied in work.

Child labour is not a new phenomenon. It has existed in one form or another throughout man's history. It is a universal fact that today's child forms an important section of labour force in almost all sectors of employment in all the less developed and developing economies.

There is a great variation in the definition of children. While the Census defines children as below 14 years, the Convention on Rights of Child below 18 years, the Constitution considers child labour to relate to those below 14 years as in section 2 (ii) of Child Labour Act 1986, but under section 2 (c) of the Factories Act, 1948 a child means a person who has not completed his 15th year of age. However, the employment of children under a specified legal age is termed as Child Labour. Lakshapathi aptly says:

> A child worker is a person in the age group of 5-14, employed for hire or reward on a full time or part time basis, or self-employed, or assisting his/her parents in their occupations for 2 or more hours a day.

The Convention on the Rights of Child (CRC) and the ILO Convention on Child Labour define children as under the age of 18 years which includes an almost entire adolescent group based on the WHO definition.

According to Child Labour Prohibition and Regulation Act of 1986, employment of children up to the age of 14 years and in case of hazardous employments up to 18 years is defined as child labour.

Magnitude of Child Labour

Estimates of the number of children employed are difficult to obtain. Such "invisibility" is greater for girls as they mainly work in the domestic sector. Statistics on child labour are elusive not only because of the practical difficulties involved in the design and implementation of child labour surveys but also because of difference in perception about what constitutes a child or child labour or child work. Even then many estimates are available. Some of the estimates made by various organisations are worth noting which will throw some light on the magnitude of the problem of child labour.

According to ILO (1995) there were seventy-three million child labourers between the age of 10 and 14 years, in the world of which, in Asia they were 44.6 millions, in Africa 23.6 millions and in Latin America 5.1 million. As reported in the 1961 census of India there were 14.5 million; in 1971; it came down to 10.8 million; in 1981 it was 13.6 million; whereas in 1987-88, according to the National Sample Survey it was 17.5 million.

According to the 1991 census estimates, out of about a total of 200 million children over the world in the age group of 5-14 years, some 11.28 million children are child labourers. However, NGO estimates of child labour in India range from 40 million to over 100 million.

According to estimates presented by Nangia children ranging from 30,000 to 1,50,000 were engaged in carpet weaving in Kashmir, Varanasi, Bhadohi and Rajasthan states.

About 50,000 children were engaged in match and firework industry in Sivakasi (Tamil Nadu). Nearly 80,000 children were working in coir industry in Kerala, and 50,000 were working in glass industry in Firozabad in U.P.; in Bidi making industry about 7,000 children were working in Tiruchirapalli in Tamil Nadu. In lead mines of Meghalaya also as many as 28,000 children worked. There are many other industries where children work as labourers.

Nature of Child Labour

The child employment is visible in almost all industries where unskilled labour and limited physical strength could be utilised.

Padmakumari (1993) divides occupation of children into four major groups:

1. Agriculture
2. Manufacture
3. Trade
4. Domestic

Child labour is believed to exist at a smaller scale in the organised sector like match factories, tea factories and mica industries, but a large number of children are employed in unorganised sector such as hotel industry including tea shops and wayside restaurants, domestic services, carpet and metal industry. They are also employed in newspaper selling, coolie work and in cottage and other small industries. Child labour can be categorised as follows.

1. *Domestic work* : Cleaning, looking after siblings, fetching water, etc.
2. *Non-domestic, non-monetary work* : Looking after cattle and sheep, collecting firewood, scaring away birds.
3. *Bonded labour*: Child pledged against a loan, bonded to work for life.

4. *Wage labourer*: Part of family labour, small or large industrial enterprises, roadside cafes, motor repair workshops, errand boys, etc.
5. *Marginal economic activity:* The self-employed child selling, newspapers, peanuts fruits, vegetables, shoeshining, collecting garbages.

Another way of classifying child labour is based on the location of work.

1. Within the family (which is unpaid) such as:
   a) Domestic tasks such as cooking, child care, cleaning of utensils, clothes, poultry, etc.
   b) Handicrafts/cottage industry based at home such as weaving baskets, leather work, woodwork, etc.
2. With the family but outside the home: Such as (a) domestic servant (b) construction work (c) mining (d) informal economy where employed by others, e.g., laundry, or self-employed, e.g., garbage collection selling.
3. Outside family:
   a) Employed by the others as (1) bonded labour (2) apprentice (3) skilled trades like carpet embroidery, brasswork, gem polishing (4) domestic servant (5) commercial shops, restaurants, etc. (6) industries or unskilled occupation, mines, etc. (7) begging (8) prostitution and pornography.
   b) Self-employed in informal sector such as (1) shoeshining (2) car washing (3) selling newspaper (4) recycling rubbish, etc.

Situation of Working Children and Their Exploitation

The situation of working children is pathetic and they are exploited to a great extent in the following aspects:

1. *Hours of work*: Generally they work for six to eight hours per day, sometimes even 12 to 14 hours. Often there are no fixed hours in certain kinds of work.
2. *Wages:* In most of the cases children are employed as family labourer, no separate wage is paid to the child. In the industries they are paid lower wages for the same work as adult. They are treated as 'apprentice' for a long period even though the actual work is being done.
3. *Health:* The element of risk is always there in whatever occupation the children are engaged. They get tired easily and the fatigue sets in due to their tender bodies. They work in unhygienic conditions having poor light and poor ventilation. The uncomfortable postures in which they work results in aches, pains, stiffened legs and joints and ultimately their growth gets arrested. In cases of extreme exploitation such as prostitution they are victims of sexually transmitted diseases.
4. *Occupational hazards:* Long hours of work may lead to accidents where, in such events, no first aid facility is available nor social security and accident insurance scheme. Children are exposed to toxic and severely harmful substances such as silica dust, pesticide, etc. In many kinds of work they are exposed to excessive heat, many a time there is a risk of being badly injured or burned.

Causes of Child Labour

The causes of child labour are many and deep-rooted and interwoven in social and cultural heritage of Indian society. It is a socio-economic problem. The International Labour Organisation has rightly observed that child labour is essentially a problem of development. It is a phenomenon deeply rooted in economic and social conditions. Some of the main causes are as follows:

1. High Population Growth
   a) Decreased infant mortality and increased life expectancy, more dependency burden on the earning member of the family.
   b) Many children produced of a couple with underlying philosophy, "Two hands to work but only one mouth to feed".
   c) Each member of the family is required to contribute to the family's purse.
2. *Poverty:* The root cause
   a) Low per capita income due to large family.
   b) Rising cost of living.
   c) To meet even basic necessities among masses of low socio-economic people, children are required to work.
3. Lack of Schooling
   a) Lack of motivation for schooling on the part of parent and children.
   b) Low priority for education by parents as they think that school education is useless, "does not equip child for his future," "education would motivate him to run away from rural home and traditional craft" etc.
   c) Parents think: "Since he has to earn his living, he may as well start as young as possible".
   d) Parent's attitude: "more fruitful use of time than spending on schooling."
   e) Lack of sufficient, easily accessible, suitable educational facilities.
   f) Girls required to take care of house and siblings while parents work.
4. Traditional craft taught to children

   While helping the parents, children are taught traditional craft of the parents which becomes a regular economic activity later.

5. Unemployment/ Underemployment of Parents

   Death/disease/illness of earning parent forces child to be in the labour force.

6. Family Tensions/Parental Apathy

   Broken homes, tensions within the homes, parental rejection lead to (i) avoidance of schooling (ii) necessitates earning and (iii) running away from home, hence earn for self-survival.

7. Migrancy from Village

   a) Family migration from rural to urban area, hence child's work needed to supplement family income.

   b) Child runs away from rural to urban area, so earn for self-support.

8. Profit Motives of Employees

   a) Child is hired on low wages than adult for the same amount of work.

   b) Does not demand benefits as per the law.

9. "Nimble Fingers" Argument

   Children preferred as workers in certain industries (carpet weaving) due to alleged "nimble fingers".

Consequence of Child Labour

Child labour has many-facet consequences.

1. *Physical Consequences:* Working conditions and environment such as excessive heat, bad inner atmosphere, dust, noise, poor light and ventilation, harmful gases, overcrowdedness may lead to skin troubles, bronchitis, tuberculosis, defects in eyes and ears, and many other diseases. Anaemia and chronic bronchitis are also common among child workers. Physical growth retardation or deformities may result because of heavy loads, awkward body positions, chronic fatigue. Over-exertion coupled with unbalanced diet may lead to malnutrition.

2. *Psycho-social Consequences:* Child labour is deprived of opportunities to play, educate himself, recreation, love and parental affection. Working children are physically, emotionally and sexually abused by their employers. Psychologically disturbed children may become ill-tempered, they may resort to lying and stealing, may start consuming drugs and may become aggressive, anti-social and delinquent. A working child is denied the opportunities of upward mobility. Illiteracy ensures that the child remains an unskilled labourer forever, with no hope of upward mobility or freedom from oppression.

Strategy for Eradication and Elevation of Child Labour

The problem of child labour may not be a basic disease. It may be a symptom and a clear indicator of the alarming deficiencies of the basic socio-economic structure of the society. But as the socio-economic development is a very long and slow process, it may take decades to abolish the child labour in the country. During the last few years, pressure to eliminate or at least reduce child labour has significantly increased, and both national and international agencies are putting in the their best efforts to achieve this. Since the problem is complex and multi-dimensional, a variety of intervention strategies at all levels becomes imperative.

After independence, the Constitution of India recognised the need for granting special protection to child workers. In *Fundamental Rights* specific provisions in regard to children have been made in part III of the Constitution. "The Directive Principles of the State of Policy" also emphasizes this aspect.

Several legislations and executive orders have been exacted from time to time. A beginning was made way back in 1881. India was one of the founder-members of the I.L.O. and was a signatory to the first convention on the prohibition of child labour in 1919. Since then a number of Acts have been passed in India the latest being Child Labour (Prohibition and

Regulation)Act, 1986. The legislation concerning child labour deals mainly with four points:

i) Minimum age for employment of children
ii) A minimum period of work per day and forbidding work at night
iii) Prohibition of certain types of work for children
iv) Medical examination of all working children.

Even this act covers only children in the organised sector and not the 90 per cent in the unorganised sector or family units.

Unfortunately the implementation of the laws is very ineffective due to lack of adequate enforcement machinery, bribing the officials by employers and lack of number of inspectors. The Committee on the Rights of the Child 2000 recommends to India that states and districts establish and oversee child labour vigilance committees and ensure that labour inspectors have enough resources to effectively carry out their work. Besides legislations and its implementation, there must be an effective monitoring system in place. The employers must keep a record of the age of children employed. But any legislation totally prohibiting child labour would amount to hardships to the poor parents and their children. Moreover, Anker *et.al.* opine that the child labour problem in India cannot be solved by elimination of child labour in one or a few industries, because many of thus displaced child labourers would move to other industries.

The National Child Labour Policy has been framed to take care of the administration and welfare aspects since mere legislation is not enough to cope with this problem. The Ministry of Labour, Government of India has recognised the area of child labour concentration in Indian states and industries and have selected them under the National Child Labour Programme for Rehabilitation. They are as follows:

1) Carpet industry, Jammu and Kashmir
2) Brassware, Moradabad, U.P.

3) Lock, Aligarh
4) Glass, Firozabad, U.P.
5) Carpet, Varanasi, U.P.
6) Precious stone polishing, Jaipur, Rajasthan
7) Slate industry, Mandsaur, M.P.
8) Slate industry, Markapur, Andhra Pradesh
9) Diamond polishing, Surat, Gujarat
10) Match and firework industry, Sivakasi, Tamil Nadu
11) Gem polishing industry, Rajasthan.

According to Wermer Blenk, Programme Manager, ILO Geneva:

> International labour Organisation (ILO) launched a world-wide "Programme or Elimination of Child Labour (IPEC)". In India it was started in 1992. It has been able to involve government, workers and employers' organisations, N.G.O.S. research organisation and social scientists and bring them together in search of a better understanding of the problem and in developing and implementing the solution.

The strategy for eradication and elevation of child labour should have the following integrated approaches:

1) *Comprehensive approach:* A collective and all-round effort from the government, N.G.O. social workers, educational institutions, researcher, etc.
2) *Goal-oriented approach:* Setting and working for long as well as short term goals for eradication and /or reduction and elevation of child labour.
   a) *Long term goals* : Eradication of child labour
      i) Reduction of poverty
      ii) Provision of adequate employment of adults

iii) Reduction in magnitude of child labour

iv) Rehabilitation programme for displaced child labour

v) Creating public awareness about child's rights and labour

vi) Compulsory primary education

vii) Adequate provision of educational facilities.

viii) Effective enforcement of law and coverage of children working in an unorganised sector under the law.

ix) Movements of trade union against employment of children.

b) Short Term Goal : Improve the quality of life of working children

i) Improve educational status of working children by providing education at a convenient time and place.

ii) Improve health status of working children by proper nutrition, regular medical check-up.

iii) Improve work conditions of children by adequate light, ventilation, sanitation, proper sitting conditions.

iv) Safeguard children against occupational hazards.

v) Provide adequate and suitable recreational facilities to prevent children driffing into delinquency, vagrancy, prostitution, drug addictions etc.

vi) Movement by trade unions to improve working conditions of children.

vii) Effective supervisory machinery of government to improve quality of life of working children.

viii) Collective effort from social workers, N.G.O., educational institutions, etc., to monitor and elevate the quality of life of working children.

CONCLUSION

Children—tomorrow's citizens and precious national assets—would learn to respect human rights if they are provided with fulfilment of their rights. One of the child rights is protection from exploitation, especially economic exploitation. The clear violation of this is involvement of millions of children in labour force as child labour, mostly in unpaid/low paid forms. Children are exposed to occupational hazards having serious consequences on their mental and physical development. The government has passed Acts and has a special policy for children but it lacks effective enforcement machinery. There is a need to combat poverty and adult unemployment being the root cause of child labour. An integrated, comprehensive goal-oriented approach to eradicate and/or reduce and alleviate the conditions of working children is required from not only the government but also from NGO, social workers and educational institutions.

REFERENCES

Annan, Kofi, A., 1998, "Foreword", *The State of World's Children,* Oxford; U.K., Oxford University Press.

Belleamy, Carol, 1998, *The State of the World's Children,* Oxford, U.K., UNICEF, Oxford University Press.

Bezbaruah and M.K. Janeja, 2000, New Delhi, *Adolescents in India—A profile,*/UNFPA, for U.N. System in India.

Charter for Children's Rights (2001), http:/www.wca.nic.in/ charter Onna.ntum.

Common Position Paper of the System in India on "Child Labour" 1998.

Economic Times, 1985, High incidences of child labour, 12:228, November 10., pp. 5.

Gupta, M. and Klaus Vol, (1998), *Course Materials on Child Labour in India,* New Delhi, Published by Authors.

Lakshapathi, P., 1993, "The Rights of Working Children in India," in *Child Labour Multi-Dimensional Problem* by K. Srinivasan and V. Gandotra (Eds), Delhi, Ajanta Publications.

Ministry of Labour, 1981, *Report of Child Labour in Indian Industries,* Simla, Labour Bureau; Government of India.

Nangia, Praveen, 1987, *Child Labour Cause-effect Syndrome,* Bombay, Janak Publishers.

New Encyclopedia Britannica, 1978, Micro Paedia Vol. II 15th Ed. p. 329.

Padmakumari, K. V., 1993, "Child Labour, its Nature and Extent of Exploitation", in *Child Labour-Multi Dimensional Problem by* K. Srinivasan and V. Gandotra (Eds.) Delhi, Ajanta Publications.

Pichholiya, K.R. and B.L. Tripathi, 1993, "Prevention of Child Labour: An Action Programme for Gujarat State" in *Children at Work: Problems and Policy Options,* Singh B.P. and M. Shukla (Eds.), New Delhi, B.R. Publishing Corporation.

Richard, Anker S. Barge, S. Rajgopal and M.P. Joseph (Eds.), *Economics of Child Labour in Hazardous Industries of India,* Baroda, Centre for Operations Research and Training (CORT).

Saxena, S.B., 1993, "A Profile of Working Children in a Village of Gujarat", in *Child Labour Multi Dimensional Problem* by K. Srinivasan and V. Gandotra (Eds.) Delhi, Ajanta Publications.

Singh Leena, 1993, "A Profile of Working Children in India: An Overview", in *Children at Work.—Problems and Policy Options* Delhi, B.R. Publishing Corporation.

Vaswani, T., 1993, "Multi-Dimensional Problem of Child Labour and Multi-Pronged Approach", in *Child Labour Multi-Dimensional Problem,* Delhi, Ajanta Publication.

Wermer, Blenk, 1998, "Foreword" in *Economics of Child Labour in Hazardous Industries of India,* Baroda, Centre for Operation Research and Trainings.

8

Politics of Human Rights and Globalisation

*—Sujata Dasgupta**

Scientific and technological advancement by way of discoveries have shrunk the world of today into a small village, where each one knows each one and any happenings in one remote corner becomes a stirring force for the rest of the world. Howsoever a country might be with the impregnable geographical frontiers, yet insecurity looms large and is subject to maddening crowd's ignoble strife. A friendly or hostile relation between those of major importance in the life of the world implies that a state of constant flux and fluctuation becomes its principal characteristics. Desires and cravings, social consciousness and fear, mutual suspicion of man against man, and other factors are behavioural foundations of what culminates into a nation.

A political system is the basis of all activities in a state, immaterial of what kind of a system it is. Once the system is introduced, those in power and authority keep on maintaining that all costs, since no one is completely beyond the reach of some kind of political system, as everyone is involved in some fashion at some time is some kind of political system, either willingly or unwillingly. In the modern days many new systems are emerging and are coming to the front, while being tested for their acceptability. India is in particular a laboratory of

* *Head of Political Science Department in B.S.V.P. College for Women, University of Banglore.*

development and change, a static society in progress, with a political system grounded in conservative traditions but nevertheless in a process of change, sometimes operations in particular ways and often strangely affected by non-political forces and development.

In the thought world of social sciences the theme of human rights has been to lift itself from an ignoble position, as its horizons have rapidly expanded, while the recent trends and ongoings have been inextricably connected with the ground realities, and to place the tenets before the readers in the drive behind this instant venture. The scope and nature of the discipline have crossed the traditional boundary, reaching wider fields of thought and probe. Unimaginable, at the beginning of the last century, to theory building, policy formulating, and even advising, in the beginning of the new millennium it is not only elevating but also has pride for the members of this generation.

The foundation of the United Nations was laid on the ashes of the League of Nations, nicknamed as disrupted daughter of a dishonourable mother after the stigma of dismal failure was attached to it. The preamble and articles of the charter of United Nations expressed the guiding spirit of the world body, also to reaffirm faith in fundamental human rights. The hope of mankind still lies in strengthening the United Nations in spite of its known shortcomings and limitations. Killing the United Nations may blow up the dam that has prevented wars from spreading, and might do the same in future, as killing it increases tremendously the chances that man may one day wipe himself off the face of the earth. No doubt, there is disturbing evidence that vital United Nations programmes are losing momentum; and continuance of such a trend may disillusion people in the Third World countries, is also a gloomy apprehension; and the United Nations must be kept from wasting away from political malnutrition.

Since the time of King John of England the idea of human rights has been known in Europe though under various names, which established principles of due process and equality before the law, as also contained provisions forbidding official misconduct. The idea of "National Rights" emerged in Europe during the eighteenth and nineteenth centuries. Rights belong to one by nature, being a human being and not by his citizenship and membership of any social group, an idea which faced vigorous debate and rejection by many a philosopher as baseless. Revolutions in the late eighteenth century in North America and France, resulted in proclamation of unalienable rights in US declaration of independence, and "Declaration of the Rights of Man" by the First French Republic.

The concept of 'nature rights' fell eventually into disfavour, but the idea of 'universal rights' took root, as the then philosophers expanded the concept. In his treatise, *Civil Disobedience* it was Thoreau who among the philosophers was the first to use the term "human right". Gandhi and King erected their concept of non-violent resistance to unethical government acts from the postulates of Thoreau, J.S. Mill's, *Essay on Liberty* and Thomas Paine's essay, *The rights of Man*, need a mention too.

Many of the issues which took centre stage in the nineteenth century, which later in the twentieth century were considered as human rights issues, in the Americas, then was known as the "Indian Problem". However, neither the emancipated American slaves nor the freed Russian serfs saw any real degree of freedom or basic rights for many more decades that followed. The last part of nineteenth century and the first half of last century human rights activism remained largely tied to political and religious factions. None the less several civil rights movements and human rights movements managed to affect social changes. Credibility stood hampered when concerns were found to be political and not-humanitarian encouraging partisan protests and more oppression, uninvolved citizens who got caught in cross-fires cursed both sides and turned deaf-ears.

The Appeal for Amnesty, 1961, in respect on the six "prisoners of conscience" from different countries and backgrounds, needs a mention, as the response to the appeal resulted eventually in the birth of both Amnesty International and the 'modern human rights movement', whose early years were rather rocky. Amnesty sticks to what it knows and not go outside its mandate, and does not take position on many issues, which many view as human rights concerns and does not endorse or criticise any form of government. It works on behalf of individual prisoners, and abolishes specific practices like torture and death penalty. Many activists felt that human rights could be better served by a broader field of action.

Over the years combinations of concerns led to formation of other groups, including those which later merged to form "Human Rights Watch", first one being, 'Helsinki Watch' 1978. 'Regional Human Rights Watchdog Groups' operated under extremely difficult conditions. Recognition for human rights movement and Amnesty International grew during the seventies of the last century.

Both, state and rights also called human rights—have acquired the status of subjects of political science, as any analysis of right cannot remain outside the political theory. Natural rights are the products of natural law, and the validity of positive laws or manmade laws are tested by their capacity to protect or implement the natural rights. The importance of natural rights and natural laws declined—the emergence of positivism was chiefly responsible for that. Concessions granted by society or the states arc not rights, since rights are products of law. Concessions can be withdrawn to the extent that the state deems such withdrawals of its recognition compatible with the interests of general welfare.

The emergence of utilitarianism and Marxism caused the eclipse of natural rights. To the Marxists natural rights have no historical perspective. Extreme libertarians and libertarian anarchists deemed rights as excessive private affairs. Rise of totalitarianism and fascism made a heavy jolt to the realisation of rights. Stress upon the need for reformulation of the idea of rights and the role of state in the field of protection, resulted in concern for individual rights which increased manifold. Rights are not asserted defensively against the action of the state, while any claim for the satisfaction of human needs cannot be called a right. A justified expectation may appeal to legal authority or law and also moral consciousness. All social people have both legal and ethical rights.

For some, rights are self-conscious claims of individuals to understand and develop moral goodness, making the individual identify with the rest of the society. We think of rights more in constructive terms and not in negative ways, as a responsible state cannot be a helpless onlooker of all the social events. Rights for few or rights for many, calls for structuring society to all its sections to enjoy the fruits of rights. Claim rights are different from favours or concessions which are awarded by authorities or individuals. Claim rights are by virtue of a law or agreement, suspendable by the holder or amendable by a rule or changeable in terms of agreement.

Laski placed individuals and state on the same plank, and called rights a social concept which are deeply connected with social life, which individuals claim for development of their best self, in which the state has primary duty to help individuals, as rights completely depend upon institutions and recognition by state through laws, which determine the character and implementation of rights. The legal theory of rights, though attractive, is highly questionable, having nothing to contribute to an adequate political philosophy. The validity of rights is not derived from recognition by state. Rights are corrective to functions, since they are implicit in rights. Recognition of individuals rights to resist, implies and admits liberal philosophy.

Mere declaration of rights is not enough for any society, without maintenance of justice. Purpose of rights is to maximise liberty to enjoy rights. Equality has to be in terms of capacity for enjoyment and exercise of rights, being legal and not social.

When goodwill, cooperation, and friendship become the basis of human relation, it is fraternity, so essential for development of personality, and so necessary for maximisation of justice. The liberal theory of rights as above, implies how people's rights can be extended or modified in the prevailing structure of capitalist society. Liberal philosophies emphasize political rights, which alone cannot materialise the ambition of individuals.

Mere announcement of equal right idea cannot absolve theorists of responsibility. Right by its very nature can consist only in the application of an equal standard. The concepts of equal rights and justice are abstract, and unrelated to real situation of society. Ideas of justice vary from time to time and place to place, and a highly volatile concept cannot be a reliable determiner of rights. The idea of external justice is misleading, in a changing world, since external means not the same to all. Marxist view of rights suffers from ambivalence.

The progress of civilisation is of prime necessity and that could be possible if maximum human progress was achieved. Rights are indispensable for the progress of civilisation, and man and the state have something to do. An expansion of state activity may extend the rights of individuals.

A widespread acceptance of the principles of human rights does not mean that there is complete agreement about the nature of such rights or their substantive scope, as some of the basic questions have yet to receive conclusive answers. Many issues are matters of an ongoing debate, and will likely remain so long as there exists contending approaches to public order and scarcities among resources. Despite the lack of consensus, a number of widely and interrelated postulates may be seen to reflect. Yet any postulates, that stand out though accurate, are fraught with questions about the content and legitimate scope of human rights and any priorities, and not without controversy. Like all normative traditions, human rights as a tradition is a product of its time, reflecting the process of historical continuity and change. All human rights form an indivisible whole, and its protection is not a matter of purely domestic jurisdiction.

India is criticised for human rights violations although it has been at pains to awaken the global consciousness, to combating international and cross-border terrorism. India has made significant contribution in setting up a national human rights constitution. Education on human rights and strategies for rights invite development. Work done by the National Human Rights Commission in India is appreciable. It handles a very substantial case load. It is quiet pathfinder for looking at individual complaints, as also trying to share ways of doing that will be effective.

India has prided itself on being a pluralistic state and is rightly admired for being the largest democracy, which is not an easy system, and needs resolution and support, yet complicated. The increasing violence unleashed by non-state actors of terrorist groups and militia, mercenary groups within the nations such as private armies, increasingly pose a problem causing worry and terrible threat.

Today's world order is getting known as 'globalisation'. The demise of the Cold War helped the emergence of a new aggressive competitive order, with negative impacts in developing societies. Globalisation is not a simple but complex set of processes that operates at the multiple level, making humanity perceivable as fundamentally one, with a common destiny that is the result of a technological revolution in information and communication and the awareness of unsustainability of the current way of life. Globalisation has substantially contributed to the intensification of debt, poverty and crisis in the developing world, creating a situation where the role and importance of nation-state is becoming irrelevant. Globalisation requires the humiliation of hundreds of millions of people keeping them in constant insecurity, pitting them against one another in competitive struggle for survival. Global corporations have replaced colonial powers, and allowed to feast on natural resources, human resources, and national wealth, displacing farmers from their land, workers from jobs, and communications from their roots. National governments are becoming the implements of orders received from the international actors. This results in creation of powerlessness of suffering, many in Third World countries, resulting in violations of rights of millions of people.

The relation between globalisation, development and human rights raises policy and legal questions. Human rights have become an integral part of the process of globalisation in many ways. Globalisation intensifies impoverishment and violates human rights and human dignity. The concept of development itself is interpreted differently and the concept of right to development is not taken seriously. Global integration of structures, processes and ideologies produce injustice, oppression, exploitation and mal-development in society. Systematic integration of the forces that are dominant in the globalisation process intensifies human rights violations. Human rights have become another arsenal of Western countries in their bid to bring recalcitrant Third World nations to heel on their New World order. A shift in policy is based on convenience rather than on ideological convictions or moral principles. Examples of double standards adopted by affluent countries that profess concern for human rights, are not of unknown antiquity. Global giant operations through earth-spanning technologies have a negative impact on human rights. Globalisation has its winners and losers.

A look at the impact of globalisation of human rights reflects that, as global economic forces shape a new world order, human rights face urgent new challenges. Uprisings, massive layoffs and protests stand reported by media as separate and distinct events, which are linked to forces of globalisation, the economic engine that is transforming the world in its own image. Globalisation and human rights take viewers on a journey that starts at a summit for corporate decision makers, while examining an emerging conflict in a new world order between those making macro-economic decisions and those struggling to cope with the impact of those decisions. At the core of the programme is the ongoing debate over whether or not human rights concerns should be linked to economic policies. Globalisation and human rights go behind-the-scenes to look at the role played by giant and powerful transnational corporations and global agencies.

Globalisation has brought in its train, great inequalities, mass impoverishment and despair. It has fractured society along the existing fault line of class, gender and community which, almost irreversibly, widens the gap internationally between the rich and poor nations, resulting in gross human rights violations for millions. The political management of the world is done through the United Nations and other global structures, networks, and forces. The relation between globalisation, development, and human rights raises many more questions. Promoted by "Washington Consensus", based on market and its logic, is the market-oriented development paradigm, which implies exploitation, making exclusion an inevitable part of progress, making expansion and exclusion happen in the same breath.

Much uncertainty remains regarding the political effectiveness of sanctions, which are questionable ethically because they impose disproportionate harm on the innocent, as suffering inflicted on vulnerable groups in the target country cannot be deemed as a legitimate means of exerting pressure on political leaders. Any sanction that goes beyond a standard, loses political and moral legitimacy. Sanctions should never deprive the civilians of the basic human right to life and survival. Mostly, sanctions are a prelude to war rather than an alternative.

Whatever may be the attitudes and policies of governments, reality of popular demands for human rights including political freedom beyond debate deepening and widening concern for promotion and protection of all fronts, hastened by the self-determinist impulse in post-colonial era, is now unmistakably woven into the fabric of contemporary world affairs.

Substantially responsible for this progressive development has been, of course, the work of the United Nations, and its allied agencies. The application of international human rights law depends for the most part on the voluntary consent of nations whose formidable obstacles attend the endeavours of human rights policymakers, activists, and scholars. The implementation of human rights prescriptions bespeaks wide.

Spread resistance and rejections. The mechanisms for the observances or enforcements of human rights are, overall, yet in their infancy. It is certain that a palpable concern for the advancement of human rights is here to stay, out of necessity no less than out of idealism.

9

'Human Rights' Chandigarh Chapter, Dev Samaj College of Education for Women

—*Satindra Dhillon**

Since its inception, human right have been a priority issue for the United Nations. According to the UN Secretary-General Kofi Annan, "human rights are at the core of the UN sacred bond with the peoples of the United Nations." We feel honoured to be a part of an institution which to the best of its ability believes in promoting one of its major human rights, i.e., the right to education. As is envisaged in Article 26 of the Universal Declaration of Human Rights, "...Technical and professional education shall be made generally available and higher education shall be equally accessible to all on the basis of merit." We are proud to say that in our college merit is given its due recognition.

Our college started the journey of spreading HRE among students by inaugurating the Human Rights Education Cell in May 1997 under the guidance of Dr. Gulab Churasia. It is our firm opinion that the training colleges of education are the real beacons of society as they bring forth and develop trained personalities who are themselves intellectually, socially, culturally, emotionally, morally, and physically made fit so that out of each sound trunk, many fruitful branches can emerge.

* *Principal, Dev Samaj College of Education, Chandigarh.*

Report of the Activities of the Human Rights Club of Dev Samaj College of Education for Women, Chandigarh, for the Session 1998-99

The main objective of the club is to spread awareness among the masses about the human rights and to educate them about these rights. The beginning is done every year with the new group of students. Lectures and discussions are held from time to time during the time period allotted in the timetable for the club activities.

Some of the members of the club visited the Mini Secretariat to meet the members of the Human Rights Commission and this proved to be a source of inspiration for them.

The student members visited various schools in the city assigned to them to motivate the students and teachers for setting up human rights cells in their respective schools. The student members were successful in setting up human rights cells in various Government high schools, government Senior Secondary schools and a few public schools. The student members gave lectures on the human rights and duties and threw light on the various articles under the Universal Declaration of Human Rights and Human Rights in Indian Constitution and Law. The school students were very enthusiastic and participated in all the activities actively. The rights of the child, especially the girl-child, all forms of discrimination against women and the right to education, etc., were emphasized in particular. Various competitions were held in the schools with the cooperation of the school teachers in charge of their respective Human Rights Cells on the theme of human rights. These competitions were slogan writing, paper reading, essay writing competitions, etc. Prizes were given to the outstanding winners in the various competitions and also to the participants so as to encourage them for active future participation in other activities also. The response of the students was very good and highly commendable.

On 10 December 1998, a function was organised to mark the 50th anniversary of the Universal Declaration of Human Rights. Prof. Pam Rajput and Dr. Mohd. Khalid were the guests on the occasion. On-the-spot poster making, slogan writing and cartoon making competition of the college students was also conducted and the distinguished guest, Prof. Pam Rajput, gave away the prizes.

The student members visited Kajheri during the N.S.S. camp from 24 to 30 September 1998. They conducted a survey and collected data related to the number of family members, their educational qualifications, monthly income, medical problems, cleanliness habits and enlightened them about their rights and duties. Writing materials were distributed to the needy children and they were also taught by our college students.

A Seminar-cum-Workshop on "Human Rights Education in Schools and Colleges—A Plan of Action" was organised by our college on 21–22nd December 1998. This was inaugurated by D.S. Mangat PCS (D.P.I. Schools and Colleges). There were eighteen resource persons in all who presented their papers in the various sessions. In the workshop. The Panel Discussion was held with Dr. R.K. Behl (Retd. Director, State Institute of Education, Chandigarh) as the Chairperson. The member of the panel included Dr. D.R. Vij, an eminent educationist from Jalandhar, Dr. Keshav Mandadi, Education Officer, Kendriya Vidyalaya Sangathan, Dr. Satinder Dhillon, Principal of the host college, (Dr. Urmila Sharma and D.S. Rani, Senior Lecturers of the college. Three groups were assigned the task of preparing the recommendations of HRE at the primary level, secondary level, and college level.

Dr. Satinder Dhillon attended a Conference on UN Decade for Human Rights Education (1995-2004) at Udaipur along with Dr. Jyoti Khanna and Manjula Kataria on 4 and 5 October 1998 and presented a paper there.

Dr. Satinder Dhillon was the Regional Representative at the "UGC British Counsel Workshop on Human Rights

Education—Challenges and Opportunities" organised at New Delhi on 30 November 1998. She had been specially invited to organise the syllabus of human rights at the graduation level.

Mandeep Grewal, in charge of the Human Rights Club, attended a lecture on human rights by Lord Lester of Herne Hill on 17 December, 1998 organised by the time Group in association with UNESCO and NHRC at New Delhi.

Liveleen, a student, participated in a conference with students and staff of Luther College, USA. organised by the Indian Council of Women Entrepreneurs, Punjab on 16 January 1999 at UT Guest House, Chandigarh.

Dr. Satinder Dhillon attended with Mary Robinson a meeting "UN High Commissioner of Human Rights" on 17 February 1999 at New Delhi.

The first women's cell in a college was set up on 8 March 1999 as part of the International Women's Day celebrated by the NSS Unit of our college. This cell was inaugurated by Prof. Pam Rajput, Director of the Women's Studies Centre of Punjab University. The issues raised during the discussion were discrimination against women, sexual harassment, female infanticide and obscenity in mass media.

In November 1999, Dr. Satinder Dhillon attended a seminar which raised its voice against the fashion shows being organised at all levels without any proper aim and utility.

Report on the Activities of the Human Rights Club of Deve Samaj College of Education for Women, Chandigarh, for the Session 1999-2000

Introductory lectures to the students of the college on the Articles of the Universal Declaration of Human Rights were delivered. Discussions were held with smaller groups of students.

During the teaching practice, i.e., 9 to 22 November 1999, the students of the college spread awareness about human rights amongst the students of different classes in the various practising schools, through lectures and discussions. The Hindi version of the articles was distributed along with the English versions to the students. Various competitions were held in the schools, like poster making, slogan writing, essay writing, etc., on the theme of human rights, specifically "Right of Life" according to the Article 3 of the Universal Declaration of Human Rights. In the age of environmental consciousness, the theme included the Right to Life for the Plant Kingdom, Save Environment Save Us, Ban on the use of polythene bags, Grow more trees, etc. Besides the stress was also on the "Rights of the Child" and "Consumer Rights".

Student members visit old people's home, orphanages, blind institute, etc., regularly.

They also visit the Consumer Forum Chandigarh meeting various presidents and conveners of different sectors of Chandigarh to gain information and knowledge about the charters and rights of the consumers.

On 14 November 1999, the noted environmentalist, Sunder Lal Bahuguna, gave a talk in our college in collaboration with Yuvsatta, Chandigarh. He stated that the young generation should raise its voice against exploitation of nature in the name of development.

On 10 December 1999 we celebrated the Human Rights Day by organising a seminar on Consumer Rights and observed the International Day of Disabled Persons, which was on 3 December. Poster making and slogan writing competitions for the college students were also held on the theme of human rights.

We intend to publish a booklet in simple language for the small children to make them aware about human rights but this is going to be possible only if we are able to get some financial support. Material for this is already being compiled.

It is true that we have miles to go but the colleges of education can definitely play a pivotal role in spreading awareness about human rights among their pupils and teachers who will further inspire their students in various schools.

10

Education and Human Rights

*Louis Vernal**

EMERGENCE OF HUMAN RIGHTS MOVEMENTS

> "Recognition of the inherent dignity and of the equal and inalienable rights of all members of the human family is the foundation of freedom, justice and peace in the world" (Preamble to the Universal Declaration of Human Rights).

Man is a social being and all members in a group agree on certain norms of social behaviour, defining the rights and obligations of the individuals and imposing restrictions for maintaining the social order. In course of time, those who held power dominated. However, there have been rallying cries of resistance to the tyranny of oppression and arbitrary rule. The understandings between the ruler and the ruled have been codified in Greek, Roman, Chinese and Indian systems of governance.

Natural law became the symbol of people's movements against despotism and the cornerstone of constitutional democracy. The Magna Carta in England, the American Declaration of Independence, the French Declaration on the Rights of Man, the Bolshevik Revolution in Russia are landmarks in the development of the concept of human rights. The twentieth century saw the emergence of new nations out of the colonial domination of the West. These were also the

* *Principal, College of Education, Goa.*

result of the aspirations of the people and the belief in the rights of man. The United Nations was established with the objective of encouraging respect for human rights within the ambit of international peace and security.

The dignity of the human being is a transcendent value and the fountainhead for any discourse on human or fundamental right. History teaches us that when we forget this truth, there is a rise in negative trends that debase mankind. Some of these are ethnic exclusiveness, racial superiority, narrow materialism not to talk of the various "isms" such as Nazism, Fascism and so on. The ravages of war and crime right from the dawn of human existence resulted from the absence of respect for man and his rights. There was a period in human history when individuals had no rights, the same being vested in the lords, kings and governments.

The two world wars and the havoc they wrought on mankind led to the Universal Declaration of Human Rights in 1948. Human rights stem from the inherent dignity and worth of a human being. All human beings without exception are equal in dignity. Human rights, whether we consider civil and political rights or economic, social and cultural rights, all are ultimately the expression of different dimensions of the single subject, the human person. Defence of the universality and indivisibility of human rights is essential for the construction of a peaceful society and for the overall development of individuals, peoples and nations. Human rights are the foundation of human existence and co-existence.

DIMENSIONS OF HUMAN RIGHTS

The concept of human rights has a secular dimension. The French Revolution was the culmination of the emergence of human rights in the philosophies of the seventeenth century. The American Declaration of Independence in 1776 declared: "All men are created equal, are endowed by their creator with certain inalienable rights."

God has created men in His own image and God Himself recognises and respects the supreme worth of what He has created. Anyone who professes to take rights seriously must accept, at the minimum, the vague but powerful idea of human dignity. If there is harmony in a community, each person would be valued. Human rights come into the picture when human dignity is denied.

Man is moral and irrespective of any religious beliefs, he has the capacity to recognise moral truths. It is possible for people of differing backgrounds to engage in moral discourse with one another on the basis of some common assumptions. Human rights is rooted in moral values. Right from the Magna Carta of 1215 to the present, rights have become enshrined in declarations, conventions and covenants that go to make up International Human Rights Law.

Natural law and basic rights transcend the laws and power of any given state government. Human beings do not have rights because they are given by and recognised by a government; all persons have rights because these are rooted in a natural law. No government can deprive any person or any group of human beings of their basic rights. Human rights is endorsed by all 185 members of the United Nations.

EDUCATION AND HUMAN RIGHTS

Human rights is a modern version of the age-old role of freedom and rationality of human kind. Human progress and prosperity is now linked to the reverence to human rights in different communities. Concern for human rights is coexistent with human culture and civilisation. Every human being has a right to live with dignity. Education has been considered to be the delivery system to realise our social and economic goals; sadly, its empowerment to realise the worth and dignity of life has been minimal.

The human right to education is aimed at securing happiness. The all-round development of the human personality makes the individual an asset to society. It is only when a nation or society is able to achieve success in creating a substantial number of such individuals, that it secures happiness. The real happiness and prosperity of any nation is directly proportionate to the number of men possessing physical, intellectual and moral strengths that it produces through proper education.

The International Congress on the Teaching of Human Rights (Vienna, 1979) emphasised that human rights education and teaching must aim at:

a) fostering attitudes of tolerance, respect and solidarity
b) Providing knowledge about human rights
c) Developing means by which human rights can be translated into social and political reality

Indian civilisation recognises education as one of the pious obligations of human society. The great Sanskrit poet Bhartruhari in the first century BC stated: "A man without education is equal to an animal". The right to education has to be treated as one of tanscendental importance in the life of an individual. This has been recognised not only in this country since thousands of years, but all over the world. The right to education occurs in as many as three Articles in part IV of the Indian Constitution (Articles 41, 45, 46) showing the importance attached to it by the founding fathers. Even some Articles in part II (Art. 25 and 30) speak of education.

Any discussion on human rights and education must consider the following important aspects:

a) Knowledge of human rights
b) Rights of the child
c) Role of education institutions

KNOWLEDGE OF HUMAN RIGHTS

The United Nations World Public Information Campaign for Human Rights was launched by the General Assembly on 10 December 1988 through production and dissemination of printed materials on human rights. Further, workshops and seminars were organised and the media utilised extensively. It also wanted the establishment of human rights institutions. The school specific measures included the development of curriculum for human rights and the revision of textbooks integrating human rights in them. Networking among educators was also to be build.

In India, the National Human Rights Commission (NHRC) is the nodal agency for promoting and fostering the culture of human rights. It has initiated the preparation by NCERT of:

a) source books by the NCERT on human rights for facilitating access by teachers and academics,
b) teacher training modules for preserves and in-service stages, and
c) revised textbooks to remove any reference which may be prejudicial to human rights and including materials aimed at inculcating genuine sensitivity to and understanding of such rights.

The NHRC also sought the cooperation of the UGC to help bring human rights at the undergraduate and postgraduate courses. Besides collaboration with the NGOs, it also aimed at sensitising the armed forces and the police. The non-formal sector is also a powerful tool for the spread of human rights education through the departments of non-formal and continuing education. There are 10 open universities, 65 centres of distance education, and hundreds of private distance educational institutions. All should imbibe the spirit of human rights.

The knowledge aspects of human rights education should be based on an understanding of the principles stated in the charter of the United Nations, the Universal Declaration of Human Rights, the International Covenants of Human Rights, the International Human Rights instruments. The focus is on the indivisibility of human rights—civil and political, economic, social, cultural rights, individual and cultural rights. Secondly, it should include the historical experience and contribution of mankind towards self-determination and elimination of all forms of discrimination and exploitation.

There is a need to develop a value system by fostering the attitude of accepting and appreciating people of different races, colours, religions, cultures and nationalities, of tolerance and respect for differences in customs, social, economic and political systems contributing towards international understanding and peace.

HUMAN RIGHTS AND THE CHILD

Many of the world's children live in poverty and are uncared for as regards to nutrition, health and education. They are also exploited for their labour or in the sex trade. A movement for the protection of the rights of the child led to the 1958 Declaration of the Rights of the Child and the 1989 Convention on the Rights of the Child. We as teachers should be aware of these rights since they concern the students in our schools. The Articles that relate to education are:

a) Article 13: "The child shall have the right to freedom of expression; this right shall include freedom to seek, receive and impart information and ideas of all kinds regardless of frontiers, either orally, in writing or in print, in the form of art or through any other media of the child's choice."

b) Article 14: "Parties shall respect the right of the child to freedom of thought, conscience and religion."

c) Article 28: "Parties shall recognise the right of the child to education and with a view to achieving this right progressively and on the basis of equal opportunity."

d) Article 29: "Parties shall agree that the education of the child shall be directed to:

   a) the development of the child's personality, talents and mental and physical abilities to their fullest potential.

   b) the development of respect for human rights and fundamental freedom, and for the principal enshrined in the Charter of the United Nations.

e) Article 31: "Parties shall recognise the right of the child to rest and leisure, to engage in play and recreational activities appropriate to the age of the child and to participate freely in cultural life and the arts.

f) Article 37: "Parties shall ensure that no child shall be subjected to torture or other cruel, inhuman or degrading treatment or punishment."

Role of Educational Institutions

The education angle has two aspects:

a) The right to education

b) Education as a safeguard for human rights

The right to education is very firmly stated in the Universal Declaration of Human Rights and in the Convention on the Rights of the Child. The right to education is crucial for the future of mankind. All schools and their teachers should provide instruction on human rights through a study of both the above documents. The rights of the child are also those of the pupils in the classroom who must be respected and have their dignity and freedom recognised. Education should be child-centred and activity-based. As such learning the rights of human beings cannot be a passive process in which the pupil is forced to follow an authoritarian teaching model.

Human rights education aims at creating an attitude of respect for other people. Knowledge about human rights should lead on to activities that promote the law and the rights. The adult behaviour exhibits, unfortunately, a gap between precepts and attitudes, between what is said and what is done. The teacher should be the role model in upholding and spreading human rights. The child's knowledge and beliefs should find expression in discussions, posters and drawings, written texts including stories, games and songs.

Social studies classes, especially civic, should focus on human rights democracy and peace since these are the foundations of citizenship. In addition to civics, all the subjects taught in school can contribute to the establishment of the concepts required for an understanding of human rights.

Every teacher training institution must lay the foundation for human rights. This can begin with an analysis of the plurality of our society, our tradition of respecting every individual for his worth, our faith in a social, secular, democratic system. If teachers are imbued with the zeal for recognising and upholding human dignity, the nation is safe since the pupils under them will imbibe the same spirit.

For this purpose, discussion on the various aspects of human rights can be integrated with topics under Sociology/ Philosophy of Education or Education in Emerging Indian Society. This aspect could be incorporated in pre-service and in-service teacher education programmes at all levels. The involvement of 50,000 teacher educators would have a deep impact. In this way the NCTE can play a crucial role in promoting education for human rights.

11

Role of Education in Creating Awareness/Sensitisation about Human Rights and Fundamental Duties

*Wasef Marashdeh**

Education is a complex process. It is the development of the complete human personality as Dewey describes. It is life in its rich meaning which has different sides. Every educational process should have a variety of deep aims.

GOOD CITIZENSHIP

The good citizen is developed and he is not created. His first education starts at the house. So part of the house duty is to produce good citizens to the nation. These citizens should know their nations' rights upon them and their duties towards it. They should do their duties to other people in their nations. So the whole country gets use of these good duties. This shows that house duties are serious in educating children to be good citizens.

**English Department, Faculty of Arts & Science, Irbid Private University, Irbid, Jordan.*

EDUCATIONAL ENVIRONMENTS : SCHOOL

Democracy of education is giving the same chance to citizens in education whatever their sex, wealth, colour, religion or any other consideration. It is the main aim of education because it is believed that the individual is the basic unit of society. Then comes the society, the nation and humanity in general. So it is the right of every individual to learn as much as he can to the extent he is able to. It is the nations right to exploit the individual's competency to serve the nation's good aims, and the right of humanity that all individuals in all countries should serve it to become a good world. We can say that these rights become fixed.

The school is an educational environment, not only a place for learning. It is interested in brain development, growing up of the body, and increasing a child's passion. So, modern school tries to be an educational environment in which the child grows up to have a healthy body, a wealthy mind, controlled passion, and a balanced personality. The individual should know his rights and duties, and he should do his work to serve himself and his nation. He should know the humanity rights upon him.

School is an Environment for Learning

In the past, the important person in a school was the teacher. The school was a place where the child went to be given some knowledge, some information, some few skills which he was required to learn by heart. Then the child repeated them in front of the teacher, who gave him the licence to be a scholar. This scholar repeated what he had learnt to his students. But nowadays a school aims to discover a childs abilities, and to give him the aims, the means, the methods with which he can fulfil his curiosity, to achieve his desires, to exploit his talents and to achieve his goals. Through all these activities the child learns.

Dewey said, "School is a place for life. The child must live, appreciate his private life in it, and to cooperate with his environment, to introduce the world through it, and to form new experiences for himself to help his normal life later on."

Due to the above mentioned, the child in a modern school becomes the most important person. Around him all the effectiveness turn, and all establishments are organised. The school environment is to serve him and to enable him to test and to learn through experience. The child is not given abstract data, but he is given the chance to learn through his communication with society and environment and his relation with them. The teacher is only a means to narrow the distance between the child and life and to facilitate the means through which he is able to live, to experience, and to learn.

EDUCATION AND WORK

There is another feature of modern school which is the connection between knowledge and work. In the past, knowledge was sought for knowledge, and knowledge was given to super class people who were not in need work. But today things are different. Nowadays we live in a scientific world. So a modern school is concerned with applying knowledge in work. The school becomes concerned with giving the child the chance to work with his hand, and to do the experiment himself, and to try.

According to these concepts, labour is built on a deep base of knowledge, and knowledge is built on a clear base of work and appreciation. Due to this, education took care to combine knowledge and work together, so learning is achieved through work and appreciation. The result of this combination is that laboratories, factories, workshops and experimental fields become part of the modern school.

In addition to that some modern schools send their students in the secondary stage to work in farms and factories part of their time to learn from these farms and factories the truth of applied knowledge.

Child Most Important in Modern School

Modern education realises that a school is established to be an environment where the learner practices his activities, and to show through its classrooms, playgrounds, laboratories his vitality and his desires. Taking this meaning in consideration, the modern school becomes another environment besides the house. Both of them organise activities, arrange works to stimulate the child's activity, and encourage him to work. They make him test where he learns new knowledge and new skills. A modern school is the place where the child shows new abilities and talents. Where he can express himself develop his desires, and gain the knowledge and the skill which enables him to reach his present life, he begins to appreciate it, and to prepare himself for the future.

The teacher's role in all this is as the organiser of the environment and the experience. He is the master who helps the child to limit his aims and desires, and to exploit his talents and get used to the school's abilities in teaching him and in training his mind. The modern teacher does not want to interfere with the child's activity unless there is a need for that, or to lead and guide him. So the teacher's work takes the form of a helper for learning and not the form of teaching and reciting. The modern school becomes a place where the child learns and is not taught.

What leads the teacher in his work in the modern school is the child's present life and his childhood. Then comes the child's future life, his needs, his position in it. This future life should follow the present life and it should be one of production.

Individual Differences

Every person differs from the others. Every person has a

separate personality. It is true that people are similar to each other, because all of them have sense and sensibility, and they do their works, but this similarity varies and differs.

The amount of passion, its type and the passionate behaviour differs from one individual to another. The way in which the individual looks at things is available to the people, but it are not available at the same form and amount. Due to that, people differ from each other according to their thinking, rules, judgements, behaviour, attitudes, and their habits. All these affairs make every individual distinguished from others. They make this distinction real among brothers and among twins. This is in addition to the distinction among foreigners. Due to that, education should take these individual differences into consideration.

Education has to look at every individual as a separate world. He has a distinguished personality. He has his desires which differ from others. He has his aims which make him different from others. He has his abilities, talents, and special needs which should be taken into consideration.

It is true that a modern school cannot give every child a special teacher, and special areas of activity, but it can arrange to give each individual to help develop a child's talents, abilities, doing the best for him to gain knowledge, experience, skills, which help him in his present time and in his future.

Self-Government

Modern education aims to enable the child to live his present life and to appreciate it, to prepare himself to the future, and to develop his ability and talents after he reveals them and when he is being ready for his future. He can be a good citizen who serves himself, his country and his nation and then humanity. By doing this, modern education gives the child his right in living his childhood, and at the same time it changes its method in teaching and learning.

From the means which are used in self-life government, that is, training the students to govern themselves, to control themselves, and to guide themselves, modern education rejects the stiff role of the teacher by describing him as a ruler or a dictator.

Modern education makes the teacher a guide and an adviser. He steps in when he is needed, and helps when somebody needs his help. By this, the student learns to control himself and to guide his work towards the direction he likes, to feel responsible in his work, to appreciate his achievements. Without doing that, the child becomes a person with a weak personality, who does not appreciate his work, or the expected results.

MODERN SCHOOL AND CHILD'S FUTURE

A school is the place where the child lives his life with his requirements. To live in a society you should interact with this society and to deal with the environment. The child affects his society and he is effected it. Then if the school a good place for the child to live in, it should allow the child to work and to think. He must deal with the people in the school, whether they are colleagues or teachers. He should take from them and give in return. This school environment should give the child the chance to reveal his talent, ability and to exploit his talents. He should develop them and guide them for his benefits and the benefit of his society, and humanity in general. Then this child will grow up to become the person who has his own life, to be a good citizen in future.

The school's duty is to take all these instructions into consideration, and a child to appreciate his present life, and to prepare him for his future life. The school should prepare the child to be a happy person and to be a good citizen, a skilful tradesman and a good worker—a person who knows his duties towards himself, his society, his nation and towards humanity.

According to this, the modern school believes in guidance, both vocational and educational guidance. The teacher in his school guides the child and prepares him for his job, for his society, and for humanity. So if the school is important in advanced countries, it is very important in developing countries. It does its duties towards children, houses, societies, and social establishments. Due to this, it is not only a place for teaching only, but it is a place for preparation, guidance, counselling and education in its comprehensive meaning.

These counselling and preparations are not limited to a certain stage of education, but they extend that to the elementary, preparatory, secondary stages and to the university.

In addition to that, there are many important duties to be done at school. One of these duties is the development of a child's personality. The school is the place which deals with a person's mind, his passion, his deeds, his social relations, his behavioural attitudes, his opinions, and his beliefs.

Modern education aims at forming the child with a balanced psychology, good behaviour, good morals, the child's appreciation, and the ability to get him to make good use of his leisure time.

EDUCATION AND SOCIETY

Societies are not frozen. They are either developing or retreating. Due to this, the new generation demands the development.

Man cannot live outside society, and society has to deal with education. There is no education outside society. This triangular truth is the contact between education and social life. The society affects with its educational system, with its past, its cultural tradition, its present status, its demands, and its future.

Finally we see that the importance of taking care of the individual should concentrate on his personality, his morals, his thinking, and his social dispositions.

REFERENCES

Baldwin, Alfred L., (ed.), *Theories of child development,* New York: Wiley.

Brickman, William W., Comparative Education, *Encyclopedia of Educational Research*, New York, 1969.

Bruner, J.S., *The Process of Education*, Cambridge, Mass.: University Press, 1960.

Elkind, D., *Child Development and Education,* Oxford University Press, 1976.

Erikson, E.H., *Childhood an Society,* New York: 1950.

Fischer, K.W. & A. Lazarson, *Human Development,* W.H. Freeman and Co.: New York, 1948.

Havighurst, R., *Human Development and Education,* New York,: Longmans, 1953.

Michael, William B., "Prediction", *Encyclopedia of Educational Research*. New York: Macmillan, 1969.

Stanley, William O. and B.O. Thancl Smith, "The History, Philosophical, and Social Framework of Education", *Review of Educational Research*, (June 1956).

PART II

Challenges of Teacher Education in Globalisation Era

12

Critical Challenges of the 21st Century: Implication for Teacher Education, Globalisation, Privatisation Technology and Ecology

*Deepa Dabir**

Everybody is acquainted with the term 'Future'. The meaning of future is linked with the concept of time, no doubt a person is concerned with the individualistic concept of 'future' but from a collective point of view 'future' is connected with social, cultural, industrial, technical life as a whole, while the process of futuristic enquiries has its root in advanced, future studies which tend to explore the probable occurrence of future events with the futuristic looks of the changes which are yet to occur. For this, a long range perspective planning is very much essential from the point of view of solving of existing sectors of social life. It is implied that futures can be designed, shaped and controlled, hence the need for perspective planning.

R.B. Baker designed that futurology constitutes an interdisciplinary, methodological system and a critical analysis of human nature, experience and knowledge with the primary purpose of understanding and developing humanities, actual

**Lecturer of Post Graduate, Department of Education, Nagpur University, Nagpur.*

and potential abilities to forecast and influence the emergence of alternative futures. It is very clear from the definition that future studies is a more comprehensive body of knowledge accommodating all kinds of probabilities occurrence of future events. It is an independent discipline. It concerns with all the disciplines with regard to changes and human development.

CRITICAL CHALLENGE OF THE 21ST CENTURY

Teacher education concerns with following important aspects:-

1. Post-industrial (pattern) society: Changing pattern of rural and urban life.
2. Changing pattern of job opportunities.
3. Change in political system.
4. Change in economic system.
5. Change in scientific and technological development.
6. Change in educational pattern, i.e.:
   - i. Open school and open university system.
   - ii. Technological innovations in educational process.
   - iii. Curriculum innovations.
   - iv. Changes in courses and training.
   - v. Changes in professional courses, etc.

The concept 'Education' itself is a developmental process. The educational system accommodates 'being' in the process 'becoming' and it is connected with futuristic visions and change process. In other words, 'Education' is an element of 'futurism'. It enables the man to be futuristic, hence there should be a futuristic educational system.

The twenty-first century in education looks for a long-term perspective planning in education, identification of a futuristic nature of education, technology forecasting and technology assessment in the context of educational development and quality development in education.

Moreover, the twenty-first century education will be strengthened with the help of:

1. Identifying future process in education.
2. Visualising alternative structures and forms of education.
3. Applying effective education technology and its evaluation.
4. Implying effective teaching models and techniques.
5. Bringing excellence in teacher education.
6. Encouraging future-oriented studies at different levels.

In the light of the above points technology of education should be based on:

1. Forecast of socio economic front.
2. Forecast on technologist—new technology should emerge in future forecasted on the basis of existing trend.
3. Scenario building—total lifestyle in a given point of forthcoming time and different paths.
4. Doing sectorial forecast to and their import on overall economy and lifestyle.
5. Literacy of women's education.
6. Food and nutrition in rural areas.
7. Implication of preferred scenario with regard to achievements, feasibility, time, finance and management.
8. Identification of desired lifestyle and its reflection in education.
9. Knowledge and skills of dealing normative, explorative and external forecasts from the necessary input of perspective planning.
10.

Inputs →	Process →	Output
↓	↓	↓
Students, teachers and teacher education	Content and feedback	Students and teachers

Taking into consideration all these above points the twenty-first century education perspective should involve:

1. Perspective planning.
2. Anticipatory management.
3. Technology and technical forecast.
4. Communication technology.
5. Inter-disciplinary approach.
6. System approach and system dynamics.
7. Computer education at all levels.
8. Internet systems.
9. Future values and value education.
10. Environmental education.
11. Vocational education
12. Education for all
13. Peace education
14. Future studies, researches, experiments and innovations in specific future—its problems, goals, process inputs and feedback mechanism.
15. Future studies and creativity—creativity being an essential prerequisite of search for future life.
16. Excellence in teacher education for quality development in education.

In the light of the above points the futurology of educational perspective, above any system, is characterised by interdependence between the elements and subsystems. Some of the major concerns are:

1. Perspective Planning

i) Identification of goals and monitory provision for attainment of goals.

ii) Textbook planning within the goals, short-term planning and long-term planning incorporates the expected future needs of the society by avoiding future crises and by adopting appropriate ways and means.

2. *Anticipatory Management*

The modern concept of management in terms of identification of goals in the context of social, economic, technological industrial, scientific and political environment with the vested alternative to achieve the objectives and goals.

3. *Technology and Technical Forecasting*

Internet, inteltech communication technology, information technology, floppies of every subject and every units. A-V aids structure of MIS computer technology forecast new coming Windows, models of MIS.

4. *Management Education*

Management information systems, futures of business, professions, technology, consumerism, modern management system identifying the direction of change, to overcome crises, to avoid the future opportunities, to accommodate future demands in the management systems.

5. *Interdisciplinary Approach*

System view, system approach and system dynamics, interaction of different components, interdependence between the elements and subsystems.

Systems approach in education: Techniques, models of teaching different methods, goals, and achievements. Qualitative and quantitative approach.

6. *Future Values and Value Education*

Science and religion in future society, humanistic values, future values should be anticipated according to the future serial change, decided future values and value education programme on experimental basis, basis values, social values, moral values and future values.

7. *Environmental Education*

   Separate subject—at all levels of education involving and anticipating futuristic environmental change, environmental pollution remedies based on forecasting.

8. *Education to all*

9. *Futures of Human Right*

   Rights of children and deprived communities, world human rights, awareness about rights, responsibilities and duties.

10. *Peace Education*

    Peace in family, community, religion, society states, regions, country and peace in the world.

11. Future studies, researches, experiments, innovations in specific future—its problems, goals, process, inputs—feedback and output mechanism.

12. *Future and Creativity*

    Creativity is one of the essential prerequisites of search for future life, creative thinking, creative teaching, creative perspective and creative education.

13. *Excellence in Teacher Education for Promotion of Quality Development of Education*

    Elements of effective teaching concept of excellence (beyond effectiveness), knowledge-based teacher education; models of teaching, models of learning to teach, methodology of teaching, skills of teaching for practice, feedback programmes, perception of teaching, interrelationships between method of teaching and models of teaching.

Management of New Concept in Teacher Education

a) Strategic management in teacher education

b) Management Information System (MIS)

c) Management of teaching in teacher education institutes.

d) Management of staff development.

e) Management of teacher education at international level.

f) Management of teacher resources.

Teacher education is facing many problems today. Teacher education and employments have become the cause and effect relationship concept, and the state of unemployment creates under-remarks on the quality of teacher education. A sound programme of education for teachers therefore is essential for qualitative improvement in education.

The above areas demand intellectual interaction of social scientists, philosophers, physical scientists, technologists and educationists and education policy makers to evolve a sound understanding and awareness about social futures and a bright future for general education and teacher education.

13

Teacher Education and Global Changes in the 21st Century

*L.B. Patted**

Education in the modern age seeks to preserve, transmit and advance knowledge, and is committed to bring a change for the betterment of society. The importance of education lies in the fact that it is considered a powerful instrument of social change and progress as has been underlined by various educational experts, committees and commissions in India and abroad. The Education Commission (1964-66) observed, "The destiny of India is now being shaped in her classrooms. In a world based on science and technology. It is education that determines the level of prosperity, welfare and security of people. On the quality and number of persons coming out of our schools and colleges will depend our success in the great enterprise of national reconstruction...." The Commission strongly recommended that the framers of Educational policy should try to relate education to the life, needs and aspirations of the people and thereby make it a powerful instrument of social, economic and cultural transformation for the realisation of the national goals.

For the realisation of the purpose of education, we have to provide the right type of education for the teachers who are ultimately responsible for shaping its destiny. The role of the

**Selection Grade Lecturer, University College of Education, Dharwad, Karnatak.*

teachers has rightly been emphasised in POA of the National Policy of Education (NPE), 1986, that the teacher is the principle means for implementing all educational programmes and of the organisation of education. It further elaborated that the principle role will always be teaching and guidance of their pupils not only through classroom instruction and tutorials but also by personal contact and numerous other ways. Teachers have always been employed for building the character of their pupils. It is expected from the teachers to undertake or promote research, experimentation and innovation. Not only this but teachers are indispensable in their role in extension and social service. They have also to participate in the management of activities which educational institutions undertake to implement their programme. This role was further strengthened in the review of NPE 1986 in 1992 that teachers would continue to play a crucial role in the formulation and implementation of the educational programme.

No system of education can rise above the level of its teachers. The strength of the educational system must largely depend upon the quality of its teachers. Howevergood may be the aims, equipments, efficient administration, the evaluation of the children is determined by the teachers. Therefore, no more important matter than that of securing a sufficient supply of the right kind of people to the profession, providing them with the best possible training and ensuring them a status and esteem commensurate with the importance and responsibility of their work. The progress of the society depends on the quality of its teachers. So a great responsibility rests on the training colleges.

For maintaining standard in teacher education at the national level, the UGC should take responsibility and at the state level, the state board of education should own the responsibility. Enough funds should be made available to the UGC for bringing improvement in the teacher education system. The UGC should set up a joint standing committees for teacher education in collaboration with the NCERT. The government of India should make provision of funds in the centrally sponsored sectors to develop teacher education.

Teaching is becoming, and eventually will become, a distinct profession. The teacher is the basic practitioner in the field of education. He is the person who is presumably qualified both by capacity and preparation to teach in a school and who assumes full responsibility for his action as a teacher. The teacher will continue to be a pivotal figure in the field of education. He will be both trained and devoted to a lifetime career in teaching.

The act of teaching is the essential act of the teacher. What he does in formal, systematic, self-conscious and responsible manner may be expressed in the form: A(im), C(ontent), M(ethod) and E(valuation.)

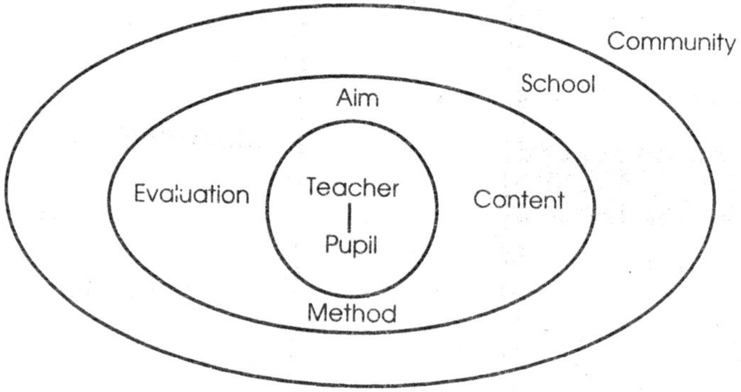

Figure 13.1: School and community relationship

The teacher provides a service (teaching) to his clients (pupils) either individually or in a groups within the environment of an institution known as school, which may be public or private, elementary, secondary or collegiate level. Teaching is a professional act consisting of essential elements which are, or should be, always present.

They are as follows:

1. *Aim*: All teaching consists of an attempt on the part of the teacher to bring about desirable changes in the behaviour

of the pupil. The teacher must take due account of the social demands. He must be skilful, strong and committed enough to be aware of the individual welfare and dignity of each pupil.

2. *Content:* In attempting to bring about changes in pupil, the teacher always draws upon content, a field of knowledge, some organised part of human experiences that represents the accumulated wisdom of the ages. The teacher must have something to teach, a content that will enable him to achieve his aim.
3. *Method:* This is the manner in which a teacher states his aim, how he communicates with his pupils, the way in which he entices the pupils to accept the aim, so that the pupils becomes highly motivated to learn the selected content. The prepared teacher approaches each teaching situation as a problem to be solved.
4. *Evaluation:* An essential part of every teaching act is evaluation, in which the teacher checks to determine the extent to which the original aim of teaching has been achieved. A teacher evaluates to determine the extent and direction of the changes that have resulted from teaching.

Other Roles of Teachers

A qualified and responsible career teacher has other roles in which to be effective. He must work with his colleagues including other teachers, supervisors and administrators in the constant improvement of the curriculum, in enforcing a high ethical standard of conduct within the profession and in bringing about working conditions to encourage effective teaching. He must also work with parents and the public to interpret what the school is attempting, to secure their evaluation, cooperation and support in developing the best educational programme. He also collaborates with the members of other professions, obtaining support and a proper division of labour where the services of education and those of the other professions overlap.

Essentials in Teacher Education

An efficient teaching requires persons of high intellectual capacity since teaching occupies a professional position of expertness in the service. The teacher education curriculum can be divided into three categories as follows:

1. General and liberal education.
2. Specialised education.
3. Professional education.

All the three are substantial and essential ingredients in teacher education and their place in teacher education noted in the following figure:

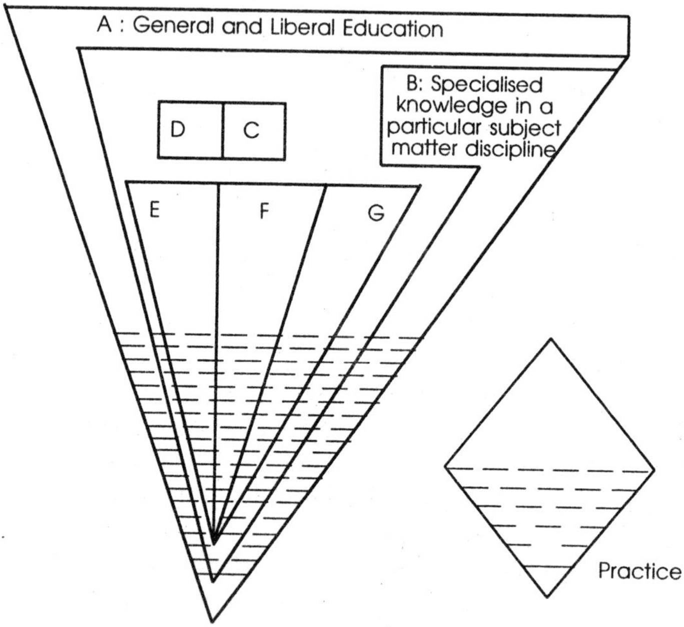

C: Relevant knowledge from behavioural science (psychology, sociology, anthropology, biology, etc.)
D: Relevant knowledge from humanity & science (e.g. history, philosophy)
E: Application to role of school in a society.
F: Educational application to behavioural science.
G: Educational application to school curriculum and methods.

Figure 13.2: A diagram for teacher education

Professional training alone will not produce professional teachers. Teachers can only function professionally to the extent that their role is professionlised. In this modern world teaching can only become truly professionlised through changes in the role and functions of the teacher. Increase of effectiveness and efficiency are related to the professional functions. Therefore, the teacher must possess both effectiveness and efficiency in the teaching process. The professional teaching involves changes in the attitudes of teachers. The teachers must possess outstanding quality in their profession through persistent work in the teaching process. The teacher should become productive and possess special skills related to an effective teaching life an other professionals.

The hallmark of the present century is the knowledge explosion and therefore there is an urgent need for the teachers to equip themselves with the latest developments in their respective areas of specialisation. The student-teachers are selected to the teachers training through an entrance test by the centralised administrative cell (CAC) in Karnataka State since 1999. A person who intends to become a teacher should be academically competent and also should have other attributes such as character, conduct, aptitude, accountability, empathy, love for children, liking for job, etc. Emotional stability, extraversion and dependability appear to be positively related to teaching skills and students' achievement. Every effort will be made to make teaching an attractive profession to which a young person of talent and commitment may feel motivated to join. The responsibility of secondary teacher education rests with the colleges of education and provide one-year teacher education programme which is not enough for educating the teachers better. The Regional Institute of Education (RIE managed by NCERT) provides four years integrated course after higher secondary stage, in addition to the usual BEd and MEd programme. The comprehensive institutions would also be provided facilities and staff for undertaking research and supplement the efforts of the NCERT in order to promote innovation and experimentation. Good colleges of education and departments of universities will also be given autonomous status. Modern methods and techniques of teaching can be used for the training of the student-teachers.

Regarding the evaluation of the teacher training course, there should be continuous and comprehensive evaluation in theory, practical and practice-teaching components which are more helpful to the skill-based programme of teacher education. Teacher education should be made creative and dynamic in order to cater to the requirements of the twenty-first century. The outdated pre-service teacher education programme should be replaced by the changed socio-economic status and needs of the country and also keeping in view the constitutional provisions, the forces of globalisation, privatisation and liberalisation which are affecting the country.

TEACHER-EDUCATORS

The quality of teacher education programme depends on the quality of teacher-educators who are the teachers of the teachers. The teacher training institutions and colleges of education should have professionally qualified teacher-educators. They should be well equipped with the latest knowledge in their subjects by undergoing orientation and refresher courses conducted by the Academic Staff Colleges at the university level. There should be strong, unified and responsible professional teacher associations for the protection of dignity and rights, competence, social status and professional growth of the teachers.

The government created the National Council of Teacher Education (NCTE) in 1975 and was given effect from 1995 which makes an effort in maintaining the quality of teacher education through planned and coordinated development of teacher education programmes throughout the country. In addition to this, there should be a close link between teacher education institutions and university department of education for the improvement of teacher education programme as reported in NPE (1986, p. 26). The I.A.S.Es' are also making efforts for the improvement of teacher education. The teacher education programme should be overhauled to meet the requirements of the twenty-first century.

IN-SERVICE EDUCATION OF TEACHERS

The SCERTs have to play a major role in planning, sponsoring, monitoring and evaluating the in-service education programme for all levels of teachers, instructors and other educational personnel. The need of in-service education of teachers arose due to changing national goals, inputs in teaching-learning system and inadequate background of teachers. The SCERTs would prepare suitable materials for in-service education of teachers, undertake orientation of key persons, and monitoring and evaluation of programmes. At the district level District Inservice Education Training (DIET) should be made an agency to conduct the programmes of in-service education for primary school teachers. Distance in-service education will be prepared and extended with the help of broadcasting agencies. The SCERTs and DIETs should be well equipped with all modern technological equipments for maintaining an effective in-service programmes.

Prospective Teacher Education for the 21st Century

The main aim of education is to bring total development of the personality of the children. The children should be made aware of the Indian culture, values, customs and traditions which instruct eternal values to the children and hold to be good at all times. India is a country with multi-languages, religions, castes, etc., which were not affected by the unity and integrity of the nation even in the past. The feeling of oneness should be developed among the children.

The children should develop first the attitude of belongingness to the country and the world community later on. They should be taught to respect all religions, culture and customs of the people who live in India. They should also to be taught to uphold the values of Indian culture through value education, and should eliminate violence, terrorism, fanaticism, and develop universal brotherhood among the children. There are tensions, clashes and a tendency of exclusion throughout the world. There is an urgent need to develop cohesion, unity, humanism, tolerance, brotherhood in the budding minds of the children. India is a country with a sovereign, republic, secular and democratic form of government. Secularism is termed as treating all religions equally. There can be peace in a society only when people learn to respect the religions and religious beliefs of others.

The modern world has adopted globalisation, privatisation, liberalisation. India is also not exception to these. Globalisation has made the whole world very small. The right people can with effort have as many as facilities as they can which they were unable have before. The life of the common people has become miserable. Especially, the globalisation has created many problems in India which are harmful to the healthy society and environment.

The rapid population growth is the root cause for all the problems. The children should be made aware of the problems of over-population. Privatisation is also one of the major threats to the common people. People may have the fear of upsetting the super class people (10%) who rule society by exploiting the common people. Common people may not be able to have higher education and other facilities of life in future as they are having now if there is privatisation.

Another important aspect is the knowledge and skill of using a computer and other electronic devices in teaching-learning process which has gained great importance now and it would become still more important in future. The computer-aided-instruction has gained more importance through the world. Therefore, the knowledge of the computer is a must for the teacher. But most of the teachers do not have the knowledge of the computer in India. There is an urgent need to include computer education in the teacher education curriculum at all levels. The knowledge of a computer, electronic devices and information technology would devise the future direction of society in all respects.

At present more importance is to be given for the protection of environment. At no other time in human history has this need been felt so deeply. The whole world is facing the problem of environmental pollution. The over-using and misusing of the environment result in the extinction of natural endowments and also are dangerous to the existence of living beings. Therefore, care must be taken for the protection of our environment.

One significant change that is noticeable in teacher education programme is the introduction of citizenship training in the practical form of citizenship camps, or what has come to be known as community life. The community life contributes more to the democratic way of living. A very great emphasis is laid on developing a real community life at the institution and in fostering close and wholesome student-teacher relationship. The community has its own role in school organisation and its managerial affairs. In some states of India primary education is shared by the panchayats and village committees. In the District Primary Education Programme (DPEP) certain functions are performed by the village committees.

In conclusion, I would like to state that the teacher education curriculum and training programme should be altered as per the changing requirements of the modern world in order to face the challenges of the twenty-first century more effectively. Teachers are the builders of the nation. They can chisel the personality of the children who are the citizens of tomorrow and they can play an important role in the development of the country. The parents and community leaders can also support the constructive work of the school.

REFERENCES

Eurich, Alvin C., 1964, *Planning for more effective teaching. 'Teacher Education: A Reappraisal*, Edited by Smith Elmer R. Harper and Row Publishers, Newyork and Evanston.

Gupta, Arun K., 1975, *Teacher Education—Current and Prospects*, Sterling Publishers, Pvt. Ltd., New Delhi.

Government of India, 1986, *National Policy on Education—Program of Action*, Govt. of India, Ministry of Human Resource Development, New Delhi.

Kakkad, G.M., 1988, *Secondary Education: New Directions and Dimensions*, Himalaya Publishing House, Bombay, Nagpur, Delhi.

Khaja, Peer M., 2001, 'The Teacher Education in the 21st Century in India—Challenges Ahead', *University News*, Vol. 39, No. 8, February 19, 2001, pp 1-8.

Mathur, V.S., 1975, *Teacher Education—Some Thoughts*, Aggarwal Prakashan, Ambala City.

Nizam, Eali, 1997,' *Teacher Education in India*, APH Publishing Corporation, New Delhi.

Panandikar, S., *Teacher Education in India*.

Robert, Bush N., 1962, *A scheme for teacher education: A Reappraisal*, Edited by Smith Elmer. R., Harper and Row Publishers, New York and Evanston.

14

Human Rights Education: Teacher Education Curriculum

*Shashi Wanjari**

Education is a means through which we can bring the changes in human life. The fundamental aim of education is to stimulate learning, to enhance thinking and to develop a personality to facilitate self-actualisation and to liberate human potentialities. Therefore, in education changes are welcome whenever there is a change in social needs, social management, etc. The curriculum of higher education should be need-oriented or need-based according to the expectations.

The document of high education came out from the first conference on higher education held in 1998 at Paris. It focuses through Article-6 that relevance in higher education should be assessed in terms of the *fit* between what society expects of institution and what they do. This requires a better articulation with the problems of society aims, including respect to cultures and environmental protection. The conference aimed at *World Declaration of Higher Education for Twenty First Century: Vision and Action* and the framework for priority action for change and development of higher education, represents an agreement between all stakeholders concerning the principle and key actions needed for the renewal of higher education in the new century.

**Reader, Post-graduate Department of Education, Nagpur University, Nagpur.*

In higher education, teacher education plays a crucial role. It is a professional programme and not confined to the presentation of theory only. Expectations from teacher education are rather different from the other professions. It is expected that a teacher educator should be able to analyse and challenge the basic assumption in his work. He should be a reflective practitioner.

According to Victor Ordonez (UNESCO) 1998 in his inaugural speech delivered in the Ninth Triennia Conference of WCCI-Cincinnati held at Bangkok, he stressed that if educational systems stay the same while the world around them changes dramatically, we will be betraying the next generation. He further said that it is clear that global trends present real dangers of distorting educational efforts, if key tensions are not recognised and basic policies are not adopted to keep the balance between the tensions. Dalor himself in the introduction says, "We have to confront, the better to overcome them, the main tensions that although they are not new, will be central to the problems of the twenty-first century", namely, the tension between the global and local, tradition and modernity, long-term and short term consideration, the need for competition and the concern for equality of opportunity, extraordinary expansion of knowledge and human beings' capacity to assimilate it and, lastly, tension between the spiritual and the material.

He summarised that it is education's noble task to encourage each and every one, acting in accordance with their tradition and conviction and paying full respect to pluralism, to lift their minds and spirits to the plane of the universe and in some measure, to transcend themselves. It is no exaggeration on the Commission's part to say that the survival of humanity depends on it.

Besides this, Dalor's "learning to do" teaches us about not only acquiring of productive occupational skills but also the competence to deal with changing life and situations.

"Learning to be", teaches us to develop a human being beyond just a thinking and working being to the fullness of his or her potential, with greater self-esteem, aesthetic and ethical sensibility and personal responsibility.

"Learning to live together", stresses on to develop heart-to-heart relationship and eradication of conflict. If we think on the futuristic views, it indicates that we are unable to reach that level which enable us to protect from living together in peace. All human beings by nature love peace. Peace makes advancement of civilisation possible. Social and economic progress can take place only in a peaceful environment. The foundation of peace rests on the basic principle of justice, equality and freedom enjoyed by all the members of the world. The basic urge of all human beings is to live, to live better and to live long in the pursuit of happiness. Everybody on the earth is entitled to the basic rights of life aimed at protecting the dignity of the individual.

The draft proposal on higher education for twenty-first century envisages the quality of higher eduction as a multidimensional concept, and institutions of higher studies must play an important role in identifying and addressing the issues that affect that well-being of the community. Among various disciplines, education is the one which produces the teachers, who build the future of the nation and hence teacher educators are the responsible components in the education systems.

As we are aware, of the time has come to accept the challenge to develop the competence to face the situation and to share the responsibility thrown on us. Teachers are the main pillars of education. Basically they are considered to be the sole determinants of its accountability. The quality of their teaching and teaching behaviour is coupled with their dedication with which they work.

Due to technological revolution, the mental world is conquered. The lifestyle has changed. Everyone is alert to his needs. Human rights are knocking at the door of education.

Being an educationist, a teacher educator should be able to equip, understand, himself be able to handle the situation.

In the words of Williams Car it is said that educational objectives depend upon a scale of value. Educational objectives are significantly related to values, without which educational work will be incomplete. Hence it is needed to know the consistency of the scale of value. The Vienna Declaration aims at "Human rights educations which should include peace, democracy, development and social justice in order to achieve common understanding and awareness with a view to strengthening commitment to human rights." By peace and democracy, development and justice, we can have access to all the objectives because values lie hidden in the elements of the above-mentioned right. Human rights and human life values are closely related. In other words, human rights and values are the two sides of a single coin. However, a difference exists in that one has form and the other is formless. Similarly, one is visible while the other is latent. All have the right to education and the proper use of this educations is value. We can attain value by blending rights and duties together. There should be relevance of values with the human rights education. Every teacher educator is bound to discharge debts towards society by performing his duties towards his pupil teachers. For this he has to obtain the enough theoretical understanding, practical knowledge of its applications, different skills of imparting it and qualitative measures to evaluate its output.

The UN Decade for Human Rights Education (1995-2004) has inspired all countries to promote human rights education. Teachers training colleges have a special responsibility of helping in achieving the goals of the UN Decade by providing proper training to the teachers on whose shoulder is the responsibility of inculcating human rights and duties given. With this importance, there is a need to identify different objectives and frame the curriculum which may definitely be fruitful to achieve the goal in the desired direction.

The following are the objectives to be considered while framing the curriculum:

1. To know the concept of human rights and human rights education and their significance.
2. To know the various declarations and their relevance to teacher education programmes.
3. To know the various organisations and their work in the direction of human rights education.
4. To know how to link human rights education with different disciplines.
5. To acquire the ability to implement the Human Rights Education Programme (HREP).
6. To know how to use resources according to the concept.
7. To enable them to inculcate values.
8. To know the professional responsibility and duty.
9. To know the commitment, competence and performance output.
10. To search and research innovations regarding effective application human rights education.
11. To equip with different skills to adopt the method, to prepare teaching materials related with the human rights education.

Looking to the above objectives, I felt that there is a need to give three dimensions while framing the curriculum in Teacher Education.

Dimension I. Integral transformation of content-knowledge about human rights in teacher education.

Dimension II. Application of different methods to implement and to teach the content with its objectives.

Dimension III. Evaluation of reflective teacher educators and their performance with reference to awareness created in their pupil teachers.

In short, the curriculum to teacher education should have a fabric of human rights and duties. Precisely the existing framework of curriculum may not undergo a drastic change the subjects of teacher education cannot change, the dimensions as specified above have to be the same, otherwise only minor inclusions in the same papers reading knowledge of human rights and education and application are to be made. In Psychology of the BEd curriculum the topic of "S-R learning theory" should be presented to the pupil teacher as the classical 'S-R learning theory' plus the values embedded in the theory. The pupil teachers must grasp every teaching theory with a coating of 'values'. The expectation of the teachers (in the making or in-service) is that while they actually do their classroom teaching in schools, these values should be reflected in their day-to-day teaching. This will have a long-drawn effect of incorporating human rights education in teacher education programme. If the teachers are able to speak the language of human rights and values while teaching their subjects in the school, the very purpose realising the drame of a peaceful future civilisation will be fulfilled.

REFERENCES

Ahlawat, S., *Human Rights and Education.*

Dhand Harry, *Teaching Human Rights, A Handbook for Teacher Educators*, Asian Institute of Human Rights Education, Bhopal.

Marshal James and Peters Michale, *Educational Policy, The International Library of Comparative Public Policy*-2, UK and Northampton M.A, USA, 1999.

Mohanty Jagannath, *Human Rights Education*, Deep and Deep Publications Pvt. Ltd., New Delhi.

Pand, B.N., Tawari A.D., *Teacher Education,* APH Publishing Corporation, New Delhi.

University News, October 13, 1997.

Victor Ordonez, UNESCO, Educating for Balance: Integrating Technology and the Human Spirit on a Global Scale, Speech delivered in the Ninth Triennial World Conference WCCI held at Bangkok (13 July 1998).

15

A Strategy to Promote Human Rights Education: Implications for Teacher Education

Vandana Talegaonkar* and *Rina Choudhary*

INTRODUCTION

Human rights are literally rights that one has, simply because one is human. This deceptively simply idea has profound social and political consequences. Human rights entered the mainstream political theory and practice in the seventeenth century Europe. Later, in the post-cold war world, nearly all states in all regions of the world at all levels of development proclaimed their commitment to human rights. In today's world, a consistent pattern of gross human rights violation is widely perceived to undermine a regime's national and international legitimacy.

Many Asian states have guarantees of human rights in their constitutions and many of them have ratified the international instrument on human rights. However, there continues to be a wide gap between rights enshrined in these documents and the object reality that denies people their rights. The socio-politico-economic-cultural forces of the larger system

**Project Fellows; Deptt. of Educational Administration, Faculty of Education and Psychology, The M.S. University of Baroda, Baroda.*

are prevalent with a barrier in this. The characteristics of the Asian states in this regard are aptly summarised by the "The Pune Declaration on Education for Human Rights in Asia and the Pacific, India 1999" which are as follows:

a) to develop attitudes and behaviour to promote respect for the rights of others;
b) to ensure genuine gender equality and equal opportunities for women in all spheres;
c) to promote understanding and tolerance among diverse national, ethnic, religious, linguistic and other groups;
d) to empower people to participate actively in the life of a free society;
e) to promote democracy, development, social justice, communal harmony, solidarity and friendship among nations;
f) to further the activities of the UN system, in particular UNESCO, the Office of the UN High Commissioner for Human Rights and UNICEF aimed at the creation of grounds for peace based upon universal values of human rights, international understanding, tolerance and nonviolence.

If education cannot promote these positive orientations, no other source can do it with the same perfection.

Role of Teacher and Teacher Training Programme in Education for Human Rights

The education system in India, a heritage of colonial system of education, has not successfully adapted to the demands of the changed times. This makes it difficult to achieve the above-mentioned aims and objectives. In order that teachers teach human rights they must imbibe the philosophy of human rights themselves and this demands changes to be introduced in the teacher education programme with respect to:

a) new approaches to education
b) new ways of dealing with students
c) new teaching methodologies.

These new approaches demand changes in the attitude of the teacher, the teacher student relationship and the school environment. This is illustrated in the following way:

a) is experiencing the adverse impact of globalisation processes, especially in the economic and cultural fields in many cases detrimental to human rights;
b) suffers from the prevalence of different societal maladies such as child labour, sexual exploitation of women and children, gender inequality, contemporary forms of slavery, discrimination of persons belonging to national, ethnic, religious or linguistic minority groups, exclusion based on social status, deprived and disadvantaged communities and other grounds which seriously impede the promotion of human rights;
c) is disturbed by the sufferings of innocent people as a result of acts of terrorism, armed conflicts and abuse of power; and
d) is experiencing serious degradation of the environment affecting the quality of life of the people and threatening the very survival of humanity.

The Asian states in the context of these realities must initiate an urgent action to implement the human rights of their citizens and residents. Education assumes an important role in this effort. The conference also reaffirms that education is a basic right and an essential precondition for the implementation of all human rights for all. This was earlier also acknowledged by the Universal Declaration of Human rights in 1948 in Article 26... *"The General Assembly proclaims...* that every individual and every organ of society... shall strive by teaching and education to promote respect for these rights and freedom..." Article 26(2).

Aims and Objectives of Education for Human Rights

The principal aims of education for human rights according to 'The Pune Declaration on Education for Human Rights in Asia and the pacific, India, 1999' are as under:

a) to strengthen respect for human rights and fundamental freedoms; and

b) to develop fully the human personality and the sense of its dignity;

a)	The attitude of the teacher towards the student	
	Authority	Democracy
	Discrimination	Acknowledgement of everyone's Rights
	Intolerance	Respect
	Lack of knowledge of students	Recognition of individual differences of opinions
b)	Relationship between students	
	Competition	Collaboration
	Individualism	Solidarity
	Frustration over individual failures	Satisfaction over group success
	Feelings of rejection by one's peer	Feelings of acceptance by fellow students
c)	Schooling environment	
	Student permanently judged	Student valued for talents and recognition of limitations
	Women are discriminated in the tasks and responsibilities that are to them	Women and men assume responsibilities with their interests
	The student must always be the subject of decisions that are made for him/ her.	The student participates and makes decisions regarding him-self/herself and his/her education.

The argument favouring, putting teacher training first, was also strongly advanced by Peter Leuprecht, Director of Human Rights of the Council of Europe. He remarked, "If such education is to be successful at all levels, it will be necessary to train teachers and provide them with proper facilities." The teacher training in this respect should include the following:

a) *Attitude Changes:* (Tolerance for various minorities, castes and religion).
b) *Value Clarification:* (Critically exploring the negative implications of the common use of "man-made" language relating to gender references in formal writing as well as in everyday conversation.
c) *Cognitive Skills:* In matters of law, government and society, e.g., learning and understanding the provisions of the Universal Declaration of Human Rights and other international instruments.
d) *Development of Solidarity Attitudes*: Concern and sympathy for people and problems related to food, health and welfare.
e) *Participative Education for Empowerment:* Enabling people to define and meet their needs.

This list is not exhaustive.

The teacher, as a professional, has certain obligations which are in tune with the fundamental duties towards the students, the institutions and the society. Much has been spoken and written on inculcation of human rights values through education in India, but either is it not translated into action or if it has been attempted, it has been attempted in a piecemeal and sporadic way. Hence, teacher education programmes must train teachers in the strategy so that teachers in turn use these competencies to discharge their function in respect of their students. Also the competency of teachers will necessarily depend upon their commitment and their confidence. The duty of teacher educators then is also to ensure that the teacher training programmes necessarily focus on developing the confidence, the commitment along with the competence.

The teacher training programmes for propagation of human rights through the medium of education can be designed by using the competencies proposed by Mukhopadhyay (2001). These competencies are as follows:

Planning: Planning of annual curricular programmes, units and lessons, setting up of laboratories and conducting the laboratory activities, co-curricular activities, examination and evaluation, etc.

Guiding: Whether officially designated as counsellor or not, each teacher helps students both inside and outside the class in academic, personal and even in cases of financial problems.

Teaching: Classroom teaching, tutorials, groups activities, home assignments, laboratory practicals, field trips and a host of such other things.

Examination: Setting papers, planning the examination schedule, invigilation duties, evaluating answer scripts, tabulating marks, and declaring the results, several times in a year.

Management: Management of curricular activities, time management, co-curricular activities, classroom management, laboratory, library, field trips and educational tours, house activities, conduct of terminal, annual and board examinations.

Human Relations: Relationship with the principal, colleagues, students and parents, supervisors, old students, other professionals (e.g., teacher educators), etc.

Professional Development: Reading, writing, lecturing, attending training programmes, seminars, conferences, extension lectures, etc.

Extension and Social Service: Lectures, writing and publications, participating in social action programmes, community development, etc.

These competencies can be classified into three categories and represented in a three-dimensional model.

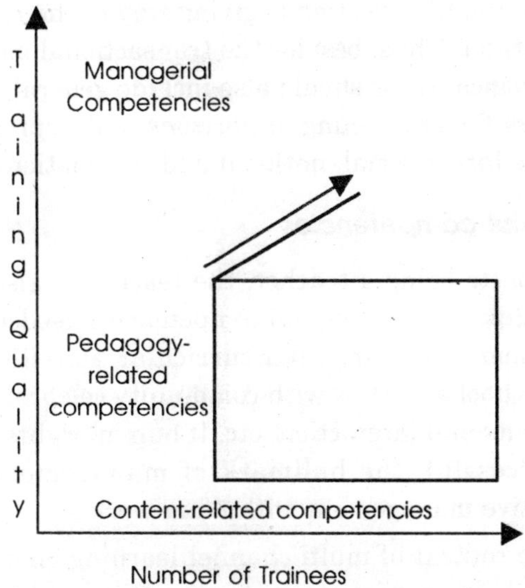

Model of training areas

Teacher Training Programmes based on Eight Competencies Proposed by Mukhopadhyay

Content competency

Recent studies on teachers indicate gross content deficiency of teachers. Refresher courses are started as in-service education for all levels of teachers to remove this deficiency. There is a need to use integrated dimensions of human rights in all subjects at all levels. NCTE has prepared self-learning nodules in this respect, which can be made use of.

Pedagogy-related competency

With globalisation and the changing scenario, inclusion of human rights in education has become imperative. In this changing scenario, the learning habits and skills need to change. Thus, the pedagogy-related competencies assume new and greater significance. The authoritarian teacher and the teacher-centered education is giving way to the role of teacher as a facilitator. Thus, besides the transactional methodologies, the pedagogical skills should also include general preparations of teachers for broadening of horizons and appreciating their role in the larger social, national and international contexts.

Managerial competencies

In addition to being a teacher, the teacher is also a manager and a leader. The managerial competencies needed for this are organisation of co-curricular/curricular activities in school, relating school activities with community celebrations, contact with parents and interaction, etc. If human rights education is to be successful, the hallmark of management should be participative management with team work.

In the context of multi-channel learning environment the challenge is in management of instruction and learning. The teacher education courses should identify the training needs of teacher related to the above, and devise training programmes accordingly.

The Asia-Pacific Regional Conference noted that a comprehensive, integrated and holistic approach is called for, to popularise education for human rights at all levels. A similar effort is also called to bring about attitudinal changes to accept positive value of human rights in education as an important element in education. Strategy needs to be worked out for motivation to bring attitudinal change. This component can be included in refresher courses to address to the teachers already working in the system

As discussed earlier, the competency parameter alone is not enough. This must be juxtaposed with commitment or willingness to perform. Based on competency and willingness component, Marmar Mukhopadhyay described four categories of teachers as follows:

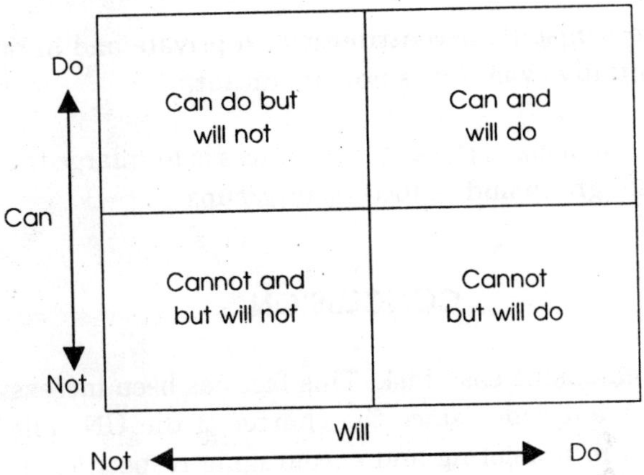

Can-do-will-do matrix

This matrix provides four categories of teachers; those who:

a) Can and will do—the safe and trusted lieutenants of the system.
b) Cannot but will do—motivated but lack competence.
c) Can but will not competent but unwilling.
d) Cannot and will not—neither motivated nor competent.

The first group poses no problem, for the second group, tailor-made programmes can be made. The major problem is posed by the third and fourth groups. The third group is very risky as they are the potential negative force in the system and the fourth group is a definite liability as they lack both motivation and competence. Strategies that may work for this are involvement and responsibility.

— Recognition—cycle (IRRC), which includes:

  — Involve them in decision making.
  — Make strategies intervention so that they accept the responsibility of their decisions and implement them.

— Recognise their contribution, in private and in public, initially even if it is not significant.

Hence, the challenge for teacher educators is to enlarge the "will and can do" group and reduce other groups.

CONCLUSION

Human rights is no easy task. This fact has been increasingly so in the five decades since the charter of the UN called for cooperation in promoting and encouraging respect for human rights and fundamental freedoms. The fundamental duty of teacher educators assumes immense significance both as pre-service and in-service trainers.

REFERENCES

Banks, D.N., *What is the State of Human Rights Education in K-12 Schools in the United States in 2000?: A Preliminary look at the National Survey of Human Rights Education.*

Claude, R.C., *Methodologies for Human Rights Education*, hie//C\WINDOWS\Desktop\humanrights.htm

Donnelly, J., *What are Human Rights?*, htpp//usinio.state.gov/products/puas/niitro/donnelly.htm.

Mukhopadhyay, M., *Total Quality in Education*, New Delhi: NIEPA, 2001.

16

Performance Appraisal and Teacher Accountability— The Need of the Hour

*Mariyamma Mathew**

Today, we have in India, a higher education system comprising about 230 universities, 8,000 colleges, three lakh teachers and five million students Except a few, many of these are just average, many more are substandard. Our universities and colleges are no longer citadels of the mind and spirit. As Prof. S.V. Chittibabu, former VC, Annamalai University, has said, "They have become shelters of academic mediocrity and choking emptiness because of vested interests".

The aim of higher education is to create "intellectually mature, morally upright, spiritually inspired and socially committed" young men and women who will be a great asset to the society. According to Gandhiji the primary aim of education is character formation. Prof. Ramaranjan Mukherrji says, "Education is not simply a process of transplanting a dead stuff of knowledge into the mind of the learners. It is a living process of character building and personality development."

Again quoting Prof. Chittibabu, "Real education consists in the teacher's conscientious endeavour to enable his students to discover themselves and their possibilities. But what is

**Department of English, Marthoma College for Women, Perumbavoor, Kerala.*

happening in the classroom today is spoonfeeding. Lessons and lectures become the substitute for intellectual exercise. Qualities of the mind like independent study, creative thinking and resourcefulness are suppressed. This type of dull and drab education produces individuals who lack initiative and imagination, self-confidence and self-reliance." Thus the very aim of higher education is thwarted.

There are various factors responsible for this alarming state of affairs. I propose to examine the role of teachers in bringing about this deterioration in standards.

Even as a student, I had great respect and admiration for the teaching community. Most of my teachers had attracted me with their sense of devotion, commitment, sincerity and hard work. I become a teacher in 1969 in a private-aided college. The teaching community in general continued to be sincere and hard-working for some more years. They had a sense of accountability. Later I realised that this was because they had no job security. The head of department kept a confidential report which was submitted to the management at the end of the academic year. If the report was not satisfactory the management had the right to terminate the service of the teacher. As a result every teacher tried hard to please the head of the department the principal and the management. The beneficiary of this process was the student. After all, colleges are meant for the students and therefore this was a healthy trend. But things changed in the early years of the seventies with the introduction of parity of pay scales for private college teachers and uniform rate of fees for students. Till that time the private college managements levied very high fees on the students and paid low salaries to the teachers. Since 1972 the managements simply collect the fees and remit it to the government and the government directly pays the salaries of teachers. This slowly led to a lack of interest and lack of control on the part of the managements. The teachers also developed a tendency to misuse this new-found freedom. They also developed a tendency to misuse this new-found freedom. They no longer had to please the management, they had job security and the majority of the teachers developed an attitude of irresponsibility and indifference, so the direct payment system along with many other reasons was mainly responsible for the fall of standards in private colleges. Many managements started to make up for the loss of income by accepting donations (which is only a euphemism for bribery) for the appointment of teachers, as a result the best talents are alienated from the field of higher education and mediocres are attracted. The capacity to pay huge amounts as donation may not combine with academic and moral excellence. At least a few private college managements use the minority rights as a shield to act as they please. Once the appointment of teachers is done neither the university nor the government has any effective control on the teachers. The teachers are not accountable to anybody. They continue to get their salary irrespective of whether they teach or not. Those who get appointment by paying huge amounts as donation, once their job is secure, start to make up for the loss by indulging in some kind of side business or by conducting private tutions to the point of neglecting their classes in the colleges.

Teachers have lost their sense of accountability to such an extent that at least a few of them evaluate answer books without even reading the answers!!! Neither the chief examiner, the chairman, nor the controller of examinations has any control over the additional examiners. They do the valuation work when they please and as they please. As a result the student community suffers and the exam system has lost all credibility.

When the UGC scheme was implemented, it was expected that the situation would change. Of course, it is certainly good to attract the best talent into the teaching profession and to encourage young teachers to improve their qualifications. But in Kerala the scheme was implemented in a very diluted form—diluted to the level of mere scales. Of course, there is a code of professional ethics for university and college teachers prepared by the task force of the UGC consisting of educational experts and representatives of the All India Federation of University and College Teacher's Organisations. It is a very impressive and comprehensive document dealing with the various aspects of higher education. It defines the goal of higher education in our country, speaks about teachers and their responsibilities, gives a list of do's for teachers regarding their relationship with students, colleagues, authorities, guardians and society. But who is there to see that this code is adhered to? Attending two refresher courses it mandatory for each promotion — to the senior grade and to the selection grade. But this stipulation has also become a farce. Many teachers attend these courses just to get a course certificate rather then to update their knowledge.

Again, according to the UGC guidelines research is as important as teaching and every teacher is expected to do research work. Oddly enough, this too is leading to a decline in standards. Many teachers now do research not out of love for the subject or out of a desire to keep themselves abreast of the latest developments in their field of study, but simply because of the prospect of getting increments and promotions. In such cases they neglect their fundamental duty which is teaching. In Australia in 1970, such a situation developed and the students there protested against this. They even insisted that university teachers should always be appointed on contract basis and students should be consulted at the time of renewal of contracts. Later they agreed to the government establishing higher education units in every university to help every individual teacher to improve his teaching ability. But in our country, in spite of so many commission reports, teachers still remain unaccountable to anybody.

Teachers should imbibe the spirit of the following quotation from the Kothari Commission Report and act accordingly:

> The destiny of India is now being shaped in her classrooms. This, we believe, is no more a rhetoric. In a world based on science and technology, it is education that determines the level of prosperity, welfare and security of the people. On the quality and number of the persons coming out of

> our schools and colleges will depend our success in the great enterprise of national reconstruction whose principal objective is to raise the standard of living of our people.

Teachers form the most powerful element of the higher education system. As Prof. Shivendra K. Verma says, "If we have the right type of teachers —willing to innovate, try out new ideas, work as members of a team— our educational system can became generative and meet the new challenges and demands of the expanding universe around us."

Teachers are the models for the future generations. Students, in addition to learning subjects from the teacher, develop their personality, shape their character and behaviour and even imitate the habits of the teacher. The personality impact of the teacher is very important. Therefore, sincere, dedicated, professionally competent, morally sound, spiritually inspired and socially committed individuals should be appointed as teachers.

In the appointment of teachers certain set norms from the academic and educative perspectives are used. But this one time measurement will not be enough for the whole career; there should be continuous evaluation. Only through appraisal and evaluation can we know our strength and weaknesses. There can be evaluation by self, peer, boss and students. The self may often be prejudiced. Peer evaluation may lack objectivity. Evaluation by boss is not always feasible because of difference in subject specialisation or lack of time. So the last resort is the student. Sometimes even overhearing students' comments can give a fragmentary feedback on teaching. But this is not comprehensive. Therefore, a systematic evaluation of teachers by students should be introduced. At the end of an academic year or a semester the students can be asked to fill up teacher evaluation cards containing parameters like sincerity, dedication, concern, love, punctuality, knowledge, competence, communication skill, moral integrity, acceptability as a model, coverage of syllabus, etc.

But great care should be taken while introducing this system. There should be absolute secrecy and impartiality in processing and using the information for improving the quality of performance by teachers. The assessment should be impartial, objective and uninfluenced by extraneous considerations like personal prejudice. To ensure this it should be conducted under examination conditions within a short time. The information should be used for the benefit of the students in a very impartial manner. The information should be passed on to each teacher confidentially so that he can improve himself. Teachers who show serious dereliction of duty should be disciplined and corrected. Such an evaluation system will go a long way in toning up the quality of teaching because lack of accountability of teachers is one of the important causes for the decline of the standard of higher education.

In some countries students' evaluation of teachers' performance is a regular feature and these are taken into account at the time of appointments and promotions. Even in our country in every other field there is scope for assessment. Politicians are assessed by voters, doctors and lawyers by their clients, bureaucrats by their seniors and even businessmen are assessed by their customers. Only we, the teachers, are exempted from any kind of assessment.

One important objection raised by some teachers to students' evaluation of teachers is that there is the danger of students being misled by caste, communal or regional considerations and being exploited by vested interests to give opinions in their favour. It is true to some extent. But if we can trust illiterate voters to assess the performance of political parties and candidates, we can certainly trust educated students to evaluate their teachers. Similarly if teachers can be trusted to examine students in an impartial manner, students also can be trusted to appraise their teachers' performance objectively.

Another objection raised is that the undergraduates are not competent enough to measure the teachers' depth in their respective subjects. But the fact is that we very often underestimate the students' ability to pass objective judgement on the level of knowledge of the teacher. They can easily fathom the depth of knowledge of a teacher by his behaviour inside the classroom. When a teacher fails to clarify their doubts or when he cannot give scientific and acceptable explanations his shallowness in the subject is revealed. In short, the objections raised are the result of our own ego, fear, insecurity and inferiority complex. When we do our task to the best of our ability, we need not have doubts about the judgement.

"To make a student aware of his own inner potentiality, to give him confidence and the ability to realise it and to give him a stimulus to perform better are what education is all about. If we are doing it, we need not resist students assessment."

("*Students' Assessment of Teachers —Why not?*", P. *Thailambal University News*, March 2nd 1998).

It is true that in our culture the students are not trained to be critical of their teachers. Therefore, proper training should be given to them to evaluate in a balanced and impartial way. They should be taught to assess their teachers without causing harm to the dignity and image of the teacher and without losing their respect for him. This critical faculty should be developed early. Thus the students also will be benefited by this process because they will learn to think independently and to express their ideas fearlessly.

I would like to conclude my observations by quoting the works of R.K. Singh (Prof. and Head, Department of Humanities and Social Sciences, Indian School of Mines, Dhanbad), 50 Years After: Challenges facing Teachers, *University News,* October 6 1997):

> Accountability is central to our existence and it is a responsibility to society that should guide the entire scope of our activities in education, research and service. We must accept a certain degree of accountability if we wish to continue to be an effective medium for social and economic progress and consequently to merit tax payers' support. We must accept responsibility for the outcome of our deeds.

17

Changing Social Realities in Indian Society and Teacher Education

*Hemlata Talesra**

Like the other Third World countries, India is passing through a fast changing society. The rapid development of social science and technology have inevitably a super culture. Modernisation which involves industrialisation, urbanisation and nationalisation is a principle process to bring about the change in the society. This paper makes an attempt to analyse the changing social realities in Indian society and the requirement of teacher education.

Indian society is a product of its own social forces and the forces exogeneous to it. In course of time its structure gets complex through a process of social change. The society consists of many groups, i.e., family, cast, class, community, religion and government. These groups constitute the social organism of the society. The role of education as a political agent of socialisation and social change assumes a crucial importance. In different countries with the passing away of traditional order, new social orders shall have to emerge. This requires the operation of institutionalisation consisting of new orientations of norms and values.

Retd. Professor and Head, Department of Educational Planning, Management and Administration, Vidya Bhawan, G. S. Institute of Advanced Studies in Education, Udaipur (Rajasthan).

FUNCTIONS OF EDUCATION TO MEET THE CHALLENGES OF SOCIETY

To meet the challenges of society education has to perform two functions: (1) Socialisation and (2) Selection. Education has to develop commitments and capacities in the process of development. In a developing society the individual has to commit himself to the common values and norms of the society. And then his further commitment is towards the performance of the specialised roles assigned to him. Talcott Persons classifies skills into two categories: (1) Skills necessary to perform roles (2) Skills to develop capacities for carrying out the role responsibility and the expectations of the group.

In a complex role society that India endures to achieve education has to train persons for effective selection of different kinds of roles.

Changing Needs of Society Require Different Patterns of Teacher Education

The existing structure of teacher education has become outdated. It is not suitable to meet the challenges of present-day society. It will need to include three kinds of curricular inputs:

1. General education is a slightly more sophisticated nature that is imparted to every youth for living a full citizen's life.
2. Principles of human development, human learning pedagogy and life adjustment along with requisite skills to help and guide children in learning development and adjustment.
3. A package of instructional material for performing their specialised job that he may opt for his teaching career.

The teacher education institutions will have to play a major role of coordination rather than direct handling all the programmes and activities of teacher preparation. The teacher of the twenty-first century will be institutions for knowledge-production and disbursement (such as universities, laboratories, libraries, continuing-education centres, mass media, data processing centres, etc.) and others will be of institutions producing goods and services (such as form, factories, radio and TV centres, railway stations, post offices, banks, hospitals, road transport services, workshops, business, corporations, sports, etc.

The teacher training institutions will have to adopt the following training strategies for preparation of teachers:

1. Teacher preparation will be made by the combination of a number of training strategies, such as, package programmes, part-time courses, short duration courses, job learning courses, distance education, etc.
2. Provide continuing education for teachers to cope with the unending race of growing knowledge.
3. Beside classroom instruction some alternative teaching learning should be provided, i.e., open learning, distance education, correspondence education, etc.
4. Under the new umbrella of non-formal education, teacher training instructions should add some inputs like skill of communications, scriptwriting for radio, preparing lessons to be telecast, handling film projectors, VCR, TV and other electronics, generating consciousness about the future using problem-solving approaches in teaching and learning.

18

Quality Assurance in Teacher Education

*V.D. Javlekar**

"What is a quality education?" A simple enough question but one that is difficult to answer. A quality education depends on what your objectives are and what you are going to do with the education.

Initial teacher education leading to BEd focuses mainly on three aspects:

1. Professional knowledge and understanding
2. Professional skills and abilities
3. Professional values and commitment.

The relationship between the content of teacher training (what is to be learnt) and the process (how is it to be learnt) is illustrated in Table 18.1. All content can be grouped under the headings, Knowledge, Skills and Attitudes, and all processes can be grouped under the headings, Theoretical Instruction, Practical Work and Field Experience.

In order to assure quality in teacher education it is necessary to determine areas of Competence, Performance and Commitment. Table 18.2 illustrates these areas.

**Reader, University of Mumbai, Vidya Nagar, Mumbai.*

Table 18.1. The relationship between the Content and the Process

PROCESS	Content: Knowledge	Skill	Attitude
Theoretical Instruction	Short Term		
Practical Work		Medium Term	
Field Experience			Long Term

Table 18.2. Areas of competence, performance and commitment

Sr. No.	*Competency Areas*	*Performance Areas*	*Commitment Areas*
1	Concept and content competency	Performance in classroom	Learns concern for all round development
2	Competency in co-curricular activities	Performance in school activities	Internal acceptance of the role and responsibility
3	Evaluation competency	Performance of the learners/ own performance	Excellence
4	Competency in imparting value education	Performance related to value-oriented education	Basic human values
5	Management competency	Performance in management of several activities including community work and parental contact	Proper coordination and control of all activities (Provider of quality service)

There are several techniques of quality assurance. The three most popularly used techniques are Benchmarking, ISO 9000 and Total Quality Management (TQM).

Table 18.3. Deming's Propositions and Implications for Teacher Education

Sr. No.	Deming's Propositions	Implications for Teacher Education
1.	Create constancy of purpose for improvement of product and service	Quality should lie at the heart of the organization's purpose. Provide quality education at the right price and through ethical means. Ensure that students are provided with relevant and useful knowledge, skills and values such that it enables them to achieve excellence in their respective fields and to grow into good human beings.
2.	Adopt new philosophy	It is necessary to recognise that we are in a new area in which an ever-increasing quality is necessary for survival. Existing defects should be eliminated. Introduce new work culture and it should reflect commitment to quality.
3.	Crease dependence on mass inspection to achieve quality	Efforts for continuous process improvement. The emphasis therefore moves to catching and correcting errors at "The source". Replace external inspection by continuous internal mechanism of quality assurance.
4.	End the practice of awarding business on price tag	Right people for right job/ task. Maintain close relationship with teachers. Develop instructional resources at the right price.
5.	Constantly and forever improve the system of production and service	Main focus is on productivity. Need to improve constantly methods of instruction, methods of assessment and methods of management.
6.	Institute modern methods of training on the job	Make sure that through training (on the job/ of the job) teachers are skilful for the jobs for which they are responsible.

(Contd...)

(Contd...)

7. Institute leadership	Managers (Principals) should realise that their role is to influence, cause, create and sustain an atmosphere within which teachers can be personally and professionally successful. Attitude should be "We do not work, we learn."
8. Drive Out Fear	Create a culture of openness, where people are not afraid of telling the truth. Encourage two-way communication. Employees must feel secure. Failure in performing innovative experiments even can be appreciated.
9 Break down barriers between stiff areas	Develop positive interdepartmental relationships. Learn from one another. Competition should be with other organisations, not within their own.
10 Eliminate slogans, exhortations and targets for the work force	Use quality improvement methods. Do it little better than before, continual improvement should be a general goal.
11 Eliminate numerical quotas	Focus on quality and not on quantity.
12 Remove barriers to pride on workmanship	Make the teachers feel that they are always being judged, ranked, and rated on the basis of their innovation, experimentation.
13 Institute a vigorous programme of education and training	Consider the needs of the staff for their own development. Plan out action programme based on development needs of teachers. Help them to achieve their own goals.
14. Take action to accomplish the transformation	The entire organisation must work together to enable a quality culture to succeed. Team work and team building should be given importance.

Benchmarking generates the indicators of quality, ISO 9000 provides a process of alternative to define acceptable level of quality, and TQM makes a unique contribution in generating organisation capacity and culture for quality assurance.

Table 18.3 shows an attempt to suggest implications of 14 cardinal principals as developed by Deming about total quality management in the field of teacher education.

Thus the above-mentioned 14 principles of TQM as given by Deming can be implemented in teacher education in order to assure quality in teacher education. One must keep in mind, at every stage of work, three fundamental principles of TQM:

1. Continuous improvement of quality.
2. Participation and involvement of teachers.
3. Developmental need-based programme for teachers.

REFERENCES

Acraro J. S., *Quality in Education An Implementation Handbook*, New Delhi, Vanity Books International, 1997.

Mukhopadhay, Marmar, *Total Quality Management in Education,* New Delhi, NIEPA, 2001.

Singh L.C., Sharma P.C., *Teacher Education and The Teacher*, New Delhi, Vikas Publishing House Pvt. Ltd.

Stones & Freeman, *Management,* New Delhi, Prentice Hall of India, 1997.

Young A., *The Manager's Handbook*, London: Sphere Books Ltd., 1986.

19

Performance Management: Conceptual Framework

Kailash Sodani* **and** ***Anita Sukhwal*****

Business thrives when people trust one another, but such "Social Capital" is under assault at many companies today. How can the company fight back? Social capital is under assault in most organisations today because of rising volatility and over-reliance on virtuality. In other words, social capital is under assault because building relationships in turbulent times is tough as volatility spawns opportunity through new technology. Secondly, social capital is under assault because few managers know how to invest in it as virtuality. Knowing that healthy relationships help an organisation, thrive is one thing; making those relationships happen in quite another.

"He who concentrates in the past or present will miss the future," quoted J. F. Kennedy. Performance management is the answer to all these problems. It helps you to:

Decide — Where you want to be in long term and why.

Plan — How to get there, with what resources and when to work out the steps on the journey.

**Prof., Deptt. of Business Administration, M. L. Sukhadia University, Udaipur (Raj.).*

***Asst. Prof., Pacific College, Udaipur (Raj.).*

Target — The results of each step that you have planned. Set Key Performance Indicators (KPIs). KPIs show what to measure to know have successful you are.

Action — Your plan.

Measure — Results constantly. Monitor the key performance indicators (KPIs) you set.

Connect — Your course, if you are not getting the planned results.

In managing at work, we are faced with change. The future is unmapped, uncertain and full of storms; whatever business, school, government, charity, etc., makes no difference. It is like crossing the Atlantic in 1606-07 as Captain Christopher Newport did, with three ships and more than a hundred people without any navigational aids and accurate charts. If your journey feels at all like this, try introducing proper performance management.

Performance management is about going around and round a loop to reach your goals. The loop spirals upwards to improve performance. This loop needs to be planned for every individual, every team and for the whole organisation. How often you go round it, depends on your circumstances, and speed of progress and change could be weekly, monthly, quarterly or annually. Of course, most organisation have measurement of result (at least financial ones). Do they monitor progress continuously? Captain Newport had to, or his fleet would have never reached America.

The Tasks, Method and Resources must link upward and downwards throughout the organisation. Each individual must knew how his tasks relate to other people or other departments and to the whole organisation, purpose and goals. To do this you need to develop process diagrams for the whole organisation.

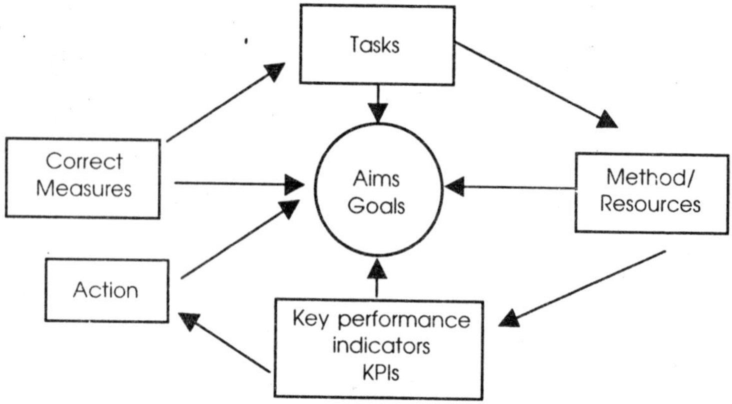

The Loop

The key performance indicates (KPIs) must be SMART, specify, measurable, agreed, realistic and time-bound. If they are not, they will be ignored. This is the hardest part of management.

Sometimes measurement shows that key performance indicators are not being achieved. What can you do? Shouting at the team or the individual is not the solution. What is needed is all the relevant acts and measurements or discussions with those who know about them and can make decision. You need to go round the loop to the plans, take account of the facts and re-plan. It is the correction of the course.

The performance management system has over 25 years of proven results. It can improve the way every organization manages its most valuable resource—the people who make everything possible. Every performance management implementation follows a time-tested process that ensures implementing success. At the same time, every performance management implementation is customised to meet individual client requirements. This combination of proven personalised care is the reason that performance management delivers improved and measurable business results every time.

Negative reinforcement generates enough behaviour to escape or avoid punishment. The improvement is usually described as "Just enough to get by". Positive reinforcement generates more behaviour then minimally required. We call this Discretionary Effort and its presence in the workplace is the only way the organisation can maximise performance. The results achieved with the application of performance management differ form 10 per cent increase in production, safety behaviour and so on to almost 40 per cent. Performance management is used in all kinds of companies—hospital, information technology, railroad, government and commercial enterprises.

I am presenting the ABC model which is the basis of performance management.

BASIS OF PERFORMANCE MANAGEMENT

ABC Model (Antecedent, Behaviour & Consequences)

Behaviour is what business is all about—why do people act the way whey do ? because consequence supports their behaviour. In a business environment many behaviours occur daily. Some of these behaviours affect our business directly (as well as positive as negative), while others are socially needed. By understanding what drives human behaviours, we can create the conditions necessary to encourage desired behaviour. The ABC model is an instrument which helps you understand the forces that drives human behaviour and applies these principles to instruments like a reward system, an organisational change, projects and so on. You can gain perspectives on why people act as they do and discover the pattern of consequences and antecedents that are associated with behaviour.

ANTECEDENT

An antecedent (sometimes referred to as activator) is something that occurs before a certain behaviour. This can be anything from a directive to the effect of the working environment. An antecedent appears both in everyday life and at workplace. Everything that prompts you to act a certain way (say switch a button) can be called an antecedent. An antecedent prompts you to take action.

In the world of business these would include policies, goals, directives, announcements, training programmes, procedure, vision, statement and so forth. All of these "set the stage" for a work behaviour or performance to take place, but they do not guarantee that it will occur. Managers are also frequent users of antecedents, telling people what to do, figuring out what to tell them to do or figuring out what to do because people did not do what they were told to do. They spend 80 per cent of their time using A (Antecedent) instead of B (Behaviour) and C (Consequences). Yes, you can say that business thrives on the use of antecedents. Although managing an antecedent appears to work, it is not the most efficient way to manage a business, sets of behaviour, actions or tasks of employees.

BEHAVIOURS

Behaviour is the centre of our universal activities. We behave in such a manner that we feel it is comfortable or just necessary. In business money making is the key goal. In order to reach this goal many actions must take place. We have to push buttons, write reports, have long meetings. Whatever we do or whatever has to be done, certain patterns of behaviour are involved. Imagine for a moment that an alien spacecraft is hovering over your place of work. Then imagine that it freezes all your employees like statues. Machines continue to run but people do not. The telephone rings but no one listens. How long will it be before your business is affected negatively. Without behaviour, no production. The same can be said about safety in the work-place, attendance, punctuality, quality and improving health in your workplace.

Behaviour is the keyword, because in business, there are so many behaviours going on. It is important to pinpoint those behaviours which directly affect the outcome of your business (process). These behaviours must support the goal and the mission of the firm. The process of pinpointing behaviour is a process done by the manager in cooperation with the employee. Helpful questions are:

a) Which actions have to take place to become an excellent employee?
b) What shows the difference between a productive and less productive employee?

One important thing is behaviour is observable so you can correct it, count it, appraise it and so manage it.

Results vs Behaviour

In business, mangers mostly focus on results instead of behaviour. They manage results, but there is a difference. Behaviours are the part of a process while results are outputs. Therefore managing results is not always as effective as it might seem.

CONSEQUENCES

What happens to us? Antecedents prompt you to act in a certain way and behaviour is an important part of business. The third item is the consequence. Consequences are powerful instruments for managers to use. They are also an instrument which is not used as frequently as it should be or used in a wrong way. For example, when a manager demonstrates what the worker needs to do, an antecedent strategy is being used (it is an instruction which prompts the employee to a specific behaviour. But, when the worker is praised for correct performance, a consequence strategy is applied.

Consequences and their Types

Reinforcement means increasing of the likelihood that the behaviour will be performed, or the intensity with which it is performed.

a) Positive reinforcement

Positive reinforcement is consequences that increase the possibility that (pinpointed) behaviour will occur more frequently in future. We can only speak of positive reinforcement, when the rate or frequency of behaviour changes in a positive way. For example, praise, bonus, giving attention, job rotation and working on projects can be the positive reinforcements. But different strokes are for different folks. Individuals have preferences. Some people prefer a pat on the back accompanied by words like "You did a fine job", while others get reinforced only by an approving look or a cynical remark.

b) Negative reinforcement

This consequence also increases the likelihood that the behaviour occurs again. In contrast to positive behaviour frequently people behave in a certain way because they have to, not because they want to. They act to avoid negative consequences, e.g., being punished by the boss. In issues like safety rules (punctuality, discipline, etc.), negative reinforcement can be effective but though is it is less desirable than positive ones. Still, they are frequently used by management.

c) Punishment

When being punished the person gets something he does not want. Punishment leads to fear and will stop the behaviour continuing. Being chewed out after launching an idea, regarding on how to optimise the business process, can inadventently stop this behaviour (to launch a new idea). Different strokes for different folks is the buzzword.

d) Extinction

In a meeting you try to bring forward a new idea and nobody pays attention to you. You try again and you are ignored once again, finally you say nothing. In the some way, ignoring withholding social reinforcement results in extinction of behaviour. Many performance problems are created not by what we do, but by what we don't do.

ABC model : A good understanding of these principles can be very profitable to an organisation. These principles can be used not only for managing behaviour but also when developing a reward system or conducting a performance appraisal.

Reinforcement

While tailoring performance management programme the manager has to choose a combination of reinforcements:

— Personal - Calling by name (personal touch)

— Sincere - Mean what you say.

— Specific - The receiver of the reinforcer must know exactly why he received a particular reinforcement (Why he is being praised).

— Immediate - "Reinforce while the employee is doing what you want".

— Frequently - (4:1 Ratio rule), one negative, at least four opportunities somewhere in the work-place to reinforce desired performance.

To conclude, managers must go to "Managing by walking around" instead of "Managing by wandering around".

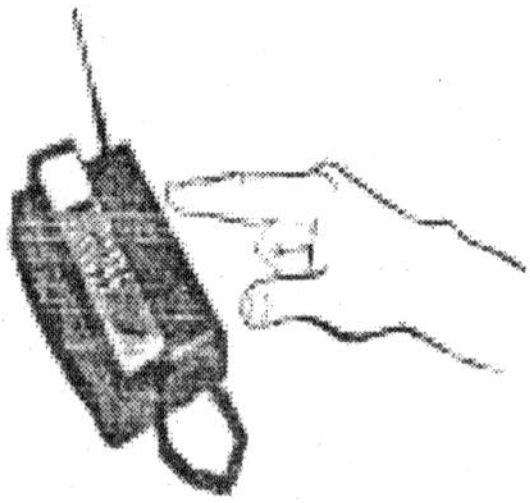

The phone prompts the man (Antecedent) to walk to it and pick it up (Behaviour). Next, he hears somebody speak (Consequence). If it is somebody he likes to speak to, we call it a positive consequence.

Good performance management is an essential tool for continuous improving of an organisation, performances. But it is not only the tool that is needed. Managers play a central role in this. All staff must be on board too. Find out why successful managers invest so much of their time in training and what they gain from that. Also, the organisation must realise that effective plan management can, and does, contribute through toxic handlers in performance management

PART III

Empowerment of Women and Education

20

A Walking Phenomenon? Women in Educational Leadership in England within a Performance Culture

*Rosalind Morton**

INTRODUCTION

The United Kingdom contains four countries, with distinct and different education systems. The focus of this presentation is the state-maintained part of the English education system. In broad terms the presentation also supports the definition of occupations as outlined by Noscow and Form as a group of people who have similar skills, who perform similar roles and these roles attract a market value which people are paid to perform. It takes the view that work is a pervasive social activity, which involves processes of social interaction with others, and which is a major source of personal identity. Whilst some research exists about the work and expectations of women teachers, there is relatively little in the UK, and even less about women in senior positions within the state system of education. In addition, earlier research may not reflect accurately the current situation: one in which there is a national shortage of teachers and headteachers it is hoped that this presentation

**Senior Research Officer, The National Foundation for Educational Research, Slough, England*

will spark a debate about the 'secret garden' of women's careers in this field. In the words of Glaser: 'In a sense a person's own career is a sensitive or taboo topic. Discussions only occur under the most private and discreet conditions."

CONTEXT OF WOMEN'S ROLES IN ENGLISH SOCIETY IN 20TH CENTURY

During the nineteenth and early twentieth centuries in England, one of women's most public, political struggles was to gain the vote. The suffrage movement in great Britain began with Chartism, but it was not until 1851 that a resolution in favour of female suffrage was presented in the House of Lords by the Earl of Carlyle. John Stuart Mill in his *Subjection of Women* (1869) was one of the earliest protagonists for the right of women to vote. Among the leaders in the early British suffrage movement were Lydia Becker, Barbara Bodichon, Emily Davies and Dr. Elizabeth Garrett Anderson. Jacob Bright presented a bill for women suffrage in the House of Commons in 1870. In 1881 the Isle of Man granted the vote to women who owned property. Local British societies united in 1897 into the National Union of Women's Suffrage Societies, of which Millicent Garrett Fawcett was President until 1919. In 1903 a militant suffrage movement emerged under the leadership of Emmeline Pankhurst and her daughters. Their organisation was the Women's Social and Political Union. The militant suffragists maintained a high public profile: for example, by heckling political speakers and through street meetings. The leaders were often imprisoned for inciting riot. In prison, many resorted to hunger strike. At the start cf World War I, the suffragists ceased all militant activity and devoted their organisation to the service of the government and the war effort. After the war a limited suffrage was granted to women of property. In 1928 voting rights for men and women were equalised.

However, gaining the right to vote was not the same as gaining equality in the workplace. The place of women in the working world was once again affected by war. In the Second World War between 1939 and 1945, women took on the work of men who were called to fight: in the factories, on the land, driving buses, in offices, as teachers. In order to carry out much of this work, they also needed to warm 'men's' clothes, such as trousers. At the end of the war in 1945, women were expected to return to their domestic duties and relinquish their places in the world to the men returning home from the armed services. But with the availability in the 1960s of the contraceptive pill, women began to exercise more choice over whether and when to bare children. That in its turn changed their perceptions of their place within the world of work. In reality, the 1950's notion of women's role being in the home as nurtures and child-rearers was of limited historical perspective. As an industrialised society, England has seen the majority of women working, for example, from the home and later, in factories, since the eighteenth century.

EQUAL OPPORTUNITIES PICTURE TODAY

A concern for equality of opportunity within the world of work has now been enshrined in law. Some of the concerns expressed by the campaigning organisations in the first quarter of the twentieth century have been incorporated into official agencies, close to government, in not always of government.

Legal Position

The Sex Discrimination Act of 1975 (SDA) prohibits sex discrimination against individuals in the areas of employment, education, and in the provision of goods, facilities and services and in the disposal or management of premises. It also prohibits discrimination in employment against married people. It is not unlawful to discriminate against someone because they are not married. Victimisation because someone has tried to exercise their rights under the SDA or Equal Pay Act is prohibited. The SDA applies to women and men of any age, including children.

The Act also defines sex discrimination, for example, direct sex discrimination is where a woman (or man) is treated less favourably than a person of the opposite sex in comparable circumstances is, or would be because of he (or his) sex. Types of direct sex discrimination include sexual harassment and treating a woman adversely because she is pregnant.

Indirect sex discrimination is where a condition or practice is applied to both sexes but it adversely affects a considerably larger proportion of one sex than the other, and it is not justifiable, irrespective of sex, to apply that condition or practice, e.g., an unnecessary requirement to be under 5' 10" would discriminate against men; a requirement to work full-time might be unlawful discrimination against women.

Campaigning and monitoring organisations

The Equal Opportunities Commission [EOC] perceives itself as the leading agency working to eliminate sex discrimination in the twenty-first century Britain. It was established under the Sex Discrimination Act in 1975. An independent statutory body, it has the following legal powers:

a) To work towards the elimination of discrimination on the grounds of sex or marriage
b) To promote equality of opportunity for women and men
c) To keep under review the Sex Discrimination Act and the Equal Pay Act
d) To provide legal advice and assistance to individuals who have been discriminated against.

The status of the EOC is as a non-departmental public body, or quango, funded through grant-in-aid. The sponsoring government department is the Women and Equality Unit at the

Cabinet Office. Although independent from the government, the EOC is responsible to the Minister for Women and Equality at the Cabinet Office. The EOC also campaigns to:

a) Close the pay gap between women and men.
b) Make it easier for parents to balance work with family responsibilities.
c) Increase the number of women in public life.
d) Break free of male and female stereotypes.
e) End sexual harassment at work.
f) Make public services relevant to the differing needs of men and women.
g) Secure comprehensive equality legislation in Europe, England, Scotland and Wales.

One the EOC's current campaigns is to increase the number of women in public life. There were 1,000 public bodies in Britain in 2001 covering 30,000 public appointments. The EOC argues that women are under-represented in public life. They make up 51 per cent of the population yet take up one-third of regional and national public appointments. They also tend to occupy the low status and unpaid appointments. Women hold few appointments paying more than £ 50,000 per annum. Black and ethnic minority women and women who are disabled may face disadvantage on the grounds of race or disability as well as on grounds of sex. The EOC believes that this under-representation of women is a major waste of the abilities and skills needed by public bodies. (cf Appendix)

The government has announced its long-term commitment to the equal representation of men and women in public appointments, a pro-rata representation to ethnic minorities and increased representation of disabled people. In support of this commitment, all government departments have published equal opportunities plans with targets and timetables. The role of Commissioner for Public Appointments has been created and a Code of Practice issued by the Office of the Commissioner for Public Appointments. The Code applies the principles of openness and transparency to the appointments process.

In another of its current research campaigns, *Women and Men in Britain: Management (Glass ceiling and sticky floor leave women the poorer sex)*, (cf. Appendix) the EOC has found that:

a) Men dominate in none out of the eleven managerial groups, the exceptions being financial institution and office managers, and health and social services managers.

b) The few sectors in which women account for 50 per cent or more of managers are in fields of work dominated by women overall, including education and health and social services.

c) Only six per cent of managers were employed part-time, and three-quarters of these were women.

d) Twenty-two per cent of managers usually worked more than 50 hours per week, and male managers (27%) were more likely than female managers (10%) to do so.

e) Women managers are less likely than male managers to have dependent children. Forty-seven per cent of male managers had dependent children. Forty-seven per cent of male managers had dependent children, and 20 per cent had at least one child under five. In comparison 35 per cent of female managers had dependent children and 12 per cent had at least one child under five.

The Fawcett Society is one of the oldest non-governmental campaigning organisations of greater equality for women in Britain. It has been in existence for over 130 years, taking its name from Millicent Fawcett, the prominent suffragist. It is a lobbying organisation which sets itself to challenge the myth women have achieved equality of opportunity in British society. In its 2001 launch of a year-long campaign, *Where are the Women?*, it aimed to show that women had not yet reached a position of equality in society with men and focused on four areas: politics, media, health and education.

For example, the society argues that there are no women Law Lords; that in November 2000, 45 companies in the FTSE 100 had no women on their Board, while the remaining 45 had just one woman on their Board. The society also argues that the pay gap between men and women has not been closed; that women working full-time earn approximately 80 per cent of the hourly wage of a man working full-time; and that this drops to 60 per cent for women working part-time. They calculate if the pay gap continues to close at the same rate it has done since 1975, it will take 40 years for women to achieve equal pay.

Professional associations for teachers and headteachers also provide campaigns for equality of opportunity. These will be mentioned in more detail within the next section.

WOMEN'S ROLE AS TEACHERS AND ADMINISTRATORS WITHIN THE STATE MAINTAINED EDUCATION SYSTEM

Many would imagine that a career in teaching and educational administration presents ideal opportunities for women. Teaching and local government posts should attract equal pay and the recruitment processes should be conducted, within the public sector, according to the law relation to equality of opportunity. However, the picture is not an unequivocal one. In this section, the profile of women's qualifications, roles in education and their pay will be outlined.

In England many responsibilities for the management of education system lie at school level. This includes the responsibility for the appointment of staff. The Department of Education and Skills (DfES) publishes statistics to show the numbers of teachers employed within the state system, but they are not necessarily accurate: especially when casual, supply and short-term contracts are considered. The DfES estimates a 10-20 per cent discrepancy (DfES website).

Teachers in Service

The following three tables show the overall numbers of qualified and unqualified teachers working full-time and in occasional service in January 2002 within English nursery and primary, secondary and special schools.

Table 20.1: Teacher numbers: 1996 to 2001 by sector and type of service (source DfES website statistical database 2002)

England: Nursery and primary schools, January 2002

	1996	*1997*	*1998*	*1999*	*2000*	*2001*
Qualified teachers full-time	198,530	198,970	197,290	198,810	202,160	204,580
In regular service	176,180	175,750	173,900	173,890	174,720	174630
On secondment	140	160	60	120	170	120
In occasional service	7,660	8,310	8,290	8,920	10,520	11,960
Teachers without QTS	1,050	1,010	1,110	1,230	1,460	2,350
Total	199,570	199,980	198,400	200,040	203,620	206,920

Numbers of Headteachers and Deputies: Male and Female

The same database shows that in English-maintained schools during the same period there were more women teachers overall than men. In primary schools there were more women than men headteachers, but more male headteachers in secondary and special schools. At deputy head level, there were more women than men. Women are better qualified overall, as measured by graduate status *(Source: Database of Teacher Records in DfES statistics website).*

Posts in Education Administration and School Improvement

The latest available information about the chief inspectors for education, who hold senior school improvement positions in local education authorities, showed that men outnumber women by two to one. The latest available information on the chief education officers, the statutory officers who work in local education authorities, showed that of 140 [out of the 154 total number of English LEAs], 118 were male and 32 female. No information was available about levels of qualifications or pay differentials between men and women.

Teachers and Headteachers' Pay

Women are clearly not equally represented within positions of authority within schools, particularly at headship level, nor at the professional and officer levels within local education authorities. Inequalities in pay emerge more pronouncedly because men tend to be the headteachers of the larger, secondary schools and within the high paid LEA positions. There is also anecdotal evidence that within the new arrangements for headteachers' pay, men are more assertive in persuading their governors of the need for annual performance pay rises.

From 1 September 1993, the government introduced a new common 18-point pay spine for classroom teachers. A teacher's position on the new spine is determined by the total number of points awarded. A relevant body, that is, in the case of a school with a delegated budget, the school's governing body, may award points under six headings: qualifications, experience, special educational needs, recruitment and retention, responsibilities and excellence. From 1 September 1996, half spine points were introduced to the classroom teachers' pay spine.

Headteachers and deputy headteachers, however, have a separate pay system with 51 incremental points. A head or deputy headteacher's pay is determined by a number of factors including: responsibilities of the post; social, economic and cultural background of the pupils attending; and the group number to which the school is assigned, that is, the size of the school.

The teachers' and headteachers' professional associations recognise issues of inequality of status and pay between women and men. The National Union to Teachers [NUT], for example, argues the educational importance for children throughout their school careers to be taught by both women and men represented throughout the school staffing structure and throughout the range of the curriculum. The NUT has a tradition of campaigning for equality: as early as 1904 for equal pay for women teachers. However, it recognises that even now, with equal pay as an established principle, the average pay of women teachers is still lower than that of men because of lack of promotion among women teachers. It campaigns particularly on equality issues which affect women:

a) fair and equal appointment procedure
b) improved professional development opportunities for women teachers
c) refresher courses, career counselling and 'keeping in touch' schemes for teachers who have taken career breaks
d) representation of women teachers in senior management roles proportionate to the numbers of women in the profession
e) improvements in the rights of teachers to maternity leave and the establishment of paternity leave, adoptive leave and other forms of family leave
f) nursery education to be available for all three-and four-year-olds
g) a comprehensive network of childcare facilities to support working parents.

Its current campaigns echo the majority of the issues outlined in the NUT's 1978 study, jointly with the EOC, *Promotion and the Woman Teacher,* raising the question of how intractable these issues are and how slow real change appears to be in materialising.

Table 20.2

Teacher numbers: 1996 to 2001 by sector and type of service (source DfES website statistical database 2002)

England: secondary schools, January 2002

	1996	*1997*	*1998*	*1999*	*2000*	*2001*
Qualified teachers full-time	191,950	192,050	191,660	194,190	196,420	200,310
In regular service	174,420	174,240	173,840	175,630	176,520	179,520
On secondment	50	40	30	40	110	50
In secondment	4,120	4,390	3,990	4,460	5,320	6,550
Teachers without QTS	1,810	1,770	1,910	2,050	2,100	2,920
Total	193,760	193,820	193,570	196,240	198,520	203,230

Table 20.3

Teacher numbers: 1996 to 2001 by sector and type of service (source DfES website statistical database 2002)

England: Special schools, January 2002

	1996	*1997*	*1998*	*1999*	*2000*	*2002*
Qualified teachers full-time	15,580	15,380	14,930	14,790	14,810	14,850
In regular service	13,490	13,490	13,050	12,880	12,810	12,690
On secondment	40	60	10	10	30	10
In occasional service	630	680	670	640	690	820
Teachers without QTS	110	150	170	230	210	300
Total	15,690	15,520	15,100	15,020	15,020	15,150

THE PERFORMANCE CULTURE IN THE ENGLISH EDUCATION SYSTEM

From a position until the 1980s where relatively little regulation existed particularly in primary education, over what was taught in the classroom, of how it was taught, the current state-maintained educational system in England is characterised by regulation and accountability, at almost every level in the system. Joan Swann, in *Language and Gender: who, if anyone is disadvantaged by what*? portrays the language of performance as a masculinisation of the education agenda: with vocabulary, for example, such as 'targeting'.

The 1944 Education Act had seen a tradition of teacher-led curriculum, especially in primary education and for pupils in the secondary modern system. Responsibility for the quality of teaching and learning had been lodged predominantly at individual school and local education authority level. There had been difficulties with this system. Most notably, statistical analyses of examination results was beginning to highlight that pupils in ostensibly similar circumstances were achieving very different standards across the country. Politically Britain was seen to be falling behind other countries in international comparisons of standards: and this was equated with Britain's ability to compete in international economic markets. There were parallel concerns about the quality of teacher training in England.

The 1988 Education Act introduced the National Curriculum divided into curriculum subjects from age five through to the end of secondary education. According to Key Stages in 1997 the national strategies for teaching literacy and numeracy were introduced; in addition to a national strategy for information technology in primary education for the first time, the national strategies saw government not only prescribing the content of the curriculum, they also its pedagogy.

Pupils

Pupils' progress and attainment are tracked and assessed from Baseline Assessment at age five, through the end of Key Stage assessments, at age seven, eleven and fourteen, (Key Stags One, Two and Three) to terminal examinations (GCSE and equivalent examinations at age 16 and 'A' Level and equivalent examinations at age eighteen). Pupils also now are given a Unique Pupils Number (UPN) by the DfES, so that their progress can be tracked as they move through the system.

Teachers

Teachers are required to teach the national curriculum, national strategies and the examination syllabi. There exists public and semi-public accountability for the standards achieved by pupils through comparison with the achievements of others via the published *League Tables*. Teachers are also inspected through the national system of school inspection by the Office for Standards in Education (OFSTED) on the quality of their teaching and management of the curriculum and assessment regime. In addition, they are assessed on their professional performance in order to qualify for continuing pay increases: the 'threshold' assessments.

Headteachers

Headteachers have formal accountability for the school's governing body for the standards achieved by pupils as well as for the school's leadership, management and administration. They are held to public account for the standards achieved by pupils through comparison of achievement against other similar schools via the published *League Tables*. Heads are inspected by Ofsted through the national inspection process according to the results achieved by the pupils, for the quality of teaching of the staff and for their general management of the school and its relations with parents and the community. The resulting inspection reports are made public by Ofsted. The headteachers' professional performance is assessed by governors, who make the decision, according to national criteria, as to whether a pay increase is justified. There are national programmes of training for aspiring heads (NPQH) and for serving heads (LPSH), which are likely to become mandatory qualification for headship in the future.

School as Individual Institutions and Groups of Schools

Individual schools are inspected by Ofsted and they are held to public account via the *League Tables* according to the end of Key Stage assessments and terminal examination results. By these means they are compared with other schools locally and nationally. Groups of schools, geographically and by cohorts are compared via the DfES' statistical analysis, according to the end to Key Stage assessments and terminal examination results. By these means they are compared with other schools locally and nationally. Groups of schools, geographically and by cohorts are compared via the DfES' statistical analysis, according to the end of Key Stage tests and terminal examinations: and via national reports on the implementation of the national strategies.

Local Education Authorities (LEAs)

LEAs are held to account by comparison with other LEAs of pupils' attainment via public *League Tables*. National website information about local education authorities provides information about LEA performance, together with case studies and opportunities for the sharing of good practice in relation to the local education authority role in the promotion of high standards and raising achievement. LEAs are also inspected jointly by Ofsted and the Audit Commission on their capacity to promote higher standards and to improve the quality of education within the maintained schools in their area. The reports resulting from these inspections are made public.

Boys' Underachievement

Such a system of high-profile public accountability affects all teachers, however, in one respect it affects women teachers more: a current public issue within this context is the apparent underachievement of boys and the possible role female teachers have in failing to combat this underachievement. The DfES statistical analysis outlines, via the Gender and Achievement section of *The Standards Site*, the following picture:

a. Boys lag behind in early literacy skills and later on in English.
b. Boys perform considerably less well than girls in the GCSE examinations; girls have been making greater progress between the ages of 11 and 16 than boys.
c. Girls continue to opt out of mathematics and science in the later stages of their educational careers. Boys still dominate science and technology at A Level.
d. In recent years there has been a virtual elimination of the gap in overall performance at A/AS Level subjects, in favour of boys.
e. Gender-related patterns of examination entry have persisted in the majority of A Level subjects for much of the last decade.

The DfES is clear within this arena that 'blanket statements about girls performing better than boys or vice versa are difficult to justify. Reference should be made to particular groups of young people, to specific aspects of the curriculum, or to different levels of performance. Moreover, it is important to remember that while gender is one of the key factors affecting educational performance, it functions in relation to other social variables such as social class, ethnic origin and local context.

However unjustified, popular media continue to associate the predominance of female teachers in primary education with the underachievement of boys, particularly black Afro-Caribbean boys. In their research study, John Gray, Mary James and Jean Rudduck of Homerton College, Cambridge, explore the questions posed by different styles of classroom learning, subject and curriculum content, approaches to assessment, peer group influence, local labour markets, phases of concern about gender-related issues and key strategies developed by some schools to combat underachievement.

What is not clear is whether the performance and accountability culture overall within the English education system affects men and women disproportionately. No evidence was available which tracks trends in appointments to headships and other senior positions, for example, in schools with serious weaknesses of LEA officers to authorities receiving critical inspection reports. No evidence was available, for example, by which to examine whether changes in women's perceptions of their careers in education are affected by a culture which emphasises outcomes and meeting target.

SETTING THE CONTEXT FOR EXPLORING ILLUSTRATIVE PERSONAL EXPERIENCE OF WOMEN HOLDING EDUCATIONAL LEADERSHIP POSITIONS

Vara Chadwick, the first woman is 1985 to win a sex discrimination case against an English local education authority, outlined her experience of organisational discrimination and gender stereotyping in the process of seeking a headship in *Equal Opportunities in the Teaching Profession—The Myth and the Reality.*

Janet Ouston, in *Women in Education Management* outlined the by-now well-rehearsed but reiterating key issues corresponding to the under-representation of women in management positions:

a. Different styles of management used by men and women
b. Women's attitudes to their careers

c. The micro-politics of the workplace
d. Women's lack of confidence in applying for senior posts
e. Women's general lack of confidence about their abilities
f. The different career paths of men and women
g. The tendency of women not to plan their careers explicitly
h. Job-related stress
i. Women's responsibilities for children
j. The issue of a new managerial paradigm needed which is more woman-friendly

Anne Gold discussed the reticence of women in recognising their careers as a legitimate subject for discussion.

In her study of women's career patterns in further education, Margaret Sanderson highlighted the ambivalence women experience in pursuing management positions within cultures they feel to be male-dominated, where they feel alienated. She also found that women's actual experience could contradict national trends, for example, in the relative disproportion of child care responsibilities between the full-time lecturers and the women in management positions.

While during the twentieth century, the search for equal opportunities between women and men has been enshrined in law, many of the issues appear to persist for women in positions of management in education.

APPENDICES

Appendix I

The Equal Opportunities Commission's current projects include:

The Views and Experiences of Parliamentary Candidates: A Gendered Perspective Research team: MORI Social Research Institute. Start date: July 2001.

Promoting Gender Equality in the Public Sector. Research team: Centre for Public Services. Start date: January 2002.

Appendix 2

EOC campaign: Glass ceiling and sticky floor leave women the poorer sex.

24 January 2002

Women will remain the poorer sex until there is a radical change of culture in workplaces across Britain, Julie Mellor, Chair of the Equal Opportunities Commission (EOC), said today. She called on all employers to tackle the long hours culture and to check their pay systems were fair.

Women and Men in Britain: Management, an EOC report out today, reveals that although women now account for 30 per cent of managers in Britain, they still earn 24 per cent less per hour than male managers. They only make up 50 per cent or more of managers in sectors traditionally associated with women, such as education and health and social services.

New figures on pay, also published today by the Office for National Statistics, show women working full-time in 2001 earned 18.5 per cent less per hour than men working full-time, compared with 19.9 per cent in 2000. The gap between women part-time workers' hourly earnings and men full-time workers' hourly earnings increased from 40.2 per cent on 2000 to 41.3 per cent in 2001.

Commenting on the figures, Ms Mellor said:

> The new figures on pay reveal the shameful truth that Britain is still failing to make any significant progress towards closing the gender pay gap. The gap between part-time women and full-time men's hourly earnings actually increased in the last year. Women will remain the poorer sex until there is a radical change of working culture in all sectors and at all levels. Routine pay reviews to check that pay systems don't short-change women are an essential part of the culture change needed.

> The dire shortage of flexible work and decent part-time work at senior levels, the long hours culture, and out-of-date ideas about 'women's work' also combine to keep women down. Men who want to spend more time with their family who work in fields traditionally dominated by women lose out too.
>
> This is not just about breaking the glass ceiling, but also about getting rid of the sticky floor that keeps so many women trapped in low-paid employment. It is time Britain's employers recognised the benefits of giving all their workers the opportunity to fulfil their potential.

REFERENCES

Arnot, M., Gray J., James, M. and Rudduck, J., *Recent Research on Gender and Educational Performance*, Homerton College, Cambridge, on *The Standards Site*.

Chadwick, V., 1989, *Equal Opportunities in the Teaching Profession—The Myth and the Reality,* in De Lyon & Widdowson Migniuoulo.

Chinoy, E., 1955, *Automobile Workers and the American Dream,* Boston, Beacon Press.

DfES, *The Standards Site,* www.standards.dfes.gov.uk/genderachievement/data.

Epstein, D., Elwood, J., Hey, V and Maw, J. (Eds), 1998, *Failing Boys? Issues in Gender and Achievement,* Buckingham, Open University Press.

Evetts, J., 1990, *Women in Primary Teaching: Career Contexts and Strategies.* London: Unwin Hyman.

Glaser, B.G., 1968, *Organisational Careers: A Sourcebook for Theory* Chicago: Aldine Publishing Company.

Gold, A., 1993, *'Women-friendly' Management Development Programmes'* in Ouston.

Hughes, E. C., 1958, The study of occupations, in Merton, R. K., Broom, L. and Cottrell, L. (Eds) *Sociology Today.* New York: Basic Books.

Lyon De, H. & Widdowson Migniuoulo, F. 1989 *Women Teachers: Issues and Experiences,* Milton Keynes: Open University Press.

Maclean, R.,1992, *Teachers' Career and Promotion Patterns. A Sociological Analysis.* London, the Falmer Press.

Miller, J., 1996, *School for Women,* London, Virago.

Morton, Rosalind, *School Development and Leadership: an International Perspective,* presentation at the University of Uppsala, 2000.

National Statistics Database: www.statistics.gov.uk/statbase.

National Union of Teachers, 1962, *Man, Work and Society: A Reader in the Sociology of Occupations.* New York: Basic Books.

Ouston, J., 1993, *Women in Education Management,* London, Longman.

Pavalko, R. M., 1972, *Sociology of Occupations and Professions,* Itasia, ILL: F. E. Peacock.

Sales, L. R., 1989, *Leadership: Managing in Real Organisations,* New York: McGraw-hill Book Company.

Sanderson, M., 1993, *A Study of Women's Career Patterns in Further Education,* unpublished thesis.

Swann, J., 1998, in Epstein, D., Elwood, J., Hey, V. and Maw, J. (Eds.), 1998; Waller, W. 1961, orig. 1936, *The Sociology of Teaching,* New York: Wiley.

21

Status and Empowerment of Women in Educational Leadership

*Hemlata Talesra**

The last hundred years may rightly be called the age of women awakening in the world. In every part of the world equality of the sexes has been ensured and various laws have been passed to improve the status of women. However, despite all changes women cannot be regarded as being emancipated from orthodoxy and the old traditions. The social and religious attitude towards the role of women in the family and society, which still have a stronghold on the minds of the people are the main hurdle in the way of social progress of women. In India and some other countries society is still male-dominated. The double standard of morality graciously provides more social freedom to men than to women. The major burden of adjustment and the household work falls mainly on the women.

Due to the above reason representation of women in top management positions in universities and other higher educational institutions are negligible. In India 30.3 per cent women educational managers are available out of the total teaching profession and they are severely represented at senior academic management positions. In a democratic process where administration demands the active participation of women and

Retd. Professor and Head, Department of Educational Planning, Management and Administration, Vidya Bhawan, G. S. Institute of Advanced Studies in Education, Udaipur (Rajasthan).

men, it is observed that the women do not contribute their best what they are capable of. The UNESCO World conference in 1998 argued that the presence of a critical mass of women in the decisionmaking process remains vastly inadequate. Generally, the men dominate the decisionmaking process. It is usually found that the educational administrators who join an institution as raw hands and with lack of any systematic training in management and administration or with special emphasis on decision making, they often find it quite difficult to take right and quick decisions.

The year 2001 being the year of 'Women's Empowerment' was an appropriate time to discuss the issues on women's leadership positions. The year 2002 should be considered for the follow-up programmes. This paper makes an attempt to analyse the status of women and suggest strategies for their empowerment in educational leadership.

Modern trends in para-psychology have declared that both men and women have common genetic abilities. For the balanced and sustainable development of society women should participate actively and freely in the process of administration. To some extent the participation of women is satisfactory in the primary and secondary levels of education. Only few women have access to higher education positions. And though the number of women teachers at college and university levels is increasing gradually, the number of women administrators at this level is very low. The data regarding the women holding various top management positions at higher education level shows that there are only 11 Vice-chancellors, 1 Pro Vice-chancellor, 3 Registrars, 66 Deans, 13 Directors and 12 Librarians among 290 universities and other higher educational institutions throughout India.

These figures reveal the fact that women are severely under-represented in top leadership positions at the higher education level in India. Whatever may be the factors responsible, whether it is due to Indian socio-cultural setup or the women themselves are responsible, the need of women participation in higher educational administration is undebatable and essential.

To face the challenges of a nation it is necessary that higher numbers of men as well as women take up leadership positions from lower to higher levels of education and participate actively in the decisionmaking process by overcoming the barriers. In order to achieve the objective of equal representation, women have to be empowered to provide leadership. The National Commission on Self-employed Women (1987-88) and the National Policy on Education (1986) Stressed the women's representation and leadership in different sectors and their equality through empowerment. There have been attempts made by many national and international organisations to impart training and skills to women for empowering them. Despite all the efforts women's representation in leadership positions is not satisfactory. This issue requires a strategic review and needs to be followed by firm action.

BRIEF HISTORY

In 1900 women did not have any formal position to influence policy and decision making. But by 1920 women intelligentsia assumed their stand on social issues and made their voice felt in the deliberations of society. They followed the tactics of lobbying for such purpose, which in fact was a male procedure adopted by them to demonstrate female opinion and influence in public decision making. Subsequently, during 1930-1950 women were concerned with four major issues:

1. Female education
2. Indenture system of female labourers
3. To vote and the right to sit in legislature
4. Legal charges concerning marriage, particularly the age of consummation.

To represent these issues, women followed three tactics: (1) resolution (2) petition and (3) meeting with Viceroy, Governor and government Committees to represent their case.

Gradually, educational institutions were established and women teachers, though very rare in numbers, also took participation in the administrative process of the institution and they proved themselves worthy of the same. In the fifties the M. S. University of Baroda, Vadodara, had the visionary Hansa Mehta, as its first woman Vice Chancellor. During the last part of the twentieth century, importance to girls education, Women's liberation movement, changes in sociocultural values, the revolutionised science and technology have contributed a lot to bring women into the mainstream. Realising the importance of women's participation in the decisionmaking process in all spheres of activities, many efforts have been put by national and international agencies, viz., MHRD, government of India, UGC, New Delhi, UNDP. But in spite of all these it is unfortunate to note that the number of women's representation in leadership positions is necessary to see the barriers that hinder the advancement of women educational leaders.

Barriers faced by Women Educational Leaders

India is a multicultural society. The behaviour pattern of women is decided to a great extent by their religion, race, region, class, etc. The women with a different background, therefore, have dissimilar barriers. Some of the barriers are as follows:

1. Age-old attitudes and customs

Age-old attitudes and customs have made women accept their position in the world of Bertrand Russell's 'Mental Prison'. Women's position at home and outside is so closely interlinked that it is very difficult to separate them. The position of women at home would refer to two aspects of a person's social position role and status role, referring to obligations and duties, and status referring to rights, privileges, power and prestige.

2. Patriarchy

In India patriarchy is a system of male domination and superiority of male control in which women are subordinate—a system of social structures and practices in which men dominate, oppress, and exploit women. This system is reinforced by an ideology that men are superior to women. Subordination destroys self-respect, self-esteem and self-confidence of the family. Religion, the legal system, the economic system and economic institutions, the political system and institutions, media and educational institutions and knowledge of them, control economic, political, religious, social and cultural institutions. All these affect negatively women educational leaders.

3. Inequality and disparity

India now has more than half a century's experience in dealing with sharp disparities rooted in several millennia. Gender disparities in educational and all other social and demographic indicators reflect the unequal position of women. We still have inequalities in caste, creed, tribe and rural urban divide. Gender cuts across all these layers making women leaders like the other women. Women leaders do more work than males but get so much less than their legitimate share in food, health, education, and resources which continue to exist. The traditional socialisation practices of a society with a marked male preference, are highly discriminatory and not only physically short changes the women on food, healthcare, education and play, but also succeed in making her believe that she is inferior and less competent than her male counterparts. Women managers come into the institution with a negative self-image and poor self-esteem. The issue of women assuming the rightful place of equality with all human beings cannot be achieved if one half of the population, that is, the male half, remains ignorant as to the rights and needs of women, the duties of both men and women. Too many of our through processes and actions have become ingrained over centuries in a milieu of social prejudice and taboo.

4. Negative Self-image

Right from birth Indian women suffer from negative-self image. Even at the higher education level women educational leaders consider themselves far behind the male workers for the same job. On the basis of my doctoral work on 'Higher Education among Women' only five per cent women leaders consider them strong to work in any part of the country; most of them consider themselves the 'weaker segment' of the society and inefficient to provide leadership.

5. Hurdle to Join leadership Job

In Indian society, there are a large number of hurdles to join the leadership positions and jobs. The overall social setup where they are born, grow, study, work and live their lives is not favourable to work in the topmost position. The type of discriminating behaviour, specifically on the social and educational fronts, puts a lot of hindrances in the proper development of their personalities. Most of the women are not able to contribute to the national development to the desired extent.

6. Traditional and Conservative thinking do not accept women leadership

The traditional and conservative society has not adjusted itself to what has happened. It has been rather a bitter pill thrust down its throat. It may not sound very convincing, but it is a fact that even today an office-going lady is looked upon with suspicion. The reason behind this may be that people will relish any scandal attached with the name of a lady occupying a responsible position.

7. Unsafe feeling

Most of the women who have occupied one chair of authority

or another are equal to men's but we will have to admit the fact that in this respect she is weaker by all means. She is still in need of security and protection.

8. Devotion for household duties

A woman who may be in the topmost leadership position devotes plenty of time for the upbringing of her children. Working women, who are out for six or eight hours a day, devote the rest of the time and energy to perform their duties at home. This has resulted in our social and domestic life becoming an anchorless ship sailing at the mercy of the waves which may drift her to a rock-bed of disaster.

9. Negative social attitude and prejudices

The more specific problems of women leaders are the result of social attitudes and prejudices. Social scientists recognise five distinct handicaps of women managers:

a) She receives lower pay for the same work.

b) The jobs of higher salary, skill and authority are closed to her.

c) Her husband's employment takes precedence over her own and thus decreases her mobility and her market.

d) Continuous advancement in her job is interrupted by her homemaking period.

e) Home making, her fundamental responsibility, offers no regular pay and gives no prestige.

NEGATIVE ATTITUDE ABOUT THE EXPERTISE IN EXECUTIVE WORK

There is a general feeling that women cannot supervise or manage educational matters effectively. Women use their feminine qualities to gain the advantages of promotions and other privileges. But modern trends in para-psychology have declared that both men and women have common generic abilities. Women have been proven educational leaders and, if enlightened, the attributes required for a woman leader in education are: sincerity, humility, gratitude, perseverance, aspiration, receptivity, progress, courage, goodness, generosity, equality and peace.

Women Leaders and Nation Building

The wide gender disparity in influential and decisionmaking positions between men and women resulted in the wasting of valuable human resources. Women's potentialities can be crucial for the developmental process of any nation. Pandit Jawaharlal Nehru, the first prime minister, and Gandhiji, the father of the nation, India, wanted the Indian women emancipated in the true sense and be given opportunities to participate in the nation-building activities. The Indian Constitution has provided equal opportunity to all, irrespective of sexes. But due to multiple barriers women have not been participating adequately. Research by Rosener (1990), Fogarty and Rupport (1971), Varghese (1990) have revealed that women are as effective as their male counterparts. They are committed, considerate, humanistic, nurturing, caring and goal-oriented, therefore, women can provide better leadership for nation building.

To provide better leadership responsibilities by women for a nation, it should be necessary to create an atmosphere in which women can realise their full identity and powers. Through this realisation women have to empower, learn to assert themselves, and participate actively in the decision-making process. They have to adopt multiple strategies to accomplish important leadership positions. These may be to envisage leadership training, motivation, skills of leadership and knowledge of managerial functions. Therefore, the vision should be as follows:

1. Women should occupy top positions and participate actively.
2. Women have to use modern techniques and approaches.
3. Networking of women leaders should be promoted throughout the world.

Strategies to Empower Women Educational Leaders

It is high time to empower women educational leaders to maximise their potential. Empowerment of women educational leaders can help to share their responsibilities in the human resource development system at all levels. One of the major strategies for the empowerment of women educational leaders in the training programme, can be imparted to different target groups with the help of different modes. Some studies have been conducted at the national and international levels to identify the training needs of educational leaders. These studies have been highlighted here to prepare a need-based training programme for leaders working at different levels of educational systems.

1. Provision of specific training

Women leaders are supposed to be well versed in different areas including teaching learning in their specific areas, communication, planning, management, administration, supervision, decisionmaking, etc. The national Policy on Education (1986) of India suggested training in financial rules and procedures, legal provisions, governing educational activities, personnel management, programme planning, data management and review techniques. The National Institute of Educational Planning and Administration, New Delhi, India, has identified 42 competencies for the training of women educational leaders.

2. Provision of concrete knowledge

There should be a concrete knowledge on the structure and

function of the specific education system, where women leaders are working. This will enable them to have a comprehensive understanding about the nature of the administrative process. It would include knowledge of educational theories, models of teaching, examples and case-studies of different educational practices, financial rules and procedure, financial control, legal provisions governing educational activities, nature of community, their behaviour pattern, resource mobilisation, quality of education, etc.

3. Developing managerial competencies and skills

Apart from the knowledge dimension, women educational leaders demand certain managerial competencies and skills, because they are the leaders, initiators, innovators, administrators, managers and institution builders. The managerial dimension would consist of the following components:

Knowledge of strategies and techniques of management

1) Knowledge of strategies and techniques of management like, brainstorming, benchmarking, quality circles, parallel learning structure, survey feedback, transactional analysis, quality of work life, systems theory, teacher's grid and many more.

Developing competencies related to HRD

2) Competencies related to human resource management, individual recognition, organisational and resource management, review techniques, remote management, managing complexity, broadening contextual competencies, record keeping and reading the situation.
3) Leadership skills require women to have the ability to lead and manage people to work as individuals and as a team towards a common goal, to initiate and manage change and improvement in pursuit of strategic objectives.

4) Decisionmaking skills and competencies require women to have the ability to investigate, to solve problems and to make decisions, to analyse, understand and interpret relevant information and data and the ability to think creatively and imaginatively to solve problems and identify opportunities, through programme planning, group/peer decision making, balanced judgement and discipline management.
5) Communication skills require women to have the ability to make points clear and understand the views of other, to evolve effective communication system in the organisation, to negotiate and consult effectively and to organise formal and informal meetings through persuasive communication, interpersonal skills and community relationship.
6) Self management skills require women to have the ability to prioritise and manage their own time effectively, to resolve conflicts within to take responsibility for their work under pressure and deadlines, to adopt self-motivational factors and to realise the strengths, weaknesses, opportunities and threats.

Attributes

The following are the attributes:

1. External attributes

A woman leader is normally criticised for the following limitations:

a) Non-availability of time while needed on overtime.
b) Over-grooming habit for developing/displaying personality.
c) Lack of assertiveness.
d) Lack of time management resulting in irregularity and unpunctuality.

e) Creating trouble for female bosses.

f) Lack of general knowledge due to commitment to family.

2) Internal attributes

a) Consciousness

b) It is usually found that the educational managers join an institution as a raw hand and for lack of any systematic training in management with special emphasis on decision making they often find it quite difficult to take right and quick decisions.

3) Right perception—awareness

Awakened at each moment, especially while on duty and generally throughout life. According to Shri Aurobindo, "Transform reason into ordered intuition, transform effort into an even and sovereign overflowing of the soul strength, transform enjoying into an even and objectless society, transform the divided individual into the world personality."

4) Handling of stress and grievances

Modern psychology has rightly said, "If the mind is quiet, the body will also be quiet, as mind is subtle matter and body materialised mind." Thus a quiet mind will result into a quiet life with ever flaming energy and will make one open, fearless and extraordinarily sensitive to make every moment of life a celebration.

5) Positive stroke—incentive

Incentive is the most effective tool for making the subordinate more creative and active.

In the end the effective women leaders should increase their power and potential for better managerial work.

REFERENCES

Briggs, D. K. & Bhagia N. M., 1985, Professional Preparation of Educational Administrators in Developing Countries. *EPA Bulletin*, Vol. 8.

Brown E., 1985, *Moving Towards Excellence: Report of the National Principal Association,* ERIC NCERT.

Department of Education, Government of India, 1986, *National Policy on Education,* MHRD, New Delhi.

Department of Educational Administration, 1995, *National Conference on Women to Assess Leadership Positions in Educational Management,* M. S. University of Baroda, Vadodara.

Fogarty, M. *et al,* 1971, *Women in Top Jobs,* George Allen & Unwin Ltd, London.

Fourth World Conference at Beijing, 1995, *Country Report,* MHRD, Government of India.

Association of Indian Universities, 2000, *Handbook of Indian Universities.*

Menon, L., 1999, *Women Empowerment and Challenges of Change,* Kanishka Publisher & Distributors, New Delhi.

Morgan, G., 1988, *Riding the Waves of Change : Developing Managerial Competencies for a Turbulent World,* San Francisco, Jossey Bass.

Peters T. and Waterman R., 1982, *In Search of Excellence,* Harper & Row, New York.

Pillai, J. K., 1995, *Women and Empowerment,* Gyan Publishing House, New Delhi.

Vinnicombe, S. & Colwill, N. L, 1997, *The Essence of Women in Management* , Prentice-Hall of India Pvt. Ltd., New Delhi.

Winship, S. L., 1993, An Analysis of Gender Differences in Positions: Paths of Community College President, *Dissertation Abstract International,* Vol .54(1).

22

Management of Women Education for Gender Equality in India

*Arun Kumar Kulshrestha**

The country now stands on the threshold of the twenty-first century. Those who are being born now will finish their elementary schooling at the turn of the century and enter into a new world. Only education can imbue people with the knowledge, the sense of purpose and the confidence essential for building a dynamic, vibrant and cohesive nation as well as for creating a better, fuller and more purposeful life. In human terms, democratic development implies the availability of equal opportunities to all people, irrespective of caste, creed, sex and religion to develop their personalities. Development of the community and group concerned in all its aspects should be directed towards the reshaping of the existing literacy, imparting of vocational skills and income-generating capabilities. These are essential means and an integral part of the process of planned socio-economic development. We should develop a broad framework of issues, around the basic understanding of citizenship building.

In India, the increase in the educational facilities and opportunities for women and the removal of traditional bars on the entry of women to particular branches and levels of

* *'Deptt. of Pedagogical Sciences, Faculty of Education, D. E. I. (Deemed University), Dayalbagh. Agra.*

education, came to be supported by all advocates of women's emancipation from the nineteenth century onwards. However, the Indian reformers of the nineteenth century wished to educate women to perform their role as good wives and mothers and not to make them as direct active participants in the process of national development.

After independence, the constitutional guarantee of equality changed the conceptual thinking, even of the traditional man in India and invited women to play multiple roles in the polity, the economy and the social functions. The educational development of women began in that direction. This is amply evident in the government's policy, the reports of various committees and commissions set up for this purpose and in the objectives of developmental plans formulated after independence. The expansion of education and health services in the twentieth century, however, precipitated a need for women teachers and doctors which results in the incorporation of these two vocations in the programme of women education.

Researches available on the education of women in India point to a number of sociocultural and socio-economic factors that influence the participation of women in the system of education. The prevailing cultural norms of gender behaviour and the perceived domestic and reproductive roles of women tend to adversely affect the learning and retention of girls in schools. The effect of gender bias varies in different social and economic groups and is particularly harsh on communities which suffer discrimination. The gender biases existing in society and domestication of girls has a direct bearing on many aspects of the educational system. The educational policy must, therefore, address itself to the larger socio-economic and cultural context that affects the education of girls. These are the propositions rendered to improve where the inequalities among boys and girls are concerned.

The Education Commission (1964-66) endorsed the recommendations of all the committees and commissions about the equality in the educational development of women. The government's National Policy (1986) also laid down, "The education system must produce young men and women of character and ability committed to national services and development. Only then education will be able to play its vital role in promoting national progress, creating a sense of common citizenship and culture and strengthening national integration."

In spite of the constitutional provision and the recommendations to the committee and commissions about the provision for the same type of education for women as for men, the traditional, limited viewpoint of women's education with a separate role for women in society has had a great influence on the planning for women's education. The new policy of education was proposed to bring the "basic change in the status of women". It did not discriminate men from women on the nature of education that was to be given in order to neutralise the prevailing distortions and anomalies. It was a well-considered edge in favour of women. The national education system was to play a positive, interventionist role in the empowerment of women. It was a considered act of faith and social justice that women's studies would be promoted as a part of various courses and educational institutions encouraged to take up active programmes to further women's development.

The last quarter of this century is marked by a series of efforts towards raising women's status, enhancing their quality of life, bringing about gender equality and gender justice. The first effort on the global level was made in 1975, the year which was observed as the "International Women's Year", and it has its motto, "Equality, Development and Peace". During the year meetings, rallies, seminars, symposia and conferences were held in all the states of India and almost all the countries of the world. As a part of the IWY programmes an international conference on women was held at Maxico in 1975. As a follow-up of the conference the United Nations declared 1976-1985 as the International Decade of Women.

The National Policy on Education with modifications undertaken in 1992, on equality of women's education, stipulated the principle removal of women illiteracy and obstacles inhibiting their overriding priority, through provisions of support services, setting of time targets and effective monitoring. Major emphasis was laid on the following points:

1. In lieu thereof recognising the holistic nature of child development, viz., nutrition, health, social, mental, physical, moral and emotional development, early childhood care and education (ECCE) will receive high priority and be suitably integrated with the child development programme.
2. Wherever possible, day-care centres will be provided as support services for universalisation of primary education to enable girls engaged in taking care of siblings to attend school and as support services for poor working women.
3. A new thrust in elementary education will emphasise three aspects: (i) Universal access and enrolment, (ii) Universal retention of children up to 14 years of age, and (iii) A substantial improvement in quality of education to enable all children to achieve essential levels of learning.
4. In the total literacy campaigns the theme of empowerment of women is receiving special focus. Since the female literacy rate in the country is strikingly lower than for men. Also in the adult education and post literacy education centres, special attention was given to enrolment of women.
5. The Mahila Samakhya was formulated in pursuance of the NPE 1986. Its overall goal is to create circumstances to enable women to better understand their predicament, to move from a state of abject disempowerment towards a situation in which they can determined their own lives and influence their environment. This presupposes that education can be decisive intervention towards women's equality.

6. There has been phenomenal expansion of educational opportunities for women in the field of higher education, both general and technical. Emphasis was laid on enrolment and retention of girls in formal and non-formal schooling.
7. Women's education at the university and college level has been diversified and re-oriented in tune with the changing requirements of the society, industry and trade. The University Grants Commission has been providing financial assistance to universities for promoting studies programmes and setting up of centres or cells for women's studies.
8. The policy of non-discrimination will be pursued vigorously to eliminate sex-sterotyping in vocational and professional courses and to promote women's participation in non-traditional occupations in existing and emergent society.

Moreover, several attempts have been made at the regional, national and global level by which the basic concept of education and equality become acceptable to the policy makers and others. The volume of resources now being devoted to development of women and children is gratifying institutional mechanism like the National Commission on Women, and others have become available. A variety of training programmes and training institutions are being implemented. There are specific schemes directed to target groups among women in respect of health, nutrition, child welfare, education, employment, self-employment, etc. Women education for gender equality is the agreed agenda for action. Hence, a rational approach has clearly stated focusing on improving the daily life conditions of women's existence and enhancing the status in family, community and society.

REFERENCES

Agrawal, S. P. & Agrawal, J. C., *Women's Education in India Historical Review, Present Status Perspective*, Concept Publishing Company, Delhi, pp. 41-42, and 87, 1992.

Anderson, M., *Improving Access to Schooling in the Third World: An Overview*, Hardward University, Cambridge, MA, 1988.

Apte, J. S., Education and Women's Empowerment, *Indian Journal of Adult Education*, 1996.

Bhandari, R. K., *Educational Development of Women in India*, Ministry of Education & Culture, Government of India, New Delhi, pp. 17-20, Publication No. 1378.

Kulshrestha, A. K., "Eradication of Sex-Discrimination in Education", *Bhartiya Shikshan*, Vol. IV, No. 4 & 5, pp. 503-505, 1994.

____________, "Elevating Women Education in India", Communicated for Publication, *In Quest of Bharatiya Shikshan*, Mumbai.

Mazumdar, V., *Women and Educational Development*, ICSSR, New Delhi, 1981.

Report of the committee for review of NPE, 1986, "Towards and Enlightened and Human Society", *NPE, 1986—A Review* (Final Report), Dec. 1990.

Singh, T., "Literacy in Women's Development", *Indian Journal of Adult Education*, April- June 1996.

23

I'm a Woman! I'm a Black! I'm a Leader: A Case Study

*Kholeka Constance Moloi**

Prion to 1994, one of the most visible legacies of education in South Africa was the fragmentation of the education system into 19 education departments that were responsible for schools. Education in South Africa was then a terrain for competing political, economic and ideological interests and contestation. The ideology of apartheid (separatist ideology) in South Africa had effectively shaped not only a strongly differentiated social structure, but also an attitudinal and perpetual separation between the various population groups in the country. The word "apartheid" means separation or apartness. Consequently, the system of apartheid, prior to 1994, stood for the separation of races, physically, politically, culturally, socio-economically and religiously. Schools were not left out in this attitudinal separation. The separation resulted in differentiated schooling systems:

1. independent schools (private schools);
2. public schools (government schools);
   a) (ex-model C) former government schools for white learners;
   b) *"township"* schools (schools for black learners); and

* *'Rand Afrikans University, Faculty of Education and Nursing, Johannesburg, South Africa.*

c) special and specialised schools (schools for children with disabilities, e.g., blind and partially sighted, deaf and hard of hearing, cerebral palsy, autism, severe behavioural problems, epilepsy, etc.).

During the apartheid era black people were clustered into designated areas or locations, which were situated far from white suburbs and these came to be known as black townships or "slum areas". In order to protect white South African political, social and economic interests, a contented black middle-class was later created which served as a buffer state between white suburbs and poor black townships. The schools that were built in these areas are commonly known as township schools. For the purpose of this paper the latter—*"township"* schools—forms the focus. These schools are in many instances characterised by a lack of sufficient teaching and learning resources and in some cases are without any buildings and, in such cases have to share space with other schools in what is termed the platoon-system. In many instances principals who had insufficient qualifications, leadership and management skills undertook leadership in these schools. It is against the background of these detrimental circumstances that the researcher conceptualises the title of this paper and intends to explore it from the perspective of a black woman, who was then even more disadvantaged than her black male counterpart in education.

INTRODUCTION

Since the advent of the new democratic government that came into power in 1994, much has changed in South Africa. The country has passed through a period of tremendously rapid and massive political transformations and economic, educational and social change. The new government has initiated a number of actions to rectify the injustices of the past. The following examples of pieces of legislation were introduced: The Labour

Relations Act, No. 66 to 1995; The Constitution of the Republic of South Africa Act, No. 108 of 1996 and the South African Schools Act. These efforts will be briefly discussed.

The Labour Relations Act, which became law on 11 November 1996, heralds a new era in labour relations in South Africa. The purpose of the Act is to advance economic development, social justice, labour peace and the democratisation of the workplace. The Constitution of the Republic of South Africa (Act 108 of 1996) was implemented during February 1997. An important component of this Constitution is the Bill of Rights, which outlines fundamental rights afforded to all South Africans, for example, the right to equality. Section 9 (2-5) of the Bill states: "The State may not unfairly discriminate directly or indirectly against anyone on one or more grounds, including race, gender, sex, pregnancy, marital status, ethnic or social origin, colour, sexual orientation, age, disability, religion, conscience, belief, culture, language and birth." One of the basic aims of the South African Schools Act is to change the different and unequal school and education systems based on ethnicity, race and colour of the past (South African Schools Act, 1997:6).

The Schools Act (1997) is aimed at the creation and management of a new national schools system. Consequently, there is currently a single national education and nine provincial departments. The provinces are further divided into districts which is made up of a number of schools ranging from five to ten schools. The curve for the past few years indicates that change is occurring at a fastly increasing pace in all sectors of life in the country. Whilst massive transformations are taking place there is still some concern about the percentage of women in leadership positions in schools, especially at the secondary level.

Research indicates that in South African schools 64 per cent of teachers are women and male teachers comprise 36 per cent of the teaching corps. However, men occupy 58 per cent of principals' posts, 69 per cent deputy-principals' posts and 50 per cent head of departments' posts in both primary and secondary schools (Gender Equity Task Team (GETT), 1997:198). Furthermore, research by Greyvenstein (2000:31) indicates that in the Gauteng Province of Education, men occupy 83 per cent of principals' posts, while women comprise only 17 per cent of these posts. This clearly indicates a preponderance of men in administration and decision-making positions.

A survey in 1990 of the top hundred companies in South Africa indicates that women form 36.6 per cent of the workforce and yet only 13 per cent are in management positions (Beijing Conference Report, 1995:24). The report further shows that women are almost invisible and voiceless. Particularly, in prominent positions such as: parliamentarian, ambassadorship, chief directorship and also in civil society, although they comprise half of the electorate of the country. Furthermore, Marshall and Thakhathi argue that "personnel and teaching are two professions that started as female specialism", however, women are not seeing an increased proportion of senior positions as these are offered to men.

Invariably, in the Constitution of South Africa Act 108 of 1996, various legal requirements to accelerate equity and equality in schools are endorsed. There are also various development programmes in place to facilitate the knowledge base and leadership skills of practising principals and their management teams in schools in South Africa. As has been stated above, the focus of this paper is on the experiences of the researcher while a principal in one of the schools in the Sedibeng District, Gauteng Province, South Africa. At this stage it will make sense to briefly look at some feminist theories and specifically black feminism to illustrate the position of women in South Africa.

Feminist Theories

According to Thakhathi there is a wide agreement that most societies prescribe different activities and characteristics for males and females, which may come to be seen as "natural" by the people involved. It then follows that feminist research in education is committed to the view that society plays a role in constructing, defining and reinforcing gender roles and gender identity. Noteworthy, there are different perspectives within feminism: liberal feminism, radical feminism, socialist feminism and black feminism.

Briefly liberal feminists argue that for women to be emancipated, they must have freedom to choose their lives, to be able to compete with men on equal terms in the professional and political world as well as in the labour market. Radical feminism focuses on patriarchy as the social system which functions in a hierarchical and dominating way, such that individual women are subordinate to individual men. They argue, "it is patriarchy that oppressed women and their subordinate position stems from the social, economic and political dominance of men in the society. Social feminism argues that inequality is the result of economic, social and political structures in which people live. Social feminists suggest that both patriarchy and capitalism have to be defeated. Weiner purports that patriarchy has a material and historical foundation in that capitalism is founded on a patriarchal division of labour. To the socialist feminists, schools play an important role in reproducing gender and class inequality. What is common though, among the various feminist perspectives, is that women are oppressed in one way or another.

According to Thakhathi in the early stages of the emergence of feminism, white feminism alienated poor and black women, as there were no potential solutions to minority women's problems. Consequently, black women saw feminism as a threat. White postulates that the juncture between anti-racist and anti-sexist struggles gave rise to black feminism. Black feminists therefore saw themselves triply oppressed on the basis of sex, colour and class, added to the list, the African culture, which is patriarchal. Thus, black feminists focused attention on the needs and experiences of black women and a critique of sexism in the black community. It is within this frame of reference that the researcher believes that with courage, resilience, fortitude, and a compelling vision, black women can contribute significantly to effective leadership in South African schools. The researcher will now take you through her journey of leadership under the most challenging circumstances ever, as a principal at Mojala-thuto Primary School for a period of ten years.

Mojala-thuto Primary School, Sedibeng District, Gauteng Province: Historical Background

Mojala-thuto Primary School is located in an informal settlement named Small-farms in the Sedibeng District of Education, Gauteng Province, South Africa. An informal settlement is a semipermanent dwelling on the fringes of black townships, which could be regarded as an illegal settlement in a prohibited area. The houses in such a settlement are made out of plastic material, wood and corrugated iron, and are mostly small in size. These settlements are densely populated and living conditions are extremely difficult because the people are to a large extent unemployed. Therefore, the community that is served by this school is very poor and the level of literacy is low. Many of the learners who come to the school have single parent (mostly mothers) and are in the care of their grandparents as their mothers are employed as domestic workers in white suburbs or elsewhere and only come home at the end of the month.

The school was opened in January 1987 with a team of 22 teachers. There were two heads of department (HODs), 19 teachers (6 males and 13 females) and myself as the principal. The two HODs were experienced teachers while the 19 teachers had just graduated from college with teaching diplomas only. We had no premises at the beginning and we had to be accommodated at a neighbouring primary school (Mosioa

Primary). This system was called the platoon system, where the host school operated from 07:00-12:00, and we worked from 12:30 to 17:00. We were hosted at that school for a period of six months. The situation at this school became unbearable in that we lost teaching time on many occasions for some reason or another. We were sometimes forced to start an hour later than the scheduled time. Again, because many of our pupils walked long distances between school and home we had to cut the periods short on many occasions. On some days we had only three hours teaching time. Apart from that we found it difficult to teach effectively from 13:00 in the afternoon and it was also difficult for the pupils to concentrate at that time of the day. All these challenges prompted us to look for our own accommodation elsewhere. At least, like all other schools we could have a decent six-seven hours normal teaching time. We owed that much to our learners! Fullan asserts that "moral purpose is about making a difference in the lives of students."

In July 1987 we left the premises and occupied a vacant school in the same neighbourhood. The area in which this school had been built was the most volatile one, where incidents of robbery, violence and atrocities of different kinds erupted on a regular basis. It was located in the heart of an area of chaos, having been vandalised during the 1984 riots. It was uninhabitable and a sight for sore eyes. Of the 14 original classrooms, only four were usable and had a door each while the rest had no doors, no windowpanes and no roof! There was neither furniture for the learners nor for the teaches. The cupboards had also been broken down. The taps were dry, as there was no running water in the premises. The toilets were in a terrible state! This was the situation when we arrived at our new premises. We saw these issues as challenges that we needed to face and resolve as a school, a team and as individuals.

Leadership Strategies for Success

Vision

Together we built a vision for our school. Our school's vision was: *"To be the best of the best"*. We understood what the vision of the school could do for us. We knew that to realise this vision we needed to collaborate and cooperate across our different functions and departments. We spoke in one spirit and focused on what was best for our learners. We focused on their work (assessment) and strove to improve our instructional practice (pedagogy and support of learning in the classroom). We were united in a common purpose, which was to do our work diligently. We had a vision and a set of common values. We knew that a vision could do wonders, if it is well understood, to become a lived experience. If the vision is strong enough it melds into shared purpose. A survey of co-workers conducted by Hagberg Consulting Group shows that women are rated significantly better than men on skills such as:

a) creating and articulating a vision;
b) setting clear direction;
c) being an inspirational model
d) setting high standards of performance; and
e) assuming responsibility.

This clearly explains the reason why we could succeed regardless of our challenges.

Collaboration

We did everything together although there were instances of resistance from the teachers occasionally. The school management team (the two heads of department and myself) saw the need to democratise educational practices within the school and this created a context to **unleash the teachers'** creative talents. **Democratic educational practices enabled us** to share ideas and information. This is critical to successful leadership in as era characterised by continuous change at the global, political and economic levels. People need to learn to cope with change and uncertainty. To be able to cope with these inevitable changes, we have to develop schools that are committed to organisational learning and collaboration. Lessons were planned together and we assisted each other in almost everything we did. We spoke of each other as teams and we forged strategic alliances across departments and in different classroom levels (different grades). Fullan and Watson contend: "the organisation of teachers' work in ways that promote professional community, has a positive relationship with the organisation of classrooms for learning and the academic performance of students." As a principal I was cautious that our human resource strategy directly supported the business strategy in attracting, developing and retaining relevant competence, which requires alignment of various resource systems.

Teamwork

The teachers grouped themselves into multi-skilled teams that ideally defined, regulated and were accountable for their work. We collaborated across all aspects of the school and mutually consulted each other in various aspects of our work. We saw ourselves as a very strong team of teachers and we were connected in synergistic ways. We could do wonders, which were admired by colleagues in the neighbouring schools. In their research HCG found that women were more enthusiastic than men in carrying out their tasks. Research by Goleman indicates that more than money motivates most high-performing teams, they seek the satisfaction of the work well done. They tend to act on their own initiative, sustain their own sense of ownership and feel accountable for their efforts. However, we tried to manage performance effectively by establishing a clear link between performance and rewards, and praise and recognition. Research by HCG indicates that women are better at motivating others. We had learnt that to be responsive to our students, we needed to build a school that had no boundaries. Focus was on teams, collaboration a virtual coordination because we had also realised that some people work best in isolation. When we make use of teams, talent moves from one unit to another in the school as needed. In the process cross-functional decisions are made through these teams and solutions to problems are tackled together. Opportunities for interactions were created and this in turn broadened professional community where teachers felt more comfortable exchanging ideas, and where a collective sense of responsibility for student development emerged. One of the successful leadership strategies is to implement different operating models centred on concepts such as processes, teams, network and strategic alliances. Research by Lambert indicates that female leaders have much to offer in the new world of teams than men because they have better social skills.

Although I was the principal, in many instances I became a team member. I led and I was led when the occasion demanded. I had learnt the skills of pushing forward and pulling back when the need arose. It is evident that women are better team members than men. We upheld the values of human rights that are afforded by the Constitution to all South Africans. One of those rights we upheld was the need for each person to be involved in the decisions that affect him. Each teacher had a sense of clarity about his roles and responsibilities, and commitment was enhanced.

Communication

The cross-boundary strategy we employed facilitated communication. Communication was multi-directional and information from the district was disseminated as quickly as possible to all the staff members. We had in place teachers who were responsible for making sure that information that came from the district office reached everyone in the school promptly. As a principal I had learnt that it is extremely important to keep the staff members informed. If teachers are given information it helps in curtailing unnecessary suspicions and mistrusts. More importantly, you create a context for dialogue, what Senge coins skilful discussion for building shared meaning within teams. Senge further observes: most teams need tools and skills to both broaden and focus the scale and scope of their conversations—to make them both more divergent and more convergent, when appropriate. People want to know what goes on around them and share their own experiences. In communication individual feelings and needs emerge and these could unravel potential areas of conflict or dissatisfaction which can them be dealt with. Research by Bedeian & Glueck indicates that distrust and suspicion affect communication negatively and may result in defensiveness and decrease the frequency of open expression.

According to Senge communication enables the team to learn to make their thought processes visible, to surface and challenge assumptions, and to look more closely at sources of disagreement. We used to talk about literally everything that concerned out work and even our individual problems. This helped us to know each other more and to understand each other's individuality although we were good working teams and got feedback from each other. HCG found that women are more expressive of their thoughts and feelings than men are. More importantly, leaders need strong feedback to be effective communicators and women are stronger than men on this aspect. HCG point out that feedback helps you to gain an understanding of your leadership style, strengths and weaknesses. Continual feedback helps leaders to benchmark progress and refocus their efforts. It also enhances the acknowledgement of the need to change in developmental areas. Lambert further reasons that there are differences between communication styles of men and women. He proffers that women communicate to build symmetrical relationships while men seek to clarify and establish asymmetries between people. It is important to clarify what these two forms of communication mean.

According to Lambert a symmetrical relationship is one that is based on equality. It is underpinned by the assumption that people are at base the same, connected and equal. It is characterised by mutual concern and a caring attitude each toward the other. Its goal is one of long-term mutual commitment, warmth and support. It is more characteristic of women than men. On the other hand, an asymmetrical relationship is one that is founded on a belief that people are unequal. People are perceived as being different and that difference is expressed in status, hierarchies and pecking orders. Communication is either a means of probing to ascertain relative status or, where relative status is clear, a way or reinforcing the differences that exist. Where sympathy exists between two people in an asymmetrical relationship it tends towards condescension rather than true concern. Such relationships are more typical, in general, of men.

Although we tried to talk to each other more openly there were incidents of misinformation through the grapevine. Bedian & Glueck define the grapevine as "all informal, often secret, means of transmitting information from person to person." The grapevine existed because of social and personal interest of teachers and not as a result of school requirements. I found it difficult to control the grapevine and did not attempt to do anything about it. On the whole, I think that the reason why we were successful in our school was because we spoke about our work, what other schools were doing and how we could learn from them and improve our instructional and professional competence. Fullan aptly states: " every leader, to be effective, must have and work on improving his or her moral purpose." He explains that moral purpose is about ends and means. In education, an important end is to make a difference in the lives of students. Consequently, we tried to find out what we could do better or differently the next time. In the process our quality of thinking improved and that in turn leveraged the quality of our work because out focus was on core instructional goals, processes and positive learner outcomes. Bredeson indicates that communication constitutes the greater part of the principal's work.

Scanning our Internal and External Environments

Lambert contends that the team looks to the leader to bring them success. He further explains that success is intimately related to the "three forces", namely, the forces in the environment, the forces in the work-team and the forces in the leader. Consequently, leadership for the emerging age is about the ability to continually scan our internal and external environments and generate ideas, knowledge and innovative capabilities. The three forces are presented below:

Forces in the environment

a) What is the nature of the task?
   i) simple or complex?
   ii) enjoyed or disliked?
   iii) novel or routine?

b) What is the present work environment?
   i) available resources?
   ii) current level of technology?
   iii) hierarchy, both formal and informal?

Forces in the work team

a) Has the team enjoyed previous success in a similar task?

b) Does the team fully understand and share the goals?

c) Are the team values implicit or explicit?

d) Has the team demonstrated commitment and the ability to meet deadlines?

Forces in the leader

a) Has the leader a track record of success?

b) What is the leader's preferred style?

c) Does the leader trust the group sufficiently to live with its outcome?

d) Is the leader under time pressures? Do time constraints exist? Does he need to function within time constraints?

According to Fullan, "commitment to the environment and to the broader global community as part and parcel of the long-term success of the school is moral purpose writ large." As a team we needed to develop a capacity for change and agility in terms of responsiveness to student and parent needs. Consequently, we needed to continually monitor our processes and procedures, structures and capabilities. The 19 teachers in our staff know each other from college. They know each other's strengths, weaknesses, talents and areas of expertise. This made my task easier because they took the initiative in allocating tasks to each other. It also created an enabling environment for development and growth as well as a sense of ownership of teaching and learning tasks, as they were in charge. This initiative reinforced the concepts of self-managing teams, democracy, transparency, collegiality and collaboration in our school. Our actual operating environment informed our shared decisions.

Pride in Our School Culture—Our Strongest Success Factor

A key to a successful school is having a positive culture, that is, a conducive teaching and learning environment. Research by HCG indicates that whether you like it or not, as a leader you are also a role model, a tone setter, a symbol of who gets ahead, a guardian or a designated change agent and a producer of culture. The research further shows that as a leader you need to understand the nature of that culture, how it is created and how it can be changed. We believed that education transformation begins with the process of cultural change within the institution. Cultural change addresses people's attitudes, skills and knowledge. We agreed on a set of values and beliefs that would guide our practice as individuals and a collective force. From shared values and beliefs we created an atmosphere of hard work but provided space for leisure and celebration. Through synergy, tolerance, perseverance, motivation and requisite skills, we established a culture of pride in our school. This did not happen overnight. It was a long and difficult process because it involved aspects such as understanding people's attitudes and valuing individual differences but simultaneously pulling towards a common goal. HCG postulate that women may be better at managing a diverse workforce because they:

a) tend to focus less on traditional values;
b) are more tolerant of differences; and
c) less bound by social traditions.

Our school culture became the nexus of our success. We were connected, valued and became part of each other. You can never understand this feeling, unless you have lived the experience. We acknowledged the unique gifts we each had as individuals, achievements and performance. This spirit reinforced our positive sides. Fullan asserts: "Moral purpose is about how human evolve over time, especially in relation to how they relate to each other." We always tried to show our best selves. We worked very hard but also had time to celebrate as a group. We would cook together and eat together while cleaning the premises. The learners were also fed. We converged even on Saturdays to clean the school premises. Labour had become part of our way of doing things at our school. It became part of our religion. Research by HCG shows that culture is expressed and transmitted in organisational systems and procedure (how things get done). Through labour, mutual love, caring, support, mutual understanding and appreciation, we managed to develop a unique culture, a culture of work, play and purpose. Fullan contends: "What makes humans different is culture. Ideas, knowledge, practices and beliefs, and the like enter consciousness and can be passed on any direct infection from one person to another." This culture still prevails to date. The culture was captured in the homes neighbouring our school. The community and ourselves came together as a neighbourhood mutually giving appreciation and reinforcement. We occasionally surprised ourselves and we marvelled at our skills.

The vision of the schools and the vision song became deeply embedded in our hearts and minds. We had deliberately entrenched a winning culture through our vision statement. This kind of culture, a unique, winning and relentless one, breeds an edge over competition. We were inspired and our perspiration become a voluntary exercise. We allowed the process of change to unfold. It was that inner strength and resolve, that made the impossible possible. As a team we had learnt to develop strategies to determine the sources of conflict, resistance and obstacles of culture change and tried to get around our problems. However, this was not easy because at times evil took the upper hand but we persevered and focused on our goals.

Strong Leadership

The principal clearly has an important role to play in motivating staff and realising the vision and goals of the school. He needs to be a visionary, leader, coach, mentor, steward, teacher, financial planner, marketer and resource provider. Research on leadership conducted by HCG indicates the women rated higher than men on traditional management skills such as hiring, coaching and developing subordinates, organising and monitoring work. Consequently, without strong leadership from the principal, the school cannot succeed. Strong leadership manifests in the following ways:

a) A strong personal vision of the school's purpose and how to actualise it
b) The ability to inspire the governing body, staff, parents and students with the vision
c) A wide knowledge base and professional competence
d) Effective planning and decisionmaking

e) The ability to build a strong partnership with the Department of Education
f) An active role in district initiatives, e.g., whole school development, sports and cultural activities, curriculum and, management development projects
g) Prompt and efficient response to the district office
h) Transparency with regard to financial management
i) An effective physical resource management system
j) A good system of peoples' management

In an effort to establish cultural change in the school staff members' contributions must be recognised and valued. The talents and skills of staff members must be acknowledged and be fully utilised to realise the school's vision and goals. Accept ideas from different individuals because each person has a story to tell and each person is a leader in his own right. Charlton posits: "The spiritual and human renaissance and demands for participation, personal growth, quality of life, family involvement, quality time and meaning are key issues in making our schools successful."

Concluding Remarks and Implications for Effective School Leadership in South Africa

What is it that brings about meaningful transformation in education? There are many possible answers to the question from different perspectives as well. However, our position is that meaningful transformation of education must be tackled from a systems and strategic learning perspective. Leaders of today's schools must cope with a unique set of challenges: globalisation, growth of strategic alliances, an accelerating avalanche of information and democratisation of access to information, increased workloads and expanding skill requirements. The earning organisation is one of the concepts used in recent management literature to make schools meaningful places of teaching and learning. A learning organisation improves a school's ability to react to, and capitalise on changes in its internal and external environment. School leaders need to learn from industry by positioning themselves strategically and creating value in their work. All organisations that focus on a competitive advantage invest in individual and organisational learning. We need to be prepared for the continuous stream of changes in education and elsewhere, new learning and teaching strategies and the changes that are happening all around us.

Ambitious Strategies

As leaders we need to develop and sustain high performance customer-focused strategies by creating networks around which teachers can work, develop and grow. These networks for learning and performing better must focus on ambitious change effort strategies for success in our schools. Mintzberg refers to strategies as emerging patterns, and views the development of strategy as a process of learning. Teachers must, therefore, be enabled to create their ideal future within a dynamic and ever changing political, economic, social and educational environment. If the school's strategy is not ambitious enough it will fail to create the needed tension to relinquish energy for aggressive action in our tasks.

Systems Thinking Approach

The new paradigm for the twenty-first century is thus, a systems thinking approach, which provides a better and holistic view of understanding living systems such as individuals, teams and organisations as they try to survive and thrive in a highly competitive environment. Systemic and strategic change means operationally that every member of the school is responsible for continuous instructional improvement in some key element of their work. Instructional improvement is not the responsibility of a select few who operate in isolation from other, but rather, a joint, collegial responsibility of everyone in the system working together in a variety of ways across all departments in the school. Mutual feedback between individuals, teams and the school is important for success. In the course of the functioning about the result of an actions, set of action or some transformation, an organisation, such as a school regulates itself in many ways based on the learning it does as a result of feedback that travels along amplifying positive and stabilising negative loops.

Knowledge Management and Knowledge Economy

Leadership for the emerging century also focuses on concepts such as knowledge management and the knowledge economy. If school leaders are able to create contexts to capture what is happening in the business environment and measure the rate and level of learning in their schools then teachers may begin to think in new and synergistic ways. We need to think differently about our work. What we do in our classrooms and in our schools has far reaching implications for social welfare, the country's economy and the quality of life within and outside the school. The new competitive economies have brought competitive changes unequalled in the South African history. In the new economy, winning will spring from organisational capabilities such as speed, responsiveness, agility, learning capacity and teacher competence. Thus, our strategies should be performance driven and be accompanied by investing in a learning culture tailored to the needs of teachers and learners as well as for the good of the whole country. As leaders we need to learn to establish core organisation, leveraging knowledge for a competitive advantage. Consequently, how schools use and leverage human capital will determine not only their success, but also their ability to survive.

Teachers must have the desire to want to perform. You, the leader can reinforce this desire to want to perform! We need to have compassion for our learners and passion for our work. Transformational leadership is not something out there. It is a change of the mindset to want to carve a niche for oneself regardless of one's circumstances. Consequently, the highest level of leadership is achieved from those who:

a) learn to be comfortable with change;
b) increase their comfort with risk;
c) share power;
d) acknowledge their limitations;
e) project a positive, upbeat, optimistic outlook even when they do not feel like it; and
f) determine what they stand for.

I'm a woman! I'm a black! I'm a leader!

REFERENCES

Bartol, K. M. & D. C., Martin, 1994, ***Management,*** London: McGraw-Hill, Bedeian, AG & Glueck, **WF 1991**, *Management, Chicago*: The Dreyden.

Beijing Conference: Plan of Action, 1995, *South African Women on the Road to Development, Equality and Peace.*

Bredeson, P.V., 1987, Communication as a measure of leadership in schools: a portraiture of school principals, *The High School Journal,* April/May: 176-186.

Bryans, P. & R. Smith, 2001, *Beyond Training: Re-conceptualising Learning at Work, Available* from:

http://www.managementfirst.com/articles/t_beyond-training.htm. (Accessed 30 May 2001).

Carrell, M.R., Grobler, P.A., Elbert, N., Marx, M., Harfield, R.D. & Van Der Schyf, S., 2000, *Human Resource Management in South Africa,* Cape Town: Pearson Education South Africa.

Charlton, G., 1999, *Human Habits of Highly Effective Organisations, The Human Race*, Pretoria: Van Schaik.

Christie, P., 1998, Schools as (Dis) Organisations: the "breakdown of the culture of learning and teaching" in South Afrinca schools, *Cambridge Journal of Education,* 28 (3), 1998.

Dessler, G., 1997, *Human Resources Management*, Seventh edition, Florida International University.

Dzvimbo, K.P., 2000, *New Millennium Challenges: A test for ZOU*, Zimbabwe Open University News, December, 2000.

Fullan, M., 2000, *Leading in a Culture of Change*, San Francisco: Jossey-Bass.

Gloeman, D., 2000, Leadership that gets results, *Harward Business Review*, March-April, 2000.

Hagberg Consulting Group, 1998, *HCG Research, Hagberg Consulting Group*, Available from: http://www.leadership-development.com/f reserch.html, Accessed on 2/20/02.

Marshall, C., 1984, from culturally defined to self defined career-stages of women administrators, *The Journal of Educational Thought*, August 19 (2): 135-247.

Measor, L. & Sikes, P., 1992, *Gender and Schools*, London: Cassell.

Middleton, S., 1993, *Educating Feminists, Life Histories and Pedagogy*, New York: Teachers College.

_______________, 1994, *Educating Feminists: Life Histories and Pedagogy*, New York: Teachers College.

Moloi, K.C., 1999, *Transforming the School into a Learning Organisation: Challenges for School Principals*. Johannesburg: Rand Afrikaans University, Published DEd Thesis.

_______________, 2002, *Linking experience with vision: Voices from a township school*, Education Africa Forum, the Fifth Edition, (Chapter).

_______________, 2002, *Schools as Learning Organisations*, Pretoria: Van Schaik (Book currently under print).

Motlhabi, M., 1984, *The Theory and Practice of Black Resistance to Apartheid, A Social Analysis*, Johannesburg: Skotaville.

Niehaus, L. & Myburgh, CPH, 1999, Predictors of strategies African school principals used to cope with daily demands, *South African Journal of Education, 19 (1)* February 1999.

Olve, N. Roy, J., & Wetter, M., 1999, *Performance Drivers, A practical guide to using the balanced scorecard*, New York: John Wiley.

Senge P.M., Kleiner, A., Roberts, C., Ross, R.B. & Smith, B., 1996, *The Fifth Discipline, Strategies and tools for building a learning organization*, London: Nicholas Brealey.

South Africa (Republic), 1997, *Understanding the S A Schools Act, What public school governors need to know*, Pretoria: Department of Education.

_______________, *Gender Equity Task Team (GETT)*, Pretoria: Department of Education.

Swanepoel, B.J. & de Villiers, A.S., 200, Establishing employment relationships and employment equity, *Managing Employment Relations in South Africa*, Service Issue 3, Durban: Butterworths.

Thakhathi, T., 2001, *Communication Strategies of Women Principals of Secondary Schools*, Pretoria: University of South Africa, Unpublished DEd Thesis.

Weiner, G., 1994, *Feminisms in Education: an Introduction*, Buckingham: Open University.

White, K., 1995, *Why Girls don't get ahead...but gutsy girls do*, London: Warmer Books.

24

Women at the Grassroots Level Politics: The Experience of Panchayati Raj

*Hemlata Talesra**

Empowerment of women is one of the major issues today. A democratic and secular India endeavours to provide the necessary conditions for greater participation of women in all spheres of life. Equal rights to women are guaranteed in the Constitution and all kinds of discrimination prohibited. Practically, women's participation in decisionmaking is low. The problems of inequality is complex and have existed because of attitudinal, cultural and social restrictions prevailing in our country for centuries. All efforts at all levels are being made to mainstream women, who have been neglected. Without their participation the integrated development of the society would be an unattainable dream. The traditional taboos which prevent and restrict the women to remain within the four walls of her home, tied down to the domestic responsibilities only, must be removed to free her from the customary restrictions of the 'Purdah system', which is a pathetic culture which cuts down the women totally from the exposure to the society.

The panchayati institution is one of the oldest institutions in India. It was conceptualised originally by Mahatma Gandhi.

"Retd. Professor and Head, Department of Educational Planning, Management and Administration, Vidya Bhawan G. S. Institute of Advanced Studies in Education, Udaipur (Rajasthan).

He believed in empowering the grassroots of Indian societies the villages. He believed that if the villages, which were the smallest social units of India, only after the family unit, were granted power to govern themselves, India as a whole could develop. This system took decades to become practical. It emerged in different states of India in different forms and was successful in Mahrashtra, Gujarat and Karnataka.

The basic element of Panchayati Raj is decentralisation of democracy, which enables the government bodies to reach far and wide to the remote areas. Today the Panchayati Raj is part of our Constitution under the 73rd Constitutional Amendment. At the village level setup, the Sarpanch is the leader who is elected directly by the village population. He is a powerful leader, who is entrusted with a wide spectrum of responsibilities for the integrated development of the villages coming under the jurisdiction of his Panchayat. The Panchas, who are like their minister, are elected directly by the villagers, who help the Sarpanch to coordinate the work effectively. There are also various committees and nominated chairpersons and members for efficient running of the various departments. This setup is there at all the three levels: district, divisional and village level. The revolutionary step taken in the 73rd Constitutional Amendment is the 33 per cent reservation of seats for women at all levels.

This paper is based on the theme 'Women at the grassroots level politics: The experiences of Panchayati Raj'. It discusses women as a part of the Panchayati Raj setup, the active role of their husbands, the emergence of women leaders at the grassroots level, women participatory development and problems faced by women leaders in the Panchayati Raj institution.

Women as Part of the Panchayati Raj Set-up

The government of Rajasthan considers empowerment of women as an ongoing process of collective struggle against the forces that oppress and subordinate women. The state policy on women lays emphasis on the empowerment of women. A beginning has already been made in this direction. This policy intended to equip women in their new role in the exercise of effective political power. Political empowerment of women has taken a lead with the new Panchayati Raj system and the representation of women. A series of significant steps are being taken to make this programme effective. For one, many of our women unused to a decision-making role, still face considerable difficulty in carrying out their newly assumed responsibilities. The main obstacle for empowerment is the dismal education level. It is an ironical situation, where even after half a century of independence, there are social groups with illiteracy rates as low as one per cent. In order to get elected, to function effectively and safeguard the interest of villages, and in particular the women and children, adequate training and authority have been provided to the women by continuous motivation and awareness programmes.

Active Role of Women Sarpanch and their Husbands

Socially and culturally, the women folk have limited opportunity for growth. Their voices were neither heard in domestic sphere nor in the society. Today, they have an opportunity to move forward in life. Strangely, in some areas, though the women were the elected members, they were asked to remain at home, so that the husband would take charge of the surpanch. There was no hesitation on the part of these men to express openly that his wife was 'made' to stand for the election for the post of Sarpanch as the seat was reserved for women, but now he would be managing the office. Natural, because not only that she was absolutely incompetent but the society would never accept her meeting the menfolk outside the family.

Gradually women have started resisting this idea. In Madhya Predesh in one of the Panchayat villages, Makura, where a woman was the Sarpanch, her husband made a seal for himself reading 'Sarpanch pati' (husband of the Sarpanch), a title coined by her husband to push her back and admitting that it was for his administrative convenience. Women want to overcome the embarrassment of 'Sarpanch Pati' and learn to take up the responsibility to contribute to their village whatever little they can. But if the power struggle begins at home they lose it when the husband and the others at home force it on her to believe and agree that the aim should be to have the power in the house, who the Surpanch is, is not so important. Some husbands want to satisfy their lust for power in the village by dictating terms and taking decision which their wives are supposed to take as the Surpanch. They are 'acting Sarpanch' in the presence of their sarpanch wives, hence the coined term 'Sarpanch Pati'.

Emergence of Women Leaders at the Grassroots Level

The introduction of women in the local self-government and the consequent emergence of women leaders at the grassroots level seems to have brought revolutionary changes in the social structures and attitudes in the rural women's life in particular and village communities in general. The Panchayati Raj institution has a definite potential to bring about positive changes in the women's status in the rural scenario. If she is given power opportunity and assistance, these can provide further strides in the development of rural areas.

Women in Participatory Work

For women to be successful in Panchayati Raj, it is essential that the rural women in general are empowered, so that there is an acceptance of women in a high position of governance. It should be ensured that women in general are encouraged to participate in the development process. In the process of my work in the villages, I felt that this can be done in the following ways:

a) Their role in the household economy should be identified and recognised. Their role should nor be just considered a part of the unorganised sector of work, it should be considered as a contribution towards the national capital wealth.

b) More employment opportunities as well as alternatives for change in employment for rural women must be made available.

c) Education and technical skills should be developed among rural women so as to empower them, because these two tools can truly help reduce gender gaps.

d) Women as well as their menfolk should be gender sensitised. Gender sansitisation can help both men and women shed their 'ingrained' gender differences to a great extent, thus bringing in equality and ensuring women's participation in the development process.

Problems Faced by Women Leaders in the Panchayati Raj Institutions

According to my study, there are some basic problems faced by these women leaders. These are:

1. Lack of education and skills among them puts them in quite a helpless situation with the bureaucrats. These women feel quite helpless. They fear to go alone to the government offices for fear of harassment. This fear cuts them off from the mainstream of governance, as they end up sending either their husbands or sons, which is a way of de-empowering them.
2. Women leaders face discrimination at the hands of other male Panchayat leaders. If she is the Sarpanch and her subordinate is a male, she is dominated by him in decisionmaking and even the rural masses in general prefer and accept a male leader. There are occasions where her participation ends in humiliation.

This situation is worse if the woman Sarpanch belongs to a lower caste (SC/ST) and her subordinate male belongs to an upper cast. Then it is the upper caste which dominates the scenario in decision making, as this culture has dominated the village scene from time immemorial. This places the women in awkward and difficult situations. Most of the lower caste people work as labourers on the farms of the upper class rich farmers. This places the elected leaders from the lower caste families in difficult situations.

CONCLUSION

Punchayats need active participation of the rural people for managing their own affairs leading to promotion of development activities best suited to satisfy the local needs. Equal participation of men and women can create an impact for an integrated development of villages. Women all over the world are concerned with the issue of gender equality through women's empowerment. The women's movement all over the world has made systematic efforts in a sustained manner to develop strategies and approaches so as to enable women to be equal partners in the nation's progress and prosperity. In India, we have completed 54 years of independence. If we take stock of the steps taken in the process of empowerment, the last five and a half decades have been momentous. The foremost among these is the provision for reservation for women, to enable women's participation in the local self-government which is a step forward towards women empowerment.

25

Barriers Faced by Women Educational Managers at Higher Education Level

*Hemlata Talesra**

The last hundred years may rightly be called the age of women awakening in the world. In every part of the world equality of he saxes has been ensured, carious laws have been passed to improve the status of women. But on the contrary inspite of all changes women cannot be regarded as being emancipated from orthodoxy, the old traditions and customs determented to the flowering of their personalities. The social and religious attitude towards the role of women in the family and society, which still have a strong hold on the minds of the people are the main hurdle in the way of social progress of women. In India and some other countries society is still male dominated. The double standard of morality graciously provide more social freedom to men then to women. The major burden of adjustment and the household work falls mainly on the women.

Due to above reason Representation of women in top management positions in Universities and other higher education institutions are negligible. In India only 30.3% women educational managers are available out of total teaching

**Retd. Professor and Head, Department of Educational Planning, Management and Administration, Vidya Bhawan G. S. Institute of Advanced Studies in Education, Udaipur (Rajasthan).*

profession and they are severally represented at senior academic management position In a democratic process where administration demands the active participation of women and men, it is observe that the women do not contribute their best what they are capable of. The UNESCO world conference 1998 argued that the presence of a critical mass of women in the decision making process remains vastly inadequate. Generally the men dominate the decision making process. It is usually fond that the educational administrators join an institution as a raw hand and for lack of any systematic training in management and administration with special emphasis on decision making, they often find it quite difficult to take right and quick decision. For such a situation whether the men are responsible or the women themselves are responsible?

BARRIER FACED BY WOMEN EDUCATIONAL MANAGERS

India is a multicultural society. The behaviour pattern of the women are decided to a great extent by their religion, race, region, class etc. The women with different background therefore, have dissimilar barriers. Some of the barriers are as follows:

1. Age Old Attitude and Customs

Age old attitude and customs have made women accept their position in the words of Bertrand Russel: 'MENTAL PRISON'. Women's position in the home and outside it is so closely inter linked that is very difficult to separate them. The position of a women in the home would refer to two aspects of a person's social position role and status role, referring obligations and duties and status referring rights, privileges, power and prestige.

2. Patriarchy

In India patriarchy is a system of male domination and superiority, of male control in which women are subordinate - a system of social structures and practices in which men dominate, oppress, exploit women. This system is reinforced by an ideology that men are superior to women. Subordination destroys self-respect, self-esteem and self-confidence. Economic, political, religious, social and cultural institutions are controlled by men- the family, religion, legal system, the economic system and economic institutions, political systems and institutions, media and educational institution and knowledge system. All these affects negatively the women educational managers at higher education level also.

3. Inequality and Disparity

India now has more then half a century's experience in dealing with sharp and disparities rooted in several millennia. Gender disparities in educational and all other social and demographic indicators reflect the unequal position of women. We have still sharp inequalities of caste, creed, tribe and rural urban divide. Gender cuts across all this layers making women managers like the other women. Women manages do more work than males but get much less than their legitimate share in food, health, education and training. The traditional gender based division of labour and resources continues to exist. The traditional socialisation practices of a society with a marked male preference, are highly discriminatory and not only physically short changed the women on food, health care, education and play, but also succeed in making her belief that she is inferior and less competent than her male counter parts. Women managers come into the institution with a negative self-image and poor self-esteem. The issues of women assuming their rightful place of equality with all human beings cannot be achieved if one half of the population that is, the male half - remain ignorant as to the rights and needs of women, the duties of both men and women. Too many of our thought processes and actions have become ingrained over centuries in a milieu of social prejudice and taboo.

4. Negative Self Image

Right from the birth Indian women are suffers from negative self image. Even at higher education level women educational managers consider them far behind the male working for the same Job. On the basis of my Ph.D. work 'Higher Education Among Women' only 5 per cent women managers consider them strong to work in any part of the country. Most of them consider themself 'Weaker section' of the society and unefficient to provide leadership.

5. Hurdle to Join Managerial and Other Leadership Job

In Indian society there are large number of hurdles to join the managerial and other leadership jobs. The overall social setup where they are born, grow, study, work and live their lives are not favourable to work on the top most position. The type of discrimination behaviour, specifically on the social and educational fronts puts a lot of hindrances in the proper development of their personalities. Most of the women are not able to contribute to the national development to a desired extent.

6. Traditional and Conservative Society

Our traditional and conservative society has not yet adjusted itself to what has happened. It has been rather a bitter pill thrust down its throat. It may not sound very convincing but it is a fact that even today an office-going lady is looked upon with suspicion. Reason behind this may be that people will relish any scandal attached wit the name of a lady occupying a responsible position.

7. Feeling of Unsafe

Indian women has occupied one chair of authority or other equal to men's but we will have to admit the fact that in this respect she is weaker by all means. She still is in need of security and protection.

8. Devotion of House Hold Duties

A women who may be in top most managing position devote plenty of time for the upbringing of their children. A earning women who is out for six or eight hours a day devote rest of the time and energy to perform her duties at home. This has resulted in our social and domestic life becoming and anchorless ship sailing at the mercy of the waves which may drift her to any rock-bed of disaster.

9. Negative Social Attitudes and Prejudices

The more specific problems of women managers are the result of social attitude and prejudices. The social scientist recognizes five district handicaps of the women managers:

a) She receives lower pay for the same work.
b) The jobs of higher salary, skill and authority are closed to her.
c) Her husband's employment takes precedence over her own and thus decreases her mobility and her market.
d) Continuous advancement in her job is interrupted by her home making period.
e) Home making, her fundamental responsibility, offers no regular pay and gives no prestige.

10. Negative Attitude about the Expertise in Executive Work

We found negative attitude about the expertise of women in executive work. There is general feeling that the women can not supervise or manage educational matters effectively. Some person feel that women use their feminine qualities to gain the advantages of promotions and other privileges. On the other hand some women workers over compensate for their femininity and work more.

The year 2001, being the year of 'women's empowerment' is an appropriate time to discuss the issues on women's leadership positions. Modern trend in para-psychology has declared that both man and women have common genetic abilities. Women has been proven educational manager and if enlightened,

the attributes required for a women leader in education are: sincerity, humility, gratitude, perseverance, aspiration, receptivity, progress, courage, goodness, generosity, equality and peace. We should see in detail how these attributes can be developed?

Following are the Attributes

1) *External attributes*—A women manage is normally criticized for the following limitations:
   a) Non availability of time while needed on over time.
   b) Over-grooming habit for developing/displaying personality.
   c) Lack of assertiveness.
   d) Lack of time management resulting in irregularity and unpunctuality.
   e) Creating trouble for female bosses.
   f) Lack of general knowledge due to commitment to family.
2) *Internal Attributes*—
   a) Consciousness

b) Decision making, 'It is usually found that the educational managers join an institution as a raw hand and for lack of any systematic training in management with special emphasis on decision making they often find it quite difficult to take right and quick decision.

3) *Right Perception-Awareness*—Awakened at each moment especially while on duty and generally throughout life. According to Shri Aurobindo; 'Transform reason into ordered intuition, Transform effort into and even and sovereign overflowing of the soul strength, transform enjoying into an even and objectless costacy, transform the divided individual into the world personality.

(4) *Handling of Stress and grievances*—Modern psychology has rightly said that 'If mind is quite, body will also be quite, as mind is subtle matter and body materialized mind. Thus quite mind will result into a quite life with ever flaming energy and will make one open, fearless and extra ordinarily sensitive to make every moment of life a celebration.

5) *Positive stroke—Incentive*—Incentive is the most effective tool for making the subordinate more creative and active.

In the last the effective women manages should increase their power and potentials for better managerial work.

26

Empowering Women Educational Managers: Strategies and Issues

Ashutosh Biswal* and *Jaishree Das*

Women constitute half of the population of our county, and in the same way, half of the available human resources. Though we talk about providing equality to the women workforce in all fields of life including service sectors, we are far from the target. Due to this, their energies and special talents are not utilised and the country is wasting human resources. Therefore, we need to deliberate on how to ensure adequate representation of women in a workplace in different positions including managerial posts.

Though teaching is considered as a suitable profession for women, still the representation of women in this profession is not up to the mark. Moreover, a substantial quantity of women teachers will be found in the elementary education set up in comparison to secondary, higher secondary and higher education setup. This is the case of the participation of women in the general education areas. While talking about the proportion of women educational managers in all levels of education, still their number will be quite low. In a male-dominated society like ours, there may be several personal, social, political, and economic problems, which may hinder the

**Deptt. of Educational Administration, M. S. University of Baroda, Vadodara.*

access of women to the managerial positions in the profession of education. What are the reasons for this low participation of women in education management? (2) What are the factors influencing women's entry to these managerial positions? (3) How can one get more women in management positions? And (4) How can one empower women working in the educational fields and make them fit for the higher positions in the educational management?

Here, 'women educational managers' refer to the school headmistress/ principals, supervisors, administrators working in the primary, secondary and higher secondary schools; women administrators working in the higher education setup like, heads of the departments, deans of the faculties; administrators at the university setup like, vice-chancellor, pro-vice-chancellor, registrar, asst. registrars; administrators working as managers in the government education set-ups like, DEOs, inspectors of schools, BEOs, and higher education officers at the state and central government education set-ups.

After the eighties, there is a lot of change in the status and position of women. Due to constitutional provisions, equity measures of state governments and central government, positive attitude of society members and many more provisions, there is a significant increase in the involvement of women in each and every field. During these years, there has also been a remarkable increase of women in the field of education. Moreover, over the last decade one of the important changes has been the entry of women at managerial positions in the educational institutions.

Our women have more rights than women of other countries, but there are large areas wherein women are suffering. One of the causes is that they are not conscious of their rights. Along with this, ignorance, non-education, attitude of society, poverty, stereotype role, etc., are the other causes of women suffering. Among women who are coming up in different managerial positions, many excel in different fields from industries to education. Even many managers in the field of education do suffer due to many factors. There is a need to empower those educational managers who are in the field, with the help of different strategies. Different strategies should be used for the aspiring women managers in the field of education. The Education Commission (1964-66) also felt a similar need nearly three and a half decades back. It stated that special training courses should be organised for headmasters. They should include short induction courses for those who are promoted as headmasters, as well as periodical refresher courses for others.

In the National Policy on Education (1986) it is stated that a very important role must be assigned to the heads of institutions and they will be specially selected and trained. In addition to specialised institutions at the national and state level, the training of educational administrators and heads of the institutions, institutes of management and other similar organisations will motivate and enable women to take up management development and training programmes, as well as policy-oriented research in these areas through documentation of case studies of real-life situation and action research for institutional development.

The Ramamurthy Committee Report (1990) also emphasized on the training of head teachers thus: "The head of the educational institution shall have a significant role to play in the effective management of the school. The role of the institutional head is a crucial factor in the management. It is in this view of the critical link between managers and institutional efficiency that training of principals have been emphasized".

All these recommendations would also be applied for women educational managers, as they are heads of the institutions. In the present paper the authors have analysed the required training needs of the secondary school principals in different dimensions, and highlighted different strategies for their training and development using different modes. Along with these training needs, the authors also highlighted the need of women managers, the need for empowering women educational managers, and some of the issues related to it.

NEED OF WOMEN EDUCATIONAL MANAGERS

There is a need of more and more women in the field of education as education is perceived to be a very suitable profession for women as nurturing and caring comes naturally to them. If women can play an important role in decision making at home, she can also play an important role in decision making at educational institutions too. So, specifically, there is a need of women educational managers in the institutions for proper and smooth management. Women managers have a sort of cold and indifferent professionalism, which had crept into education, and is now being replaced with a more human and nurturant sort of educator-educand relationship in the family model of education.

Women managers can formulate a rare combination of concern for tasks and concern for people for the management of education is considered as a synchronised blend of task and people because education is a blend of arts of education and science of learning. Their imagination and gut feeling can be effectively used in situations that defy or boggle rational thinking. Creating an environment conducive to women's success in positions of educational managers will require committed efforts on the part of the individual woman, the family and the organisation in which she works.

In Asia, women's education levels have improved dramatically in the past decade. In some Asian countries, women achieved higher level of education than men. As a result, women are increasingly well prepared to assume positions of authority in politics, business and society. In Thailand, education is the single most important route for women's advancement into managerial positions. In Singapore, more than 80 per cent of women with university education were active in the labour force. What's more, these women are usually better educated than their male counterparts.

The present management pattern of educational institution perceives dysfunctional aspects for the creation of future organisation with prevailing male leadership style. The modern organisation calls for features like flexibility, higher empathy, collective and shared responsibilities in the administration, which demand proper emotional quotient and a proper balance of feminine quotient. This suggests a shift from system and style focusing on control to those which mobilise and empower and need a shift to more involvement of women educational managers. Thus women managers ought to develop their unique leadership style, which would encompass their womanly attributes. Researches also proved the potential of women managers in the field of education. Here is the finding of a research, which says as:

a) A higher percentage of schools with women as their heads have an open climate than men as their heads.
b) There is no evidence of any real association between male and female heads of schools as regards the autocratic leadership style, democratic leadership style and laissez faire leadership style.
c) There is no evidence to show that the organisation climate is significantly independent of gender.
d) The leadership styles of women heads of schools affect the school climate.

Due to the following points it can be said that there a need of women educational managers in the present-day educational system.

NEED FOR EMPOWERING WOMEN EDUCATIONAL MANAGES

Comprising half the population, and half the human resources, if women have to contribute significantly towards development, they need to be in positions of proper management leadership to influence policy and decisionmaking. Women already in the management positions should be enriched, encouraged and motivated. Now, the focus of women empowerment has shifted from development of women to women in development. There is need for new strategies in these directions. In the immediate future, women will also continue to face conflicts in their decisions to play the role of wife and mother on the one hand, and of manager and leader on the other. They need the support of family, society educationists and planners to overcome the future conflicts. Well-planned and properly designed strategies can help a lot to make women managers effective, and empower women to be women mangers in the field of education.

STRATEGIES TO EMPOWER WOMEN EDUCATIONAL MANAGERS

It is high time to empower women educational managers to maximise their educational and management potentials. The empowerment of women educational managers can also help to share their responsibility in the human resource development, which can enhance the development of educational systems at all levels. One of the major strategies for the empowerment of women educational managers is the training programme, which can be imparted to different target groups with the help of different modes. Here the authors highlighted the required training needs of the women educational managers.

Adequate research has not been done in the area of training need of women educational managers, but few studies have been conducted at national and international levels to identify the training needs of managers in the general fields and of the educational managers like school principals. Some of these studies have been highlighted here to prepare a need-based training programme according to the specific educational managers working at different levels of education systems, irrespective of the experience, locality and physical denominations.

Dimensions of Women Managers' Training

Women managers are supposed to be well versed in different areas including teaching-learning in their specific areas, communication, planning, management, administration, supervision, decision making, etc. In terms of skills, she should be acquired with skills of teaching, managing, decisionmaking and leadership.

The National Policy on Education (1986), suggested in the light of the required training needs of the head teachers and the mode of training that, for heads of institutions, training in financial rules and procedures, legal provisions governing educational activities, personnel management, programmes planning and data management, and review techniques will be considered essential. Pre-induction training will be prescribed as an essential requirement for personnel selected as heads of institutions. This can be generally applicable for women managers like women principals or head teachers.

Regarding different dimensions of training programme—Morgan identified nine competencies for managers in companies, which are also found relevant for women managers to some extent. These were (1) reading the environment, (2) promoting productivity, (3) headship with vision, (4) human resource management, (5) promoting learning, innovation and creativity, (6) skill of remote management, (7) using information technology as a transformative force, (8) managing complexity and (9) broadening contextual competencies.

In 1988 the Mississippi State Department of Education developed a 40-hour module for training the principals and central office staff of state-accredited elementary school with dimensions like (1) definition and development of appropriate curriculum, (2) use of learning centres as an instructional setting, (3) use of assessment measures to strengthen a comprehensive programme of instruction and (4) development of a practical plan for implementing a comprehensive instructional programme.

Principal's training programme "Moving Towards Excellence" developed at Texas, US was based on the perception that the measure of an effective principal as the instructional leader of the school can be found in the perception and implementation of curriculum development. According, the programme, principals' training would include four domains of instructional leadership. Prerequisites for the first domain, i.e., Formative domain, are (1) the role of the principal is to support the philosophy and goals of the concept of education for all (2) the decision-making process should include faculty and staff and (3) the knowledge base to be developed. The second domain, i.e., Planning domain includes (1) a thorough knowledge of state curriculum requirements an alternatives (2) organisation and effective use of staff, and (3) provision of opportunities for teacher improvement and development. The third domain, i.e., implementation domain includes (1) staff hiring (2) setting teacher performance standards (3) instilling a lesson model for teachers to follow (4) ensuring teacher familiarity with the essentials of their curriculum, and (5) providing a specific model for lesson plan writing. The fourth domain, i.e., evaluation domain includes (1) teacher evaluation (2) student evaluation and (3) public evaluation. Similar types of programmes may be applicable to women educational managers.

The National Institute of Educational Planning and Administration, New Delhi, has identified some 42 competencies for the training of principals and educational managers including women educational managers, and arranged them in eight broad categories: (1) academic areas of management, (2) personnel management, (3) financial management, (4) school plant and infrastructure, (5) linkage and interface, (6) student service, (7) method and procedure and (8) managerial excellence.

Similarly, Shaw identified the six major areas of competencies: (1) personnel management (2) self awareness (3) human relations abilities (4) techniques of administrative leadership (5) instructional leadership and (6) community relationship for educational managers.

On the basis of the discussed related literature survey, details of the proposed dimensions required for the training of women educational mangers are proposed which is as follows:

Knowledge dimensions

The women education managers need to possess a concrete knowledge on the structure and functions of the specific educational system where they are working. This would enable them to have a comprehensive understanding about the nature of administrative process in the educational set-up. The following are the key areas in knowledge dimension:

a) *Philosophy and value system of Indian society*: It would include philosophical and sociological foundation of Indian education including Indian philosophical and sociological thoughts.

b) *Educational policies, commissions and committees in India:* It would include philosophical and sociological foundation of Indian education including Indian philosophical and sociological thoughts.

It would also include the policies and reports related to the right and privilege of women like the National Committee on Women's Education (1957-59). The committee should include awareness about women's rights like constitutional provisions, directives and amendments.

a) *Educational principles and practices:* It would include knowledge of educational theories, models of teachings, examples and case studies of different educational practices.

b) *Financial and legal provisions:* It would include financial rules and procedures, financial control, legal provisions governing educational activities, legal supports, etc.

c) *Emerging issues at the educational level:* It would include the nature of students and their behaviour pattern, resource crunch and the need for resource mobilisation, community partnership and community mobilization, application of advanced technology in teaching-learning and administration, quality and standards of different levels of education, staff appraisal and promotion, vocationalisation of school and higher education, etc.

Managerial dimension

Apart form the knowledge dimension women educational managers demand certain managerial competencies and skills because they are the leaders, initiators, innovators, administrators, managers and institution builders. The managerial dimensions would consist of the following components:

a) *Management strategies:* An effective and competent woman educational manager should know the strategies and techniques of management like, brainstorming, benchmarking quality circle, parallel learning structure, survey feedback, transactional analysis, quality of work life, system theory, teacher's grid and many more. She should know different management theories and practices like classical theory, scientific theory and democratic theory. Apart form these she should go through SWOT analysis and t-group training for self-management.

b) *Managerial competencies:* It would include competencies related to human resource management, individual recognition, organisational and resource management, review techniques, remote management, managing complexity, broadening contextual competencies, record keeping, and reading the situation.

c) *Leadership skills, competencies:* It requires the ability to lead and manage people to work as individuals and as a team towards a common goal; to initiate and manage change and improvement in pursuit of strategic objectives; to devolve responsibilities, dilate tasks and monitor practice to see that they are being carried out; and to command credibility through the discharge of their functions and to influence others. Apart from these abilities the women educational managers should be familiar with different leadership styles and tested leadership skills to lead students, teachers and the community members. They should also be acquainted with staff development and motivation, headship with vision, delegation, and promotion of learning innovation and creativity, democratic and moral dimensions of leadership including social justice, praxis, pluralism and inquiry.

d) *Decision-making skills and competencies:* It requires the ability to investigate, to solve problems and to make decisions; to analyse, understand and interpret relevant information and data; and the ability to think creatively and imaginatively to solve problems and identify opportunities, thorough programme planning, group/peer decision-making balanced judgement and discipline management.

e) *Communication skills and competencies:* It requires the ability to make points clear and understand the views of others, to evolve effective communication system in the organisation, to negotiate and consult effectively, and to organise formal and informal meetings through persuasive communication, interpersonal skills, and community relationship.

f) *Self-management skills:* It requires the ability to prioritise and manage their own time effectively, to resolve conflicts within, to take responsibility of their own professional development, to manage stress and work under pressure and deadline, to adapt self-motivational factors, and to realise the strengths, weaknesses, opportunities and threats.

Professional dimension

A woman educational manager should be a professional in, mind and spirit. She should possess professionalism in teaching management, administration and each and every activity. Professional dimension includes the following components.

a) *Professionalism related to internal environment:* It includes the abilities to develop strategic plans for curriculum development, to develop professionalism among teachers and students, to pursue the information and update the knowledge, to create healthy professional/ work environment, and the ability to understand and manage micro-politics in the institution and the community, institution climate and institution effectiveness measures.

b) *Professionalism related to external environment:* It includes the ability to be the liaison between the educational system and government agencies, to understand the present political philosophy and to manage macro-politics, to strengthen the educational system by mobilising the external environment and the ability to maintain public relation.

Information technology dimension

In the age of third wave change, i.e., social change due to information technology, women educational managers should not be away from information technology revolution. To cope up with the changes in the field of education, she should have the minimum skills to work with computers, internet, e-mail, management systems, data management and some useful computer packages. For this, training should be organised related to information technology to use information technology as a transformative force.

MODES OF TRAINING

The in-service women educational managers would prefer the self-study mode, distance mode and virtual mode of training, whereas, with the help of formal mode of training the aspiring women educational managers would get training beforehand. Husen and Postlenthwaite have emphasized both pre-service and in-service training for women educational managers in their study. According to them, pre-service training is a must, and in-service training is needed for professional development. Leithwood and others argue for a long-term in-service training for the development of educational managers using Managers Profile Method. In this context the training programme of women education would be imparted using a modes like in-service mode for working managers, pre-service mode for perspective managers, self-study mode for interested working managers and distance mode for both in-service and pre-service educational managers.

CONCLUSION

No doubt there is a need for properly rationalised, well-structured strategies including training programmes for the empowerment of women educational managers. There is a proper need even to discuss some of the available strategies and one has to see whether these are helping to empower women managers or to overpower them in the process. Before training is initiated, the objectives of the training programme for various categories of women educational managers will be defined in terms of job profiles at various levels and the required expertise, skill and institutional development. For a perfect training programme the assessment of training need for those educational managers and their job assessment is essential which would clarify and justify the type of training programme needed. Once the different types of requirements and capabilities, roles and responsibilities of different categories of educational managers are identified, perfect curricula for training programmes for educational administrations at various levels may be developed properly. Let us hope for a better future with more empowered women managers in the field of education through proper strategies.

Women only manage to shake off centuries-old bondage in recent decades. There are now role models for the women of the future. Everyone can become a pioneer. There is a wide spectrum of possibilities: becoming an entrepreneur, a professional manager, a wife and social activists. The time has come for thousand flowers to bloom.

REFERENCES

Briggs. D. K. and Bhagia, N. M., 1985, "Professional Preparation of Educational Administrators in Developing Countries", *EPA Bulletin*, Vol. 8.

Brown. E., 1985, Moving Towards Excellence: The Principal, Paper presented at the annual Meeting of the National Association of Secondary School Principals, New Orleans. Jan. 1985, *Source: ERIC Database: 1982-91.*

Department of Education, 1986, *National Policy on Education-1986,* New Delhi: MHRD.

Department of Education, 1992, *Programme of Action on National Policy on Education 1986,* New Delhi: MHRD.

Government of India, 1990, *Towards an Enlightened and Humane Society: NPE, 1986, A Review*, New Delhi.

Grace, C. and Howard, E.., 1989, Training Principals to Develop Comprehensive Early Childhood Programmes: The Mississippi Model. Paper presented at the annual meeting of the Association for Supervision and Curriculum Development, Orlando, US, *Source: ERIC Database: 1982-91.*

Institute of Education, 1997, *Information for Candidates—Prepare for Headship,* London, University of London.

Leithwood, K., *et al.* 1984, Training Principals for School Improvement, *Education and Urban Society,* Vol. 17. No. 1. 1984. U. S. *Source: ERIC Database: 1982-91.*

Martis, A., 1995, Gender Differences in Leadership styles of the Heads of Secondary Schools as Perceived by their Teachers, Paper presented at the National Conference on Women Access to Leadership Positions in Educational Management, Department of Educational Administration. FEP, M. S. University of Baroda, Vadodara.

Ministry of Education, 1953, *Secondary Education Commission 1952-53*, New Delhi Government of India.

Ministry of Education and Youth Services, 1971, *Education and National Development: Report of Education Commission 1964-66*, New Delhi: NCERT.

Morgan, G., 1988, *Riding the Waves of Change: Developing Managerial Competencies for a Turbulent World.* San Francisco, Jossly-Boss.

Naisbitt, J., 1996, *Megatrends Asia—The Eight Asian Megatrends that are Changing the World*, Nicholas Brealey Publishing, London.

Perers, T. and Waterman, R., 1982, *In Search of Excellence*, Harper and Row, New York.

27

Strategies for Empowering Rural Women Educational Managers

*Mukesh Chandrakar** and *Ashutosh Biswal***

INTRODUCTION

Women constitute almost half of the nation's total human resources. Without planned and proper utilisation of half of the human resources, no nation can hope to move towards the goal of all-round development of the society. In Indian society, the position and status of women has been continuously changing in the course of time. As compared to the women in the Vedic period, the position and status of present-day women, particularly in the rural areas, is declining. After the UN declaration of 1975 as the Year of the women, momentum has been gathering all over the world, demanding gender equality and push for equal representation of women in different spheres of life. After independence much emphasis has been given in the forms of constitutional provisions, special rights and equity measures for equality for women's development and participation in all spheres of life—social, political, economic and educational. Indian women had shown their capabilities and excellence in different fields like politics, economic

* *M.Ed. Student, Department of Education, Faculty of Education and Psychology, The M.S. University of Baroda, Vadodara.*

***Lecturer, Department of Education, Faculty of Education and Psychology, The M.S. University of Baroda, Vadodara.*

development, sports, arts, etc. Apart form their achievements in other fields, their contribution in the field of education is quite huge. They start their role as tutors of children from home to the educational institutions. During last decade, there is a remarkable involvement of women in the field of education cutting across different levels of education in different positions like teachers, researchers, activists, administrators and managers. Participation of women in the field of education is increasing due to their superior ability and potentials to excel in that field, and a demand of the teaching profession of more and more women educators and managers. Women have proved their superiority over men as educational managers from the grassroots level of society, i.e., home to national and international level, executing their duties effectively and efficiently. Women have proved their superiority over men as educational managers form time to time whenever given chances to prove it.

There is another very compelling reason for women educators to prepare themselves for managerial roles in education. Psychologists tell that women are more nurturing and better at sharing than men. Men bond together in ways which make them feel more powerful, and one way of achieving that is by excluding people. Historically, women and minorities have been excluded from many male-dominated organisations, and certainly form the vast majority of leadership roles in education. By encouraging and supporting more women leaders in education they may be, in practical terms, leaders of tomorrow, which, hopefully, will be a diverse and equally empowered group.

It cannot be denied that India lives in villages. About 70 per cent of our population lives in rural areas. More than 60 per cent of our educational institutions, particularly schools and colleges, are located in rural areas. The excellencies of women in education are more inclined to the urban denomination. The women's participation in educational management is higher in urban areas in comparison to rural areas due to the different environment and opportunities. Their participation in the management of education is very low in the rural areas due to several barriers that hinder their participation. Some of them are social impositions, low education level, lack of exposure, and many others imposed by social, political and economic ethos of the society.

Largely, women educational managers in the rural areas refer to the women school heads in the name of headmistress and principals. Currently, a handful of women are working in the rural educational institutions, facing a large number of problems while performing their duties. Fortunately or unfortunately, after the enactment of the 73rd and 74th constitutional amendments which have set the stage for greater decentralisation and enhanced the role of local bodies, the problem of women educational managers have increased a lot. Many educational managers do not want to serve in the rural areas and always try to get a chance in the urban areas. These are some areas of concern, which need the attention for discussion in the national forums. There is a need to empower women managers in a different approach, particularly those serving in the rural areas. Even provisions and scopes should be created by the authorities to attract more and more women managers to serve the rural educational institutions.

In the present paper, the authors have discussed the status of rural women managers, problems faced by them in rural areas, their empowerment and the needed strategy to empower them.

STATUS OF RURAL WOMEN EDUCATIONAL MANAGERS

Women who wanted to teach, historically, faced the same struggle as women who wanted to vote, and today they want to become tail-hook pilots, or want to join the top echelon of leadership in education. Just as throughout the rest of society, in education patriarchal systems prevail, and male models for leadership dominate. The laws may exist on papers, but in the real world, support often evaporates, and those making it to the top are a token minority of the capable women available for those positions which will shape the future of education, and ultimately, the future of the country. The picture is quite hazy in case of rural women managers in the field of education. In India, many of the women mangers working in the rural educational settings are from urban areas. Indian rural women need lots of empowerment and scope to show their adequate representation in educational management.

Teaching is a challenging and complex profession requiring high level disciplines, skills and practical knowledge. Despite this, a large number of teachers do not generally receive either adequate support or pay. The capable women who are entering the teaching profession do not get a proper scope to prosper and to become managers in the fields, as it needs experience and exposure along with knowledge and skill.

Women in educational management at the beginning of the century are an issue that demands serious attention and a new urgency. In the West, particularly Western Europe and North America, although women constitute almost 45 per cent of the workforces, they occupy only 10 per cent of the management positions (*World Almanac*, 1997; USIS, 1996). This figure is much lower in the senior management positions. The figure in India is quite similar to the quoted studies and it is quite negligible for the rural women educational managers. There is a strong need to streamline the women managers in the educational system, particularly in the rural areas. It is high time to study and analyse different problems faced by women educational managers in rural areas and to plan and design some specific strategies to empower rural educational managers which can be implemented in a phased manner.

PROBLEMS FACED BY RURAL EDUCATIONAL MANAGERS

Problems of rural educational managers are many. They face problems from the family, the society, and from inside and outside the organisations where they work. In general, women educational managers and professionals in the rural areas face resisting forces like limited opportunities to higher education, discriminatory appointment and promotion practices, traditional attitudes of male managers towards working women, role conflict, male-dominated domain, male resistance to women in management, implementation of proper policies and legislations to ensure participation of women in management positions, of professional networking, lack of female role models, of professional management development programmes, lack of sufficient number of quality day-care centres, dual responsibilities of traditional and professional roles, balancing traditional and professional roles, and family obligations as a wife and a mother for child-bearing and child-rearing. Here, some of the major problems faced by rural women in general and rural educational managers in particular are being discussed.

1) *Social unacceptability:* The ancient cast system and the traditional patriarchic family system of Indian society have created a special status for women which is typically applicable for rural women. The rural people viewed women only as mothers, sisters, daughters and wives in society. Practically they have created a mindset where they cannot see a woman in any higher position other than traditional positions. Many of them have the view that women are born to serve the male. Seldom are they viewed as managers, decision makers, leaders, and administrators. Thus, when rural people see women as the managers of educational system, they, particularly the fellow males, are not ready to accept them as managers.
2) *Portrayed self-image:* In rural areas educated women working in the educational set-up have a very low self-portrayed image of themselves. This self-negative image of women hinders them to reach a proper place in the educational management.

The inferior self-image of women becomes difficult to overcome considering that it is ingrained and conditioned in their upbringing and social development. In traditional patriarchal societies, the feminine gender is subordinate, while the masculine is superior and dominant . Generally, men are held responsible for providing the necessities of life thus to work outside the home. On the other hand, women are expected to serve their husbands and children at home, especially since they are not required by the Islamic law (Sharish) to financially support the family. In this subordinate position, women become victims of their own gender. Hammoud's dynamic study on the role of women in higher education management in the Arab region confers that the most fatal obstacle which prevents women from realising their utmost professional achievement is the self-image of a woman portrayed as inferior to men, incapable of being socially and financially independent, and hence depends on the man to care for and protect them.

3) *Role conflict*: Women educational managers and even women professionals have conflicting roles of being a domesticated wife and mother, and that of a professional woman.

4) *Unaccepted by male colleagues:* Male teachers have wrong notions regarding the capacity and talent of women teachers. They attribute all the good qualities to men and attribute all the weakness to women. Male teachers believe that women cannot play an important roles in decision making in the management activities. Thus, women are not accepted by their male counterparts.

5) *Prejudice about women's leadership:* Prejudice about women's leadership and management capacity in education is another important factor that influences their position. These biases are based on views about their emotionality, and doubts as to their ability to take charge in a tough situation. It is also assumed that women

exercise a type of maternal leadership, valued in certain positions, but which competes with the great advancement power of those exercising the expert leadership style.

6) *Traditional attitudes and stereotypes:* Attitudinal change needs action at the forefront. Traditional attitudes and stereotypes received the highest attention by the rural people as it was unanimously considered a primary resisting force to women in management positions in rural areas in general and in the educational field in particular.

Although gradually changing among the more educated modern arab/Islamic societies, conservative Arab societies hold traditional socio-cultural stereotypes and attitudes about the role of women. These conservative and traditional attitudes highlighted in the literature of women in the Muslim world portray women's primary role as a wife and mother. Women are not necessarily looked upon as having the abilities and potential for developing professional careers. They are portrayed as being inferior to men, naturally emotional and unsuitable for leadership positions. Such conservative attitudes negate the concept of professional working women in traditional Arab societies. The idea of women working is degrading and a disgrace to some Arab men who consider that it is their responsibility to provide for their wives and family.

Therefore, traditional Arab/Islamic societies maintain that first and foremost, women should prepare themselves for a domestic career of being a wife and a mother. Work should only be considered as a last option under extraneous conditions and circumstances.

The above attitude tends to have a spillover effect at work, whereby male employers regard women as being less capable than men and unfit for responsible positions, claiming that their family obligations take priority; and hence, subjects them to lower productivity and absenteeism. This negative attitude and traditional stereotype towards women in Arab/Islamic societies have been, and still are, a major resisting force to the progress of professional working women, particularly for those in management. The condition of rural women in India is not quite different from that of the Arab women.

7) *Family problems:* In our prevailing rural as well as urban societies some of the family problems, mainly in the name of unmarried female members, contribute negatively towards the empowerment of women. Some of the problems are related to marriage, dowry system, security, etc.
8) *Lack of facilities:* In the rural areas, there is a lack of facilities like the unavailability of proper institutions to study, impediment to intelligent girls to progress and to be empowered. Educational institutions and training programmes which perpetuate male role models and male-oriented behaviour assure that male patriarchies will continue to dominate and exercise control in the educational system.

EMPOWERMENT OF RURAL WOMEN EDUCATIONAL MANAGERS

Women empowerment is a process which changes existing power relations by addressing itself to the three dimensions of material, human and intellectual resources. It is a process which must challenge and change ideology, the set of ideas, attitudes, beliefs and practices in which gender bias or social bias like caste, class, regionalism and communalism are embedded.

The empowerment of women has to operate at two levels. There has to be an extrinsic process where things in the outside environment are changed, by which is meant women's greater control over resources but just as important and much more critical is the intrinsic process, the change of the ideological environment. There is a need to increase women's self-confidence. This makes women gain strength and motivation to sustain their empowerment. The women have to be aware of their capacities. Otherwise they are conditioned form birth to uphold male power, privilege and prestige. The change in the intrinsic level is critical in any process of empowerment. In practice you cannot separate the two levels, extrinsic and intrinsic; they are best addressed in an interwoven way. In an example from South Asia, women always say "The men do all the work, that is why they need to have all the prestige." Empowerment is thus not only an external process, but a process that has to bring about these intrinsic changes, not only in women but also in men. If the empowerment process is sustainable and long term the intrinsic changes has to be a part of the design.

STRATEGIES FOR WOMEN EMPOWERMENT

Some of the strategies to empower rural educational managers and to prepare a scope for rural women to be educational managers are discussed here.

1) *Creating consciousness:* The process has to start with consciousness rising about the empowerment of women to leadership positions in education. Mobilising and organising different programmes are also important as it is nearly impossible for individual women to break out of the gender system in the rural areas. When groups of women do this process together they reinforce each other's strengths. These collective efforts then become an alternative, a non-traditional environment, where women can think creative thoughts and have revolutionary ideas, and the activists working with the women can give them access to information, knowledge and skills. They then go through a process of identifying their own priorities and the strategies they want to use to struggle for change, whether it is to struggle for resources or for changes in gender relations at home. They act and they analyse the

actions, what worked and what did not work. This is a sphere where a woman can raise her consciousness to a new level and then continue to new actions, new struggles and so on. Experience shows that while women often start to identify a need outside the home such as, for example, health care for the children or a community need, success in their struggle makes them gain confidence to also address the situation in the households.

Since power and control are central issues in the management, and no one gives these up voluntarily, it is up to women educators to take the initiative to see that changes are made in the way leaders are trained and selected in order to give women a level playing field to reach leadership roles in education. It needs a type of revolution on the part of women society to show their identity.

2) *Gender equality:* Equality should be emphasized irrespective of the gender. Professional careers should be viewed according to individual merit, i.e., aptitude, attitude, skill and qualifications and not on the basis of gender. Special efforts are needed to modify these attitudes through social awareness programmes promoting a woman's legal right to study, work and participate in all aspects of development at all levels. Similarly, the concept of equal opportunity for men and women, and of shared family responsibilities should be emphasized in the educational system beginning from the elementary school. Proper steps should be taken along these lines.
3) *Changing social attitudes:* The social attitude towards women should be changed. It should be started from the family and should be echoed in every part of the society. They should be viewed as equal as the male members in the society. Instead of viewing women's leadership as maternal, it should be considered as democratic and participatory, facilitating the formation of teams that are

more creative, committed, and thus more efficient in their work. For a woman coming up in life as a leader from the educational field it needs more of participation, more of encouragement, more of devotion and facilities from the society.

4) *Equity measures:* To provide equality opportunities to the female population in the educational field, the policy of reservation for women should be implemented properly for their proper education and training. It is inadvisable to empower women through their reservation in the government services. Reservation can be usefully harmful while using it for a job. Can we think of reservations beyond SC, ST, SEBC, PH, and EXS? Now the latest move is that there should be reservation for women in government jobs. Perhaps it is the time when India needs to prepare for reservations for all. It is high time that we do away with categorisation. The role of each entity needs to be properly defined. Here more emphasis should be given to other equity measures other than the reservation in the government jobs which again may create categorisation between male and female.

5) *Networking and discussion on women educational managers:* There is a need to foster the creation of female manager's networks in different fields including education at local, regional and national levels to share their views which can strengthen the process of empowerment. Seminars and the activities of similar nature on career development of women managers in education and negotiation permit a joint examination of the obstacles women face and the strategies designed to overcome them.

6) *Organising training programmes:* Training programmes with different dimensions for women empowerment in educational management could be organised at different levels. The following components could be part and parcel of training programmes:

a) *Management strategies:* An effective and competent rural woman educational manager should know the strategies and techniques of management like, brainstorming, benchmarking, quality circle, parallel learning structure, survey, feedback, and transactional analysis, quality of work life, system theory, teacher's grid and many more. She should know different management theories and practices like, classical theory, scientific theory and democratic theory. Apart form these she should go through SWOT analysis and t-group training for self-management.

b) *Managerial competencies:* It would include competencies related to human resource management, individual recognition, organisational and resource management, review techniques, remote management, managing complexity, broadening contextual competencies, record keeping, and reading the situation.

c) *Leadership skills, competencies:* It requires the ability to lead and manage people to work as individuals and as a team towards a common goal; to initiate and manage change and improvement in pursuit of strategic objectives; to devolve responsibilities, delegate tasks and monitor practice to see that they are being carried out; and to command credibility through the discharge of their functions and to influence others. Apart form these abilities the women education managers should be familiar with different leadership styles and tested leadership skills to lead students, teachers and the community members. They should be acquainted with staff development and motivation, headship with vision, delegation, and promotion of learning innovation and creativity, democratic and moral dimensions of leadership including social justice, praxis, pluralism, and inquiry.

d) *Decision making skills and competencies:* It requires the ability to investigate, to solve problems and to make decisions; to analyse, understand and interpret relevant information and data; and the ability to think creatively and imaginatively to solve problems and identify opportunities, thorough programme planning, group/peer decision making, balanced judgement, and discipline management.

e) *Development of communication skills*: Women educational managers in rural areas lack proper communication skills and so it should be a component of training programme. As centralised leadership gives way to flattened hierarchy and employee empowerment, managers in education will be expected to have good communication and interpersonal skills, the ability to listen and relate to others, and be capable of working in self-managing teams.

f) *Management by heart:* It is a special management skill where women can do well. Showing appreciation can go a long way in boosting the morale of the employee and give them a professional environment to work in. A simple example of management by heart would be giving a smile to your co-workers instead of maintaining a stern demeanour and being open to listening. Moreover, everyone in the workplace can be a VIP, V stands for Validation, I for information and P for participation with the use of this strategy. Validation and acknowledging one's coworkers and treating people as equal and intelligent human beings will create a cooperative and positive work atmosphere and a win-win situation for both managers and co-workers. It is quite necessary for rural educational institutions.

g) *Developing a killer instinct:* Being a human resource professional, the women educational managers in the rural areas have to develop a killer instinct in human resource management at the organisational level as she has to work inside a pool of problems of different types. This will bring about a collaborative environment, for the benefit of the co-workers as well as the institutions.

7) *Balancing stereotyping and modern role of educational managers:* There should be a proper balance between the stereotyping and modern role of rural women educational managers. Mere stereotyping and ultra modernisation are both extremes. Ultra moderns need to be stereotype, whereas stereotypes need to be transformational. Working women need to modernise their stereotype roles. Stereotype women may not be lacking originality and individuality. The manifestation of their originality is more a matter of the environs they get. Mere stereotyping is compromising, whereas mere modernising is mechanising. The functional requirement is the equilibration of both the roles.

8) *Role of civil society in women's empowerment:* The actors of civil society should contribute in organising women, building public awareness, training and gender sensitisation, providing services to those in remote places, public policy watching, market watching, public information, monitoring violations, public information, autonomous research, innovations and experimentation, advocacy and advisory work. Organisations at the grassroot levels like women's organisations and NGOs have a role to play in this process. The end product of this synergetic process is a convergence, between the enabling conditions of the state and the grassroots organisations and community, household and individual changes in a sense fusing together to create a more gender just society.

9) *State and centre's role:* The state and the centre have general enabling roles in the process of women's empowerment. The states have to remove structural barrier and biases in their own policies and programmes

to provide a sound base for the empowerment of women educational managers. It has to create space in the design, implementation and monitoring of its programmes and policies. More access for rural women educational managers in governmental institution has to be ensured by the state government. The state has to reform the legal system and the judicial systems to remove the inequalities that are enshrined and embedded in law. Equal access for women to public resources and services provided by the state has to be ensured. The most important role of the state, a critical role that the state has to play, is to implement and enforce the agreements and the protection of women's rights. Moreover, the greater visibility of women in decision-making positions encourages other women to opt for such positions, and can contribute to changing the social manifestations and images of gender.

The actual processes of empowerment has to occur at several levels. The transformation has to give changes in the ideological system, in access to resources and in institutions and structures at several levels, such as the family and the household, the village and the community, the state and the market.

10) *Empirical research work:* In order to undertake effective actions in the area of women empowerment in rural educational set-ups, there is a need to substantiate strategies with facts. For this reason, there is a need of research studies.

Investigations should be conducted in concrete practices that slow women's career development within the firm in the context of the organisational changes being produced by the current re-organisation of the labour market (forms of contracting, subcontracting, technological changes, etc.). Investigation is needed to know how the different forms of work flexibility affect women's career development, and performance indicators for a system to measure the level of gender equity can be designed. Study of the specific characteristics that leadership training programmes for promoting female leadership with different sectors can be encouraged.

CONCLUSION

There is a great need for the empowerment of rural educational managers to share the available human resources optimally to the maximum success in the development of education and society. It is high time to start the process in an effective way. There is a need of deep involvement of each and every person in the process as one learnt how by being deeply involved in what you are doing you can actually allot a lot of value to it.

One has to think of these developmental perspectives, considering the real problem of rural educational women managers, and then planning and implementation can be proper.

One has to think of things from the other person's perspective. Great ideas are in plenty but they are successful only when tested out there in the real work.

Someone in the management had said, "Success is to walk the last mile with a smile on your lips and a song in your heart. There should be a sense of fulfilment and achievement in whatever you do." It is the starting of the big marathon. We have to utilise our resources in this processes maximally and optimally in a planned way to achieve the objectives of empowering rural educational managers.

28

Environment Education and Protection: Women as Leaders in 21st Century

*Maneesha Shukul**

Women, to a great extent, are the influencing force in the whole world—from the family circle to the policy decision maker. Their role as an agent of social change is comparatively less known or sometimes completely ignored. According to Dehlot, "Women's role as 'wife', 'mother', 'housekeeper' and 'income-earner' are the most well known and agreed upon worldwide; but the role of 'community organiser' and 'family kinship maintainer' has been rarely considered by the government and planners when introducing new programmes in the community. Women's role as an agent of social change and her leadership must be realised as well as utilised for environment education and protection.

NEED FOR ENVIRONMENT EDUCATION

One of the global challenges in the twenty-first century continues to be a resource and environmental crisis as was in the past century; no doubt the magnitude has increased.

* *Reader, Home Management Department, Faculty of Home Science, M. S. University, Vadodara.*

Recently the world has recognised the urgent need for the balance and harmony between humanity and the environment due to the increasing deterioration of the environment. Recommendation 96 of the Stockholm Conference on Human Environment called for the development of environment education as one of the most critical elements of an "all-out attack" on the world's environmental crisis. The goal of environment education is "to develop a world population that is aware of and concerned about the environment and its associated problems and which has the knowledge, skills, attitudes, motivations and commitments to work individually and collectively toward solution of current problem and the prevention of new ones."

Environment education with its aims of promoting an awareness of and responsibility for the environment should be a lifelong process in order to improve and protect the environment now and in future. If individuals are environmentally educated the society and government are only an extension of an individual. An environmentally literate country is more likely to adopt an environmentally sound programme. Hence it is essential that environment education should reach all sections of the population through the use of both formal and non-formal techniques.

LEADERSHIP OF WOMEN IN THE FAMILY

Women are an important link in the goal of achieving a satisfactory balance between nature, natural resources and human activities because of their central role in the family as managers of production and as consumers of scarce resources. They are directly or indirectly in close contact with the environment, may be as producers, consumers, managers of fuel fodder-food collector for the family. They are most affected by the environmental degradation.

Environmentally aware and concerned women influence the

entire family circle, especially children in their perception, values, attitudes, behaviour and in ethical considerations. They influence all the family members in the use of natural resources, energy consumption and in waste recycling. Thus the family is the first, most effective and close-link place where most of the women are working as a leader in imparting environment education to the whole family.

LEADERSHIP IN THE COMMUNITY

To date, women have not really been perceived to be a part of natural environment conservation scene. They are often seen as a part of the problem, seldom as a part of the solution. But because of various roles women play, they can prove to be most suitable leaders for environment education and protection.

Women as the Most Suitable Leaders in Environment Education and Protection

Women are at present, and in future will continue to be, the most suitable leaders in environment education and protection. Empowering them with appropriate environmental information, training and employment opportunities can increase their number. They must be reinforced with a positive attitude and motivation to work with commitment for the more equitable and sustainable development of the planet as well as for the healthier environment.

Women have the ingredients of leadership. They have the ability to use power effectively and in a responsible manner. They have the fundamental understanding of people. They have an ability to inspire followers to apply their full capabilities to a project and to act in a manner that will develop a climate conducive to responding to and arousing motivations.

Women are effective in formal education but are more effective in non-formal education. They are a great influential

31

Open and Distance Learning— The Cornerstone of Lifelong Learning for the Information Age

*Janet Jenkins**

DISTANCE EDUCATION—THE CONTEXT

Distance learning is at a turning point—in the scale of its use, in how it operates, and in what it is used for. In the last quarter century or so it has changed beyond recognition. From correspondence courses for significant but relatively small numbers seeking an alternative route to formal or vocational qualifications we have moved on to a methodology which forms the basis of operation of the world's largest universities, its open universities. This enormous expansion has been boosted by the emergence of new information and communications technologies which help to extend educational opportunity to an ever increasing proportion of the world's citizens.

Attitudes too have changed. Distance learning is no longer the last choice for the excluded but has instead gained an important place in national and international plans for educational development. As early as 1986 India's National Policy on Education stressed the importance of the then new national open university and of distance education. Other

**Consultant in Distance Education, Swatchways, The Quay, Wivenhoe, Colchester, UK.*

countries have similarly recognised distance learning in education policy. More recently international consensus on its value has been reflected in such documents as the Delhi Declaration on Education for All and the European Treaty of Union, while UNESCO has developed a policy document on open and distance learning.

Interested in distance leaning is not simply because it can reach large numbers of learners. It is also because it can be used for a great variety of purposes. Its potential to deliver new knowledge and skills has caught the imagination of many concerned with lifelong learning. This is reflected in the broad merit often attributed to distance learning in recent education policy statements.

Flexibility, accessibility, openness—these are words we often hear associated with open and distance learning reflecting genuine qualities. They indicated recognition of its potential to meet new learning needs and yet much distance education continues to take place within a relatively constrained and inflexible framework. In practice it is still used mainly by universities and not just open universities. As in India, many traditional universities across the world offer courses for distance students in parallel to their coursed for residential students.

Why has open and distance learning been slower to catch on in other sectors? This is partly a matter of comparison with its rapid spread in the university sector to help meet popular demand for mass higher education. But it is also because of the substantial barriers to access to education, distance or otherwise, for adult learners, such as illiteracy or poor basic education, distance, time constraints, poverty. Distance education in its traditional form can overcome some of these barriers, but, with the partial exception of higher education, does not yet have mass appeal.

Now new delivery strategies, enabled and supported by new technologies, are changing the face of distance education. Traditional tuition by correspondence can be combined with more opportunities for other individual contact and group support. Such interaction has always been a part of good distance education, but is much easier to provide using new interactive technologies.

As open and distance education becomes more flexible, accessible and interactive, its interest as tool for lifelong learning increases. The scope, content, modes of delivery of lifelong learning for the information age are today the subject of much debate, with strategies still under development, initiatives only just beginning. In the discourse on such matters, open and distance learning has a presence, but not yet a high profile. I want to argue in this paper that it is time to change that, and suggest what that change might look like.

I want to focus on routes to lifelong learning that use open and distance learning in three sectors—basic (school-level) education, higher (high skills) and post-basic vocational education and training. I will use the examples to suggest how open and distance education can be used more comprehensively in the future as an integral part of strategy to meet demand for lifelong learning.

BASIC EDUCATION

The use of distance learning for basic education is growing, although it remains contentious. For children it has a long and respectable history, starting with schools of the air—radio and correspondence—for children in the Australian outback and other countries that have large rural terrain and isolated farming families. Such schools continue today, providing models for partnership between parents and children at home and a remote school.

More recently open and distance learning has grown in popularity as an alternative route to formal education for children otherwise excluded from school, frequently because of pressure of numbers on national education systems. Examples can be cited from countries as different as Namibia and Brazil, Malawi and Indonesia, as well as India with its National Open School. In open schooling, new approaches to delivery of learning are increasingly used, such as "multichannel learning" or technology assisted approaches for isolated children.

In the eyes of many, distance education for children is perceived as second best, an alternative for those who cannot get access to "normal" school. Whether one agrees with these perceptions or not, this rather negative view is paradoxical when we come to basic education at a distance for adults. What is seen as second best for children is presented as a beacon of opportunity for adults who received incomplete formal schooling.

Open schools are indeed a wonderful opportunity for adults, but if designed for young people they are unlikely to meet all their needs and may also use an approach not well suited to their maturity. Most adults who want to improve their basic education have complex needs which may not all lie at school level, and may not fit well with the divisions into subjects and courses that apply to school courses. Many, for example, may be literate in their mother tongues but novices ("at primary level") in English, a language which they may want to learn as it becomes increasingly important for much employment. Others may have an uneven record of achievement at school long ago—good maths , poor communication skills, for example, while many simply failed to complete primary school. The pattern of need for basic education is thus varied indeed, and much lies at as level below secondary education. To increase the attraction to adults of basic level distance education, greater flexibility of approach, sensitive to their requirements, is necessary. Two contrasting developments points to an imminent breakthrough in this respect.

The age of information technology has, paradoxically, seen renewed emphasis on face-to-face and interpersonal contact as a component of good open and distance learning—the recognition that while most people can do most of their learning at a distance, learners generally do better with a rounded learning support system which includes some personal contact. Increasingly, distance leaning systems are designed to accommodate this kind of interaction, both incorporated within courses and associated with the learning environment. With guidance on course selection, thorough orientation of self-study and well-planned support, disadvantaged adults with a low level of basic education can study effectively at a distance. Even totally illiterate people can learn effectively, for example, in study groups listening to the radio, with trained group leaders. The importance of interpersonal contact is manifest in the appearance in many contexts of Open Learning or Distance Education Study Centres—places where individuals can meet tutors and counsellors, self-help, and tutored groups can meet, and all learners can consult reference material and other resources.

Secondly, new information and communications technology applications in education have given an immense boost to open and distance learning all over the world. Their immediate attraction lies in their ability to make more learning available at the same time as increasing interactivity in the absence of a teacher, through, for example, multimedia applications and electronic communication. But such learning is available only to the minority of adults, those who have easy access to computers and know-how to use them.

A network of study centres for distance learners can change the picture. It is becoming the norm to equip study centres for open and distance learning with up-to-date information and communication facilities. This potentially results in an expanded range of learning opportunities for those with access to the study centres, improved learning and teaching, and altogether more attractive learning environment. A study centre, for example, might at any one time cater for many categories of distance learner--young unemployed adults learning enterprise skills; young school leavers completing secondary-level courses; older, employed adults in the caring professions doing work-related courses in health sciences; adults learning basic English, information technology or basic number skills; yet others following university level courses. Many would use such centres in familiar ways—for regular meetings with tutors or to find material for their correspondence assignments. But there will be many other uses, which depend on access to information and communication technology. Some would use the Internet to communicate with their teacher or to download reference material. Some would use multimedia course material available in the centre, for example, numeracy material on CD-ROM. Some would take part in audio-conferences or video-conference with fellow students in other study centres.

This kind of vision shows how, even in countries which are not yet technology rich, new technologies harnessed with traditional ones can be brought into play to make education accessible to many more people. To provide learning on a large scale for the most disadvantaged remains, still, a major challenge to be tackled over the long-term with well planned initiatives. But study centres can offer flexible accommodation and support for distance learners. The flexibility offered by open and distance learning goes beyond what is possible in any class for adults, offering greater choice of subject, time, pace and place of study. Information and communications technologies enhance this potential as well as underpinning high standards in teaching and learning. Paradoxically, machines (computers) help to transform distance education from being relatively impersonal to becoming more responsive and personal.

HIGHER LEVEL DISTANCE EDUCATION

A second important type of lifelong learning is at the university level. In the information age higher level education—skills and knowledge—is essential for balanced development, both at the national and the individual level. We place importance on an ever greater proportion of young people proceeding to university. In several of the most economically successful countries, a third or more school leavers go on to higher education. There is no need to stress the immense value of open universities in opening access to higher education. There is no need to stress the immense value of open universities in opening access to higher education of those who cannot gain entry into conventional institutions, or who take up university study as adults. The "mega-universities" of our era—those with over 100,000 students—are all distance teaching universities.

But also of emerging importance is specialist higher level education and training, particularly in high level skills and knowledge applied to work. There has been a recent explosion of distance education courses leading to applied degrees, including many in the newer disciplines of applied sciences and even more in management and related fields. Most of over 100 universities in the UK now offer at least one distance-taught programme of study, and almost all of these are postgraduate courses. Such courses are normally prepared in response to demand, are often relatively small scale, and in their design are sensitive to circumstances of learners.

Higher level open and distance learning is also playing an important role elsewhere in Europe, in the development of the emerging economies of Central and Eastern Europe. Eleven counties of the Baltic region and the heart of Europe have clubbed together in a major programme of economic and social development supported by the Europen Union and known as PHARE. An important component of PHARE is its multi-country programme in distance education, intended to provide the working citizens of these newly independent countries with an opportunity to gain the new knowledge and skills necessary for change, growth and national productivity. This programme may be the first wheel of distance education which is recognised as a key tool for nation building.

This major task is being approached through a long-term strategy. First, the creation of an infrastructure of distance education, then the development of new courses. In the first phase of PHARE, just completed, each country established and equipped a national distance education study centre and trained key staff. Most of these centres are attached to a major university, and in each country there are several other study centres—40 in all over the 11 countries. This groundwork was undertaken in close partnership with distance teaching institutions in the European Union member countries, which provided advice, models and training. A few readymade courses were imported from elsewhere in Europe, translated, adapted and offered on a trial basis.

In the second phase, just starting, courses are being developed. The European Union has made funding available, for courses which meet strict criteria. The courses must be needs-based, usually in one of 12 agreed priority subject areas (these include European languages and teacher education). The model of partnership introduced in phase one is strengthened—every course will be developed by a consortium of at least three partners, two from eastern and central Europe, one from a member country of the Europeon Union. Once developed and tested the course will be available (with necessary translation) to any of the 11 PHARE countries.

The PHARE initiative has several features of interest to other countries. First, distance education courses are being developed to complement those offered face-to-face. Although the programme is regional, the choice of course is national, based on specific local need. Each distance education centre in each country decides what courses to offer on the basis of market research. The determinant of choice is demands of the national economy, with initial priority given to higher level education, where suitably trained personnel are in particularly short supply.

Partnership is critical both for course development and for delivery. Partnership operates at several levels—international, national and local. Internationally, the key linkages are between peers in educational institutions. Nationally and locally, distance education centres are expected to involve business and major employers who will use the course. This should help to ensure a market.

Technology has an important role. In many distance education courses today, computers and associated technologies form an increasingly important part of the teaching and learning system but in the PHARE countries few people have computers at home, and individual access to computers for learning is not a realistic proposition. The Distance Education Study Centres are equipped with state-of the art-technology. These centres initially form the basis for access to learning, while wider national distribution of technology builds up.

This may at first sound like putting the cart before the horse—using the technology before the users are ready. But from the point of view of these emerging economies, this is not the case. People understand that competence to use information and communication technology are essential today. The use of flexible combinations of traditional and new median for teaching and learning, together with access to distance education centres for those who require it, provides a way of leapfrogging over the barrier of individual ownership and providing these learners who want it with experience of using new technology.

The flexibility in learning that accompanies new technology applications is also important. The PHARE distance education programme looks to the long term, to creating a lasting system of lifelong learning for national benefit. But it also marks an important transition. The PHARE countries are in the midst of a process of rapid change, moving from a heavily centralised political system to a market economy. That has implications for distance education, just as much as for other aspects of society—the shift from traditional correspondence courses for mass education to distance education which is flexible, personalised, responsive. The focus on the needs of the market is replacing monolithic correspondence education with a different style of teaching and learning.

Technical and Vocational Learning at a Distance

In many industrialised countries, distance education has long been used for training working people. In some countries New Zealand and Australia, for example—its use for technical training is long established, with delivery through public distance teaching institutions at the national or state level. The UK started later, but developments seen over the last 15 years in open and distance learning provide a stimulating example of how new types of partnership between employers and education agencies, and between public and private-funded institutions, are helping to generate new, more comprehensive opportunities for people at work.

In the 1980s the government launched a programme of vocational and technical training for working adults known as the "Open Tech" programme. While very few of the projects funded under the programme survived, the programme was indirectly very influential. The idea of "Open Learning" spread amongst employers and employees, new forms of organising learning for people in work developed, and there was much innovation in applications of technology to learning. Several major employers turned to it as a major training tool for in-service training. The business sector experimented with the use of new technology for training, overtaking universities and schools in the use of innovative teaching and learning methodology. Open and distance learning using technology caught the imagination to such an extent that several major employers turned to it as the ideal means to provide continuing training to their employees. At the start of this decade, for example, British Telecom, then the national telecommunications agency in Britain, announced that its normal method for in-service training for its employees would be distance education. A further seal of approval came with the 1993 Mastricht Treaty of European Union which cited open and distance learning in the context of vocational and technical training.

From Education and Training to Learning for Life

But already we have moved on. The matter of learning for the information society is different from vocational and technical training for the age of industry. A thorough basic education is the acknowledged foundation for employability. But school learning is not enough. Working adults need new, more, different knowledge and skills throughout their working lives. Not just because their jobs change and develop, but also because our knowledge-based society needs better educated people to work productively in it. Education for adults is being transformed into something new—learning relevant to life and work woven together with any necessary completion of school learning. The traditional distinction between education and training is fast becoming blurred. In discourse, as the new agenda for basic education for adults emerges, they are now often bracketed together to signify their close relationship—"education and training" going together like "bread and butter".

A number of major employers in the UK have not only recognised the need for continuous leaning amongst their employees but have also themselves taken responsibility for providing learning opportunities. Ford, for example, has a long-established Employee Development Programme, and Unipart, the car parts manufacturer, runs Unipart University for its staff. Rover, the car manufacturer, uses open learning as the basis of its scheme of in-company education and training, open in the sense that employees are offered a wide choice of learning opportunities which may be delivered in various ways, including distance learning. Rover began using open learning in 1982. Now, over 20,000 individuals (about two-thirds of employees) follow individualised learning programmes, a very high level of participation in learning. Since 1990, every employee has had access to up to £100 a year to spend on learning anything they like which is not related to their job. The company recognises the importance of a balance between education for personal development and work-related learning.

Why not launch such a scheme nationally? That is precisely what the new Labour government in Britain plans to do, with its proposed University for Industry. The University for Industry has been described as "the hub of a national learning network". Emerging as a "virtual" institution itself, it will draw together national resources for learning to meet needs in each locality. Whether people are at work or at home, employed, self-employed, unemployed, well-educated or not, the University for Industry will provide opportunities to learn more. It will target particularly those with lower levels of skills and knowledge, and those in small and medium firms less in touch with mainstream learning opportunities or large in company schemes like Rover's. Its chief (though not exclusive) means of operation is likely to be open and distance learning—the best way to take learning to work.

The University for Industry is at an early stage of planning. A Design and Implementation Advisory Group was established only in August 1997, and since the concept is entirely new, there are many issues to be resolved. The constitution of the group reflects one important perspective, the linking of business and education: the group is chaired by an industrial leader, the Chairman of Motorola Ltd. Planning will be informed by pilot projects. The first was launched in September 1997 in the North East region of England, an area previously economically depressed and with high unemployment, but now being reinvigorated with new employment opportunities. The demand for lifelong learning in this area, which contains an extensive rural area, is potentially great. The project will help to identify the nature of that demand—what courses people actually want to take—and to explore modes of study. One way in which the pilot aims to make learning more accessible is the through "Learning World", a learning "supermarket" in one of Britain's largest shopping malls. The "Learning World", set up by one of the region's universities, Sunderland University, in association with local businesses and other education institutions, is an example of the kind of innovative arrangements that will form part of the national network for lifelong learning that will emerge, as the University for Industry takes shape.

CONCLUSIONS

The developments I have outlined give some idea of how the scope and methods of distance education are changing, to meet new demands for learning. The initiatives sketched out offer models of how these new open and flexible methods, supported by new technology applications, can widen access to learning. There are no miracle solutions. But in the new open and distance learning, the methods developed for mass education through our open universities are being turned toward widening participation in learning. Starting with need, building on partnership, drawing on national and increasingly global resource, using new technology as the servant of a new teaching and learning, distance education is becoming ever more diverse in its forms. With the learner and learning process increasingly central, "distance" in learning is an issue that may die with the century, giving way to lifelong learning "open" to all.

32

Management of Education of Weaker Segments

*Prabha Vij**

According to the Indian Constitution, everyone has the fundamental right to be educated. Therefore, all sections of population, whether advantaged or disadvantaged, rich or poor, gifted or handicapped, rural, tribal or urban, male or female must be provided educational opportunities. But according to Chanana the disparities between the disadvantaged groups, viz., women, Scheduled Castes (SC), Schedule Tribes (ST), Other Backward Classes (OBC) and minorities and advantaged groups have continued. With this in mind, there is need to provide special care, and advantage groups have continued. With this in mind, there is need to provide special care and educational opportunities to the weaker section of the population which stresses egalitarianism, social justice and economic development for all sections of societies.

From the view point of education, informal and non-formal education can be provided to the weaker segments particularly, women. Both types of education are beneficial to the learners but different kinds of knowledge gained from education vary from age to age. Non-formal education refers to planned educational activity but not always short term and non-

**Centre for Adult Continuing Education & Extension, Panjab University, Chandigarh.*

certificated such as nutrition education at a health clinic or driving lessons. It is often defined in terms of its relevance to the needs of the weaker segments, its flexibility in organisation and method and its specificity of objective. Informal and non-formal education are part of adult education provision and practice, and are distinct from formal education. As with all forms of education, adult education is concerned with the development of particular attitudes, values, skills and knowledge among the adult population. Brazilian educationalist, Paul Frerie, describes that adult education aims to challenge injustice and oppression, that is why it is called 'community education,' 'education for change,' liberatory education', 'transformation education' and 'education for empowerment'. Adult education and its related fields are used as over-reaching terms of informal, non-formal and formal education for learners of the weaker segments. This paper first lays emphasis on why the need was felt to educate weaker segments and then it takes into consideration from what angles the education of the weaker segments must be looked at. In accordance to that educational objectives for the weaker section are laid and last of all to achieve the said objectives, management measures at various levels are considered.

NEED OF THE SITUATION

Given the background of the learners of the weaker section, it would be easy for us to secure the services and programmes for them. The need for educating the weaker section arises the following reasons:

a) *Continuous denial of education*—Inequality in case of Schedule Castes/Schedule Tribes is accentuated by continuous denial of education and other facilities over a long span of time.

b) *Psychological morass*—Due to low socio-economic status the weaker segments of population are isolated from the mainstream of growth, so this segment of population perpetuates itself, and as a result, it has set up a kind of psychological morass for itself.

c) *Slackened pace of vertical socio-economic mobility*—The distinguished characteristics of Scheduled Castes/ Scheduled Tribes are: rurality, illiteracy, economic backwardness and social retardation. All these characteristics add to the inequalities faced by the weaker section. Further, the vicious cycle of poverty, backwardness and absence of facilities of modernisation of traditional skills or acquisition of new skill slacken the pace of vertical socio-economic mobility of weaker segments.

d) *Children as financial assets*—Poor people perceive children as financial assets. On an average a Scheduled Caste/Scheduled Tribe couple has four to five children.

e) *Disproportionate large numbers of illiterate women*—According to UNESCO (1993) estimates, there were 873.9 million illiterate adults in the developing countries in the year 1990, of whom 567 million or 64.9 per cent were women. UNESCO further highlighted that the factors that impede access of poor women to literacy programmes include poverty, family responsibilities, opposition by husbands, lack of time, physical distance to literacy classes and lack of motivation.

f) *Gender disparities in 15+ age group*—Female-male literacy disparities in India are due to social and cultural norms of practices. UNESCO (1993) estimates that the total number of illiterate population in India in the year 1990 was 280.7 millions illiterates in the age group of 15+, out of which 173.6 millions were females. This means that 61.8 per cent of the female population was illiterate in 1990.

g) *Lack of regular income*—Due to lack of regular source of income the people of weaker segments have to struggle daily for their day-to-day earnings.

HEARING OTHERS?

In an attempt to understand, ways in which context agree, what type of education of weaker segments should be, our initial hypothesis is that contextual factors must influence the education of weaker segments.

The Education Commission (1964-66) observed that one of the important social objectives of education is to equalise opportunities enabling the backward and underprivileged classes and individuals to use education as a lever for the improvement of their conditions. Every society that values social justice and is anxious to develop a lot of talent must ensure equality of opportunity to all sections of people.

The National Policy on Education states, "The new policy will lay special emphasis on the removal of disparities and equalise educational opportunities by attending to the specific needs of those who have been denied equality so far." It seeks to remove inequalities based on gender, race, region and religion with an improvement of quality.

Lokhead and Verspoor traced how a mother's level of schooling is correlated in terms of infant and child mortality. They further found that with the increase in mother's level of education, there was a gradual decline in infant and child mortality rate.

Bown found that there exists a relationship between women education and socio-economic changes.

Summers discovered that basic education for girls is a must for reducing the fertility, child and maternal mortality. He further averred that education for girls is a must for preventing the spread of AIDS.

UNCESCO, in its results of "World Fertility Survey 1980", indicated that wider availability of schooling provides a tendency for girls to marry later.

The United Nation Population Fund conducted a "World Bank Study of 200 Developing Countries" and found that countries which allocated substantial resources to female primary education experienced higher economic productivity, lower fertility rates, lower infant mortality rates and improved levels of life expectancy for both men and women as compared to the countries with lower levels of women educational attainment.

UNESCO organised an international seminar on "Women Education and Empowerment" and come to a conclusion that education is a must for women empowerment.

The ANC'S Policy Framework for Education and Training, Reconstruction and Development Programme (RDP), the National Women Coalitions' Women Charter for Effective Equality, as well as the Implementation Plan for Education and Training (IEPT) emphasised that inequality of women cannot be understood by looking at women alone. It must be based on fuller understanding of the relationship between men and women and how societies are structured along gender lines. They further stressed that men and women occupy different unequal positions in society. They have different roles and responsibilities. Consequently, they have also different needs which policies, plans and projects must address. A gender approach must recognise the particular problems and needs of women in any educational system.

OBJECTIVES OF EDUCATION FOR WEAKER SEGMENTS

The National Policy on Education 1986 has resolved that the National Literacy Mission (NLM) 1988 shall strive to achieve the national goals such as alleviation of poverty, national integration, environmental conservation, observance of small family norms, promotion of women equality, basic health care, women empowerment, etc. Keeping this in mind, the NLM accordingly envisages the following objectives of adult education:

1. Achieving self-reliance in literacy and numeracy;
2. Becoming aware of the causes of the deprivation of the weaker segments and moving towards amelioration of their conditions through an organisation and participation in the process of development;
3. Acquiring skills to improve the economic status and general well being; and
4. Imbibing the values of national integration, conservation of environment, women equality, observation of small family norms, etc.

MANAGEMENT CONCERNS IN EDUCATION FOR WEAKER SEGMENTS

What matters most in the field of education is proper management. Management, as we know, is the process of planning, organising, leading and controlling the work of organisation members, and of using all available organisational resources to reach the stated organisational goal. It is getting things done through other people. As the managerial concerns of education for the weaker segments depend largely upon the changing objective realities and targets, therefore, they can be broadly categorised into :

i) Management of campaigns.
ii) Management of identifying the needs of weaker segments of population.
iii) Management of educational goals such as: remediation, continuation, application and communitisation.
iv) Management of post-literacy and continuing educational programmes such as: Equivalency Programmes (EPS), Income Generating Programmes (IGPs), Quality of Life Improvement Programmes (QLIPs) and Individual Interest Promotion Programmes (IIPs).

v) Integration with development departments, educational goals such as remediation, continuation, application and communitisation.

Management of Campaigns

A multidimensional approach and a host of other measures are simultaneously required to eradicate illiteracy from the weaker segments because one approach or one campaign is not sufficient in India to remove the stigman of illiteracy because of its vastness with respect to different religions, languages, races, cultures and customs.

Social and political commitment of government and a positive role of leaders are very much essential for the success of a campaign. For example, the Total Literacy Campaign in India was successfully launched in the state of Kerala and the union territory of Pondicherry because of the full involvement of government machinery.

Involvement of the community is a must to promote the campaigns. If campaigns are launched with the involvement of various sections of society like political leaders, teachers, retired persons, literate and non-literates, the learners can be easily identified.

Technical resource support by the State Resource Centres, the District Institute of Education and Training governed by the State Council of Educational Research, the Zila Sakshartha Samitis, and voluntary agencies can help to promote a campaign.

Strong leadership is required to make any campaign a success. Committed workers, committed volunteers and instructors are needed to bring positive results from a campaign.

Massive environment building must form the basis of a campaign to generate the demand of literacy among the illiterates. According to Rahi, *mera jathas, nukkad nataks* will not generate the demand for literacy because people do not recognise their self-interest. To create a demand for literacy among people we must encourage new social demands.

Voluntary associations, including community-based organisations, non-governmental organisations (NGOs), social movements, trade unions, religious organisations and political parties must play a significant role in eradicating illiteracy among weaker sections.

Tandon et al stressed that the campaigns should be techno-managerial in nature. They are of the view that strengthening managerial structures will ensure equitable participation of women and girls in the educational process. Techno-managerial aspects help girls and women to overcome barriers to education like family and cultural constraints, lack of time, shortage of female teachers and lack of child care services.

Integrate or link national literacy programmes with campaigns like Education for All, Health for All, Small Saving Campaigns, Food for All, Campaign for Gender Equality, Freedom from Hunger Campaign, Action for Development and so on.

Local area planning is a must to launch any campaign. Effective management at this level can benefit the majority of the population.

Management of Identifying Needs of Weaker Section of Population

Kala jathas should form the main feature in mobilising the participation of women. *Kala jatha* is the powerful medium with packed messages in the popular cultural idiom forms. But more than forms the messages themselves serve to link literacy with a number of basic livelihood problems and even with questions of exploitation and discrimination against women.

The visible presence of the collector and the participation of the government machinery give some legitimacy in the eyes of the conservative sections of people.

The participation and leadership of the Bharata Gyan Vigyan Samitis (BGVS), NGO's and other voluntary organisations gave the programme credibility amongst the people, especially amongst village level intellectuals who had to be motivated to provide the village level people's leadership that is essential to make it a people's campaign.

Organisational strategy can act as a strong strategy of mobilisation in campaigns. It was followed in Pondicherry for studying women responses in terms of what gains they had made with literacy. Repeated references were found that wife beating became less by adopting this strategy.

The instructor chosen to carry literacy activities must be a familiar person who can come and teach as learners wanted.

Educational programmes for Scheduled Castes and Scheduled Tribes are actually the programmes of empowerment, so special attention must be paid to women. Here, the Mahila Samaykhya approach should become an integral part for mobilising women participation in education and development.

Local vested interest must be given due importance in motivating the people.

Public investment in women education and education for the disadvantaged members of the societies are highly desirable. There is a substantial evidence from a wide range of countries that if increased female education is linked to improvement in health, lower fertility and other benefits, the investment in female education can yield a high social rate of returns.

Religion, mythology, cultural taboos, rewards, punishments have been used to socialise girls and to make them accept and participate in their own oppression and subordination. Here the need arises for social and cultural revitalisation. Social and cultural revitalisation is part of the literacy movement, so there is need to constantly upgrade the educational strategy to create products (songs, films, dramas) to meet the challenges given by customs and traditions.

Malika suggested that for identifying the needs of disadvantaged section it is desirable to have links with mass organisations. Mass organisations of women work collaboratively with the government, whose stated objective is to empower women. She further added that if links with mass organisations are sustained and intensified the results are always positive. As in the case of anti-arrack agitation of Nellore district of Andhra Pradesh, this agitation spread soon to the other districts of Andhra Pradesh. In this agitation the rural women of Andhra Pradesh scored a massive victory, when in early 1993 the Chief Minister announced that attack should be banned in Nellore immediately.

Input of local and national issues should be used as attracting agents in identifying the needs of weaker segments.

Medical facilities are accessible in the urban areas but they are not available in the rural areas. A majority of Scheduled Caste and Scheduled Tribes live in the rural areas. They are deprived of medical facilities. Opening of health centres in their area in collaboration with Health For All campaign or the health department of the state can motivate them in joining the literacy campaign.

The media play a vital role in creating awareness about small family norms and quality of life, but a report of a survey conducted by UNESCO reveal that 90 per cent Scheduled Castes/Scheduled Tribes people have no access to TV programmes as they do not have the capacity to purchase even small black and white TVs. Here, the need arises to have community centres with TV in rural, tribal and slum areas.

Management of Educational Goals

Post-literacy programmes of adult education have to be developed in the context of lifelong education. The four major goals of education are remediation, continuation, application and communitisation.

Remediation: Remediation means making efforts for those learners, who are not able to complete their literacy. These learners initially got enrolled but dropped their studies due to different reasons and situations. As the learning needs of these learners cannot be ignored, management at this level calls for:

a) Mopping up operation of short duration courses to correct learning deficiencies of the learners.

b) Provision of basic literacy to the learners who have not participated in the total literacy campaigns because of reasons like migration, inaccessibility to the remote villages, and family circumstances.

c) Diverse approaches of non-formal education can be used under remediation. For example, all the districts of Karnataka have planned to cover the neo-literates in the age group of 9-35. It is assumed that the learners of younger age group would like to re-enter the formal educational stream. To provide non-formal education to learners-books are prepared in four parts which need four semesters for completion.

Continuation: This function of education refers to retention, reinforcement, stabilisation, upgradation and improvement of functional skills. This stage is a must for the learners, otherwise there are chances of learners to relapse into illiteracy. Management at this level calls for:

a) Provision of a wide range of reading materials according to the needs and interest of neoliterates;

b) Provision of structured courses, unstructured reading opportunities for neo-literates so that learners can practise their literacy skills. Here, opening of mini libraries or J. S. N. or mobile libraries are suggested in remote rural and urban areas;

c) Installation of black and white TVs or colour TVs at community centres, Jan Shiksha Nilayams (JSN) or Panchayat Ghars;

d) Technologists, administrators, scientists and other persons with relevant expertise should talk to neo-literates for imparting necessary information to them;

e) Organising study tours and excursions for neo-literates to gather first-hand information.

f) Use of village parliament in imparting information to the neo-literates. This novel and successful method was used at a village in Bilaspur district and Gaon Kacheri in Pune district.

Application—This stage calls for applying acquired skills for improving the quality of life of people. The quality of life of an individual can be improved by tapping different areas of life and livelihood. Here management lays stress on:

a) Organising community programmes under the headings, nutrition and health, responsible parenthood, role of environment in everyday life, use of science in everyday life, equal rights for women, role of the Panchayat in the upliftment of people;

b) Representatives of different mass organisations, especially of students, youth, women and ICDS workers should be included in Saksharata Samitis, and in Panchayat ward committees;

c) In collaboration with the existing programmes, e.g., in the area of health, the literacy programmes should also collaborate with the existing programmes such as health care services of district, health programmes, primary health centres, maternal and child care programmes. Similarly for the purpose of imparting legal literacy, the institutions like police department, courts must familiarise the people with the laws, minimum wages and consumer protection.

d) Formation of Legal Advise Resource Group or Core Group at the district level with respect to health, legal and environment. A core group must be formed at the district level consisting of lawyers and social activists. This group will identify the areas to be taught to weaker sections and prepare the materials required for imparting legal literacy.

Communitisation—Under this goal, neo-literates must be told how to secure services under programmes related to health, family welfare, child care, nutrition, agriculture, animal husbandry . This function is very much important for the learner to bring social and economic change in the country. Effective management at this level asks for:

a) Communication and coordination among Saksharata Samitis and committees at different levels.
b) Organising awareness camps for enlightening the people of their democratic rights and duties under the panchayati Raj system. The purpose is not only in making people aware of their role but also making them self-confident to exercise their rights;
c) Urging non-government organisations to involve themselves in the total literacy campaigns and post-literacy campaigns;
d) Whole-time workers must be engaged at block/ district level to provide organisational and management support.

Management of Post-Literacy and Continuing Education Programmes

According to the Directorate of Adult Education continuing education is an indispensable strategy for human resource development and creation of a learned society. Continuing education and post-literacy programmes should be given due importance while managing education for the weaker segments because of the growing realisation that formal education alone is a small component of lifelong learning. Formal education alone cannot lead to human resource development. Further, Walters suggested that only through informal and nonformal education, we can find a remedy to the structural inequalities of the society. Continuing education provides a second chance to the masses who have missed formal education and is responsive to specific needs and interests of weaker segments. The post-literacy programmes aim at providing four basic skills like life skills, survival skills, communication skills and vocational skills. A broad classification of such programmes as suggested by NLM are given below:

i) Equivalency Programmes (EPs)
ii) Income Generation Programmes (IGPs)
iii) Quality of Life Improvement Programmes (QLIPs)
iv) Individual Interest Promotion Programmes (IIPPs)

i) *Equivalency Programmes (EPs)*—Equivalency Programmes provide an opportunity to adults and out-of-school children who have acquired basic literacy skills who have completed primary education and who are willing to continue their education beyond elementary literacy for acquisition of competencies equivalent to primary or secondary level of the formal system. EPs are designed with sufficient flexibility and innovativeness, so that neo-literates can continue education of their choice at their own pace. Besides, these programmes are very cost-effective. Effective management of these programmes lays emphasis on:

   a) Integration of equivalency programmes with general and vocational education programmes. Integration will make equivalency programmes real-life oriented.

   b) Equivalency programmes must be developed as non-formal alternatives. For this, three types of delivery systems are simultaneously required. They are learning centres, self-paced learning distance education and open learning system.

c) The effective management and implementation of EPs calls for a collaborative effort between Zila Sakasharta Samitis, state resource centres, national and state open schools.

ii) *Income Generation Programmes*—Income generation programmes are those vocational and technical programmes which help the participants to acquire or upgrade vocational skills and enable them to conduct income-generating activities. IGPs are the special strategies which equip economically and socially disadvantaged people with knowledge, skills and values so that they can improve their capacity to generate income. To make these programmes a success, management of them requires:

a) Designing of IGPs as a component of continuing education which should involve the development of a variety of innovative, locally relevant, employment-oriented vocational courses.

b) Income-generating programmes could be delivered in multiple non-formal modes such as-detect contact sessions, demonstrations, study visits, self-learning modules, on-site training, apprenticeship training, distance learning or combination of any of these.

c) Management of income-generating activities should be done keeping in view the employment opportunities.

d) Networking and coordination mechanism must be given due importance, while designing and implementing IGPs because only then can these programmes benefit learners for whom these programmes are targeted.

e) The functionaries working under the schemes such as TRYSEM, DWCRA, JRY, IRDP, Krishi Vigyan Kendras, Farmers Training Centres must be fully involved in the preparation of training modules and for conducting these programmes.

iii) *Quality of Life Improvement Programmes (QLIPs)*— These programmes aim to equip learners and the community with essential knowledge, attitudes, values and skills to enable them to improve the quality of life as individuals and as members of the community. QLIPs programmes are designed on quality of life indicators categorised as biological, social, economic, humanistic and environmental. Development programmes covering different elements of quality of life such as family welfare, health, nutrition, drinking water, sanitation, population education, communal harmony and transportation can be designed under them. Management under this calls for :

a) structured learning centres, public education campaigns, self learning and printed materials;

b) QLIPs programmes should be framed while keeping in view the national goals and values.

iv) *Individual Interest Promotion Programmes (IIPPs)*— These continuing programmes aim to provide opportunity for individuals to participate in and learn about their chosen social, cultural, spiritual, health, physical and artistic interests. The main objective of IIPPs is personal development of individuals and enabling individuals to work towards personal goals and gain a sense of fulfilment and achievement. Management at this level calls for :

a) Provision of a wide range of learning activities to cater to the range of diverse interests in the society.

b) Designing appropriate courses according to the genuine needs of local weaker section of the community.

c) Involvement of a variety of agencies to provide special interest activities to the weaker sections.

d) Ensuring success implementation of these programmes, agencies which provide these programmes must be known to the potential beneficiaries.

e) IIPPs can be delivered by methods such as contact sessions at learning centres, in individual self-paced learning, distance education, group discussions, practical workshops, study tours.

Integration with Development Departments

Each literacy programme should be suitably integrated with programmes of other development departments. These departments would provide facilities for location of the learning centres, and impart training to the beneficiaries of the programme. Management under this calls for integration with development departments such as:

a) Schemes/programmes of TRYSEM, IRDP, DWACRA, ICDS, JRY, DPAP, SCYTES should be suitably linked with post-literacy and continuing education so that the facilities under these schemes are available to the neo-literates of the weaker segments.
b) The employers, trade unions and government departments/undertakings should provide facilities of reading rooms along with working places.
c) State resource centres, voluntary agencies and the private publishers should be encouraged to bring out books of common interest to the learners of weaker segments at subsidised rates.
d) The education institutions should pursuade the learners of the weaker segment to use facilities of their libraries.
e) Radio, TV, films should be used for weaker segments to sustain literacy. Serials showing gender equality, health, nutrition, small family norms should be developed and aired on the TV and radio.

LESSONS FOR THE FUTURE

What are the lessons for the future? What can one generalise about the type of education for the weaker segments? The first lesson is that illiterates, particularly belonging to the weaker section, can only be made literate through literacy campaigns. As history reveals, the Ernakulam experiment, spearheaded by the Kerala Sastra Sahitya Parishad and involving voluntary agencies actively supported by district administration, created a mass-upsurge for literacy and gave birth to the concept of total literacy campaigns. This experiment has not burgeoned into a major people's movement, that is why it spread only to 368 districts in the country. The second factor is that literacy campaigns are not targeted at the 19-35 age group only but also cover children in the age group 9-14 in the areas where there are no non-formal education centres. So, it is only through campaigns that we can educate weaker segment population.

Further, adult educators must shift their concern from equal accessibility and opportunities to equal outcomes for women, restructuring the learning environment to empower all kinds of learners. Caffarella says, "Women's education is not just gender related but also rooted in class, race, age, sexual orientation and family status." Lastly, only through collaborative and co-operative ways can we educate the weaker segments.

REFERENCES

Caffarella, R. S., 1992, "Psychological Development of Women", No. 350 Columbus : ERIC, Clearing House on Adult, Career and Vocational Education (ED 354109).

Chanana, Karuna, 1993, "Accessing Higher Education—The Dilemma of Schooling : Women Minorities, Scheduled Castes and Scheduled Tribes in Contemporary India" in *Higher Education Reform in India*; Suma Chitnis *et. al*, Sage Publication, New Delhi.

Devanoor, Basavaraga, 1995, "A Critical Review of TLC/PLC/CE in Karnataka" Published in *Journal Literacy Mission*, Edited by Tiwari, et al., Vol XX, No. 5-12, May-Dec. 1996, Sponsored by NLM.

Sundaraman, Sudha, 1996, "Literacy Campaigns Lessons for Women's Moment", Published in *Journal Literacy Mission*, Edited by

Tiwari, et al. Vol. XX, No. 5-12, May-Dec. 1996, Sponsored by NLM.

Rahi, A. L., 1995, "Literacy for the Oppressed", in *Journal Excellence in Literacy*, Edited by Nishant Farooq, Published by NLM Sponsored by SRC, J. M. Islamia, New Delhi.

Singh, Tarlok, 1995, "Women's Literacy and the Girl Child", in *Journal Excellence in Literacy,* Edited by Nishant Farooq, Published by NLM Sponsored by SRC, J. M Islamia, New Delhi.

Report of Education Commission, 1964-66, MHRO, Government of India, New Delhi.

National Literacy Mission, 1996, "Strategies for Post Literacy", Edited by Tiwari, H.O. Sponsored by NLM, Directorate of Adult Education, Government of India, New Delhi.

Gupta, Shailbal, 1996, "Literacy Programme in Hindi Heart Land" Published in *Journal Literacy Mission,* Edited by Tiwari, et al., Vol. XX No. 5-12, May-Dec. 1996, on (UNESCO), 1993, World Education Report, Paris, UNESCO.

Walters, Shirley, 1993, "Training Genders—Sensitive and Feminist Adult Educations in South Africa : An Emerging Curriculum", *Perspectives in Education*, Volume 15, No. 1, Summers 1993-1994, pp. 115-132.

Freire, Paulo, 1972, *The Pedagogy of the Oppressed*, London : Penguin.

National Policy on Education, 1986, Updated, 1992, as Programme of Action, Government of India, Ministry of Human Resource Development, New Delhi.

National Literacy Mission, 1988, Ministry of Human Resource Development, New Delhi.

Summer, 1993, "*Perspectives in Education*" Published in *International Womens Encyclopedia*, 1996, Quoted by Anita Dighe.

National Literacy Mission, 1996, "*Schemes of Continuing Education for Neo-literates*", Published by Ministry of Human Resource Development, Department of Education, Govt. of India, New Delhi.

33

Education of the Weaker Section of Our Society

*A. B. Phatak**

Equality of opportunities is one of our constitutional commitments. Our national leaders have also been repeatedly claiming that their sincere desire is to provide equal opportunities to all the sons of the soil. The election manifestoes of all the political parties promise that the upliftment of the weaker sections of our society will get top priority in our country's planning. How far these promises get fulfilled when a particular party comes to power is altogether a different matter.

It will however be unfair if some of the commendable efforts of the central as well as state governments to improve the lots of the socially and economically deprived sections of our society are not acknowledged. Still some people sincerely believe that the fruits of the process of development have been enjoyed by only a thin strata of our society. A major section, especially the have-nots, have remained outside the impact of our developmental efforts. Somehow the rich have become richer and the poor have gone much below the poverty line. Why it has happened is a question which research workers should probe into. One of the reasons might be that sometimes with the best of our intentions the schemes we plan for the upliftment of these weaker sections of society do not deliver the

**Ex. Principal, Shah G. L. Kabra TT College, Jodhpur (Rajasthan).*

goods. On paper these schemes appear to be very sound but when put to practice, they operate in a different way. The result is that a well-intentioned scheme does not fully achieve the purpose for which it was introduced. Researches need to be taken up to evaluate the implementation of every welfare scheme.

The author had an opportunity to work in a progressive residential school as a Principal where a number of scholarship holders from weaker sections under various welfare schemes of the state and central government come every year for study in the institution. Some of the problems mentioned here are based on experience gained during this period. The government bears the entire expenditure of their education which incurs so much expenditure on these noble schemes, but takes little pains to undertake systematic follow-up studies to find out the shortcoming of these schemes as well as problems faced by the beneficiaries. It needs to take up appropriate steps to remove these shortcomings, and the purpose for which the schemes are launched would be fulfilled. In this paper the author has tried to list some of the problems noticed by him with regard to these schemes. The money spent can yield much higher returns if systematic researches are taken up to see how best we can help the weaker sections of our society to get education.

NEED FOR WIDER PUBLICITY

The schemes meant for helping the weaker sections of our society should be given a wider publicity. The facilities provided to the children from tribal areas, Scheduled Castes and Backward Classes are many times not known to the parents. A study taken up by a Ph. D. scholar working under the author has substantiated this fact. Studies on a wider scale would throw more light on the fact. The parents who are literate, better off or have some relatives in the education department come to know about these facilities and take full advantage of them. Ways and means will have to be searched to see that illiterate parents from weaker sections of our society located in remote rural areas also come to know about the schemes and derive maximum benefit from them.

INITIAL DIFFICULTIES IN ADJUSTMENT

Sometimes students from remote village school, when placed in some of the prestigious institutions of the state or country, face an initial difficulty in adjusting to the new school situations and the hostel life in the residential schools. Researches are needed to find out the adjustment and other problems faced by the students from weaker sections. Merely giving financial assistance in not enough.

FEELING OF INFERIORITY

How students from higher castes and classes look at these students from the weaker section is also a matter of investigation. There are dangers of these students developing a feeling of inferiority. They have certainly many good qualities which need to be located and nurtured, e.g., tribal students are found to possess a high degree of athletic and leadership potential.

PROBLEM OF ALIENATION

A major problem likely to be faced by these students in that of alienation. After studying in a public school or a prestigious institution for seven or eight years their lifestyle undergoes a complete change. The students get accustomed be bed tea, breakfast, a fine course of dinner and other Westernised ways of life. What must be the condition of his family and the new way of life acquired by him? Sociologists should undertake a research to study how he looks at his own family and kind. Is there any alienation from his own culture? Does he face any problems in marital life? These are some of the vital questions which must be answered. It is not sufficient to finance the education of students from the weaker sections, but an attempt must be made to see that they become well adjusted citizens without having any sense of inferiority about their own culture or family.

PROBLEM OF DROPOUTS

Once a student of weaker section is selected for scholarship he is placed in a good residential school. His entire expenditure pertaining to school fees, boarding and lodging, books, clothes, other equipment and even pocket money is borne by the government. From poverty he is placed in affluence. In some public schools or prestigious institution this expenditure ranges between Rs. 3000 and Rs. 6000 per annum or even more. Though most of the students make the best use of this facility, there are some who forget the purpose for which they have been provided this facility. Instead of concentrating on studies, they develop undesirable extravagant habits and become spendthrifts, ultimately failing to secure the required percentage or retain of their scholarship. Once the scholarship is discontinued their parents are not even in a position to continue their education. From an affluent condition they come down to a condition where they even find it difficult to get two square meals a day. What a tremendous frustration! We must follow-up these dropouts and see how they settle in life. Can we do something to help them?

TIMELY RELEASE OF SCHOLARSHIPS

A rupee given in time is far better and valuable than a thousand rupees given too late. This applies to any help we wish to extend to a person. The children who are awarded scholarships should know about it in June so that they can join the institution in which they are placed right at the beginning of the session. Many times it has been observed that the list of students getting scholarships are announced as late as August. The result is that the students lose two months of studies. This in turn affects their performance in the final examination. If they got poor marks in the final examination their scholarships are discontinued. If properly planned, it should not be too difficult for the Department of Education to inform the awards in time. Some investigations could be taken up to find out bottlenecks and red-tapism in the award of financial assistance to these students.

These are some of the challenges which must be faced when we talk of a plan for the education of the students of the weaker sections of our society. Every welfare scheme that is launched by the government must be closely monitored and systematically evaluated after two or three years of its implementation. Then alone can it bear the desirable results. A detailed follow-up of the beneficiaries of these schemes is essential for the improvement of these schemes.

It is hoped that the shortcomings of existing schemes will be investigated and improved upon. At the same time many new schemes should be launched by the government for the education of the children of the weaker sections of our society.

34

Educating People for India's Response to Future Military and Diplomatic Strategy

*E. D'Souza**

Strategical thinking is all embracing and is futuristic in concept reflecting the ability of a nation to think ahead to enable it to structure its policies in a manner whereby it can face confidently any challenges to its integrity. In short, it is productive and Not a reactive process as is our wont. This calls for pragmatic leadership in a democracy where the military is subordinate to the civil authority represented by the elected members of our parliament. In the present scenario in India, strategic thinking calls for an integrated political/military chain of command with clearly defined and realistic mandates. Thus, the political and military strategic planning process must, *inter alia*, consist of improved mission guidance, a policy for the sharing, use of and dissemination of information and intelligence and the indigenous capacity to build the sinews of war based on a sound economy.

This presentation has been structured to cover three aspects: firstly, a brief review of the security scenario today; the second part arising from this scenario, is what needs to be done to hone and fine-tune our ability to meet these security concerns or India's response at the diplomatic and military

**Major General (Retd), PVSM, Leslie Sawhney Foundation, Mumbai.*

levels; and finally a discussion on this presentation leading to acceptable recommendations of what needs to be done within the parameters of achievability, and to provide those involved in governance and our planners involved in national security some ideas based on the wealth of expertise present at this seminar.

The views expressed are my own based on an ongoing association with the armed forces and national security since 1943, participation in World War II, the post-World War II Japanese occupation, and active involvement in three post Independence conflicts against Pakistan in 1948 and 1971, and the Chinese on the high altitude Sikkim, Watershed in 1965/66, three years in London from 1952 to 1955 where part of my duties involved acquisition of intelligence, an ongoing involvement with the World Consultative Association of Retired Flag Rank Officers (WCARGA) since 1982 including a week's meeting in March 2000 in Colombo, a 3-day interaction with nine Chinese Academicians at Manipal in November 2000 including two senior serving Chinese Flag Rank Officers, and a day's seminar in London on "Just Defence". In addition to writing and speaking on matters relating to national security and the armed forces for over 20 years in the national and international media, I trust that I have established my credibility to speak on this vital issue so succinctly presented by the previous speaker, Mr. Aspi Moddie. To many of the 'heavyweights' participating in this seminar, what I have to say may seem old hat. I do so to refresh your memories and also that the background for my presentation is understood.

The National Security Concerns (NSC) today include six major elements: the external aspect to ensure the integrity of our international borders; the internal security to ensure economic progress in a stable environment; the third that may raise eyebrows is environmental, the importance of nature and the natural resources to ensure a reasonable quality of life; the fourth is terrorism in all its avatars that is the buzzword today; the fifth is the bearing the infotech age has on the shaping of events; and the last, the growing power of the media as evidenced during Kargil and now in Afghanistan.

"The Elephant In The Room" was raised at the WCARGA Biennial Meeting at a presentation made by this writer. The Elephant pertains to the subcontinent's nuclear weapons. This aspect of the national security will be considered in detail in Part II in relation to the oft-repeated Western view of the dangers of a nuclear standoff between India and Pakistan. The Room is Southern Asia. There is not one but four elephants in South Asia.

India's national security set-up today, and I stand open to correction, consists of the Defence Committee of the Cabinet, the National Security Council, the Joint Intelligence Committee, and the Ministries of Defence, Home and External Affairs. There is today a variant of the Chief of Defence Staff (CDS), and the three Service HQs. Based on past experience and, regrettably, and this is open to discussion, the general attitude to defence planning has been invariably reactive. Thus the aim of this seminar is to examine and recommend what can be done to ensure that we do not face another 1962 war, Sri Lanka, Kargil *et al*.

India's geopolitical importance in Asia cannot be denied in the power equation of that continent. It is so located, be it on land, sea and air, that it presents a convenient and plausible balance with a growingly strong China. This fact has been recognised by the superpower USA and even by ASEAN countries not only as a potential market but also in the area of security. India's main strengths lie in its secular fabric, reliable armed forces, perhaps the second largest in Asia and the fourth largest in the world, and its relevance to the movement of oil and trade from West to East. Globally, though not immediately apparent, its stature as a major player in Asia is gaining recognition.

What then are the possible threats to India? Externally, China is the major player followed by Pakistan, both in conventional and nuclear terms. Internally, terrorism is a major factor in India's multicultural and pluralistic society, especially now that the situation in Afghanistan is being resolved, added to which must be included our own domestic brand of terrorism like the Naxalites, PWG, ULFA, Akalis and the LTTE.

PART II

The first and most important step that needs to be taken is to determine where our national security interests lie. As of now it would appear to be Pakistan-centric arising from continued cross-border terrorism, and the Afghan crisis. This is an attitude that needs to be monitored carefully because by so doing we tend to forget the Sleeping Dragon sitting on our border. More about this threat anon. This leads one to the National Security Council and its effectiveness to date in guiding governmental policies on defence. There is no visible proof to this end judging from the knee-jerk reactions to various situations that we need to discuses. For such an apex body, it is an enduring mystery why this Council is headed by a bureaucrat who wears three very important hats and who claims that he is competent to do so because he has the ears of the Prime Minister! This tendency of dual responsibility is enhanced by the fact that on September 11, 2001, External Affairs and Defence were being handled by the Foreign Minister. At the diplomatic level there can be little doubt that our efforts need to be focused on countries surrounding us. Recently, on August 9, 2001, at a meeting convened at Dhaka, on "Security in South Asia: National and Regional Perspectives", Lt. Gen. Satish Nambiar, who was present, brought to notice some very serious issues. For instance, a subtle message was conveyed by the President of Bangladesh, who quoted Rabindranath Tagore when he stated: "Power *has to be made secure NOT only against power but against weakness; for there lies the peril of losing balance. The weak are as great a danger for the strong as quicksand for an elephant. The people who wield absolute power are apt of forget that by so doing they generate on unseen force which some day rends that power to pieces."* Was this a subtle message for us from Bangladesh? The fears expressed by the minnows living on our periphery and in the shadow of India's size and dominance, viz., trade blockades imposed against Nepal; support to the LTTE; and sharing of river waters, are some of the issues and fears expressed by Nepal, Bangladesh and Sri Lanka. Surely the geopolitical situation dictates that we have the best of relations with these smaller neighbours. This must be a priority for our External Affairs Ministry (MEA). Other issues that surfaced were: the discontent in the northeast could be reduced by bringing the whole region under one unit; the Sino-India confrontation and the attendant hazards, with Bangladesh seeking a far more meaningful interaction with China as an insurance against Indian dominance; Lt. Gen. Javed Khan, Commandant National Defence College; Pakistan's reference to India as a regional power attempting to become a global one and suggesting the need for India to switch over from a confrontational and conflicting role to a cooperating mode; and to include China, Iran and Myanmar in SAARC are significant. Let us be honest enough to admit that we have failed diplomatically to exploit the enormous goodwill created when Bangladesh was born 30 years ago. The general impression at this meeting pointed to the Indian propensity to ignore the feelings of others. This also points to the need to pay more emphasis in our diplomatic efforts in West Asia, our main source of oil, NW Asia with the new dispensation in power in Afghanistan, Palestine, Myanmar, Tibet and countries in the Indian Ocean littoral, which are very much our immediate national security concerns.

At the armed forces level we need to take some very positive steps. Take the army, the largest of the three services on the *qui vive* since 1947. There can be little doubt that it has been overstretched and used for the simple reason that when all else is lost, it is the rule rather than the exception that the army is called in. If we have to have a lean and mean army we must divest it of such responsibilities like disaster relief, internal security and counter-insurgency operations. We need to equip it with state-of-the-art equipment to enable it to operate in deserts, jungles, high and super high altitudes and riverine terrain. In view of the possibility of marine operations it must also be trained and equipped for amphibious operations so that the Tri Service Command is operationally prepared. We seriously need to address ourselves to the overriding problem of the shortage of suitable officers, especially in the infantry arm. We tend to sweep such problems under the carpet or resort to hocism by attaching officers from other arms and services for a period of two years to the infantry. The induction of the MBT needs to be speeded up and essential force multipliers required to give the army more teeth needs to be examined.

The necessity for a blue water navy cannot be doubted with countries like China and even Thailand expanding their navies. It is encouraging to note that our navy has recently commissioned three indigenously constructed guided missile destroyers. The major deficiency is in aircraft carriers. With the decommissioning of the *Vikrant* we are left with *INS Viraat* now under refit awaiting final trials to rejoin the fleet. With our maritime responsibilities, especially now with the turbulence in West Asia, the need for a second carrier becomes inescapable. In fact, there is a need for a third in the 22,000-ton class air defence ships so that at any one time there will always be two such ships available. To those sceptics who question the utility of such mobile air platforms let me quote Admiral Arleigh Burke, USN, the erstwhile Chief of US Naval Operations. When questioned about the need to discard aircraft carriers he is on record as saying that such an answer would emerge only when such ships fail in war. The use of three US navy carriers including the *Kitty Hawk* and *Enterprise* in the ongoing conflict in Afghanistan is proof enough of the utility. To reinforce the importance of this weapon, especially for a maritime nation, the UK has invested in two carriers for as much as £ 8 billion, to be inducted into service in 2012 and 2015, and Britain has no immediate threat as we have. The establishment of the first ever Tri Service Command in the

Andamans has come not a day too soon. Although the acquisition of the Russian Admiral Gorshkov, a very expensive 'free' sift thrust upon us is under negotiation, the need for indigenisation as advocated by Admiral Bhagwat assumes significance. The ideal would be for a large carrier for the Western Fleet and two ADS, one each for the Eastern Fleet and the Andamans Tri Service Command. Let us not forget the need to show the flag in the Indian Ocean littoral and ASEAN, not in an aggressive but in a reassuring posture.

At the Air Force Commanders meeting just concluded stress was laid on the need for multipliers to make the air arm more effective for its multipurpose roles, like the acquisition of AWACS. The indigenously converted AVRO for this purpose was unfortunate as it crashed in its proving flight. But what is a matter of concern is that no visible efforts have been made to carry on with this project. We have delayed interminably the induction of the AJT for over 12 years causing the attrition rate of MiG 21 pilots to spiral. Likewise, the introduction of the home produced ALH. Our defence planners do not seem to realise the importance of remedying this problem and encouraging, like the navy has done, indigenous designing and manufacture of these important requirements. Yet another area in which we seem to have lagged behind is to complete the final trials of the prototype to the LCA. Now that there is a change in the US attitude to the release of parts for this project, we need to display greater urgency in the completion of such projects. The Air Chief is on record that the next war will be decided in the air and so there must be an increase in the number of operational squadrons. This is debatable given the areas where we are likely to operate and the financial commitment. There can be little doubt that so far as India is concerned its security will very much be a Tri Service affair. In view of the distance involved related to the threats we face we need to expand our transport fleet to move troops and for humanitarian aid, and for international commitments. There needs to be a sharper relationship between the army and the air force to cater for say a sudden attack across the border on terrorist camps. Out pilots need to be fine-tuned for this purpose. Based on prevailing experience this quick inter-service reaction to sudden threats across the border to stamp out terrorist camps is an area that needs to be addressed with more urgency. In short, to make our air force more effective the need for force multipliers needs to be given greater thought.

Our paramilitary forces under the Home Ministry have an important role to play in ensuring internal security. As of now there appears to be no rationale in the deployment of these forces. A classic example is the Border Security Forces—raised, equipped and trained for the protection of our borders. Except for very strategic sections of our international border rightly made the responsibility of the army like in J & K, this force must be used exclusively for the purpose that it has been raised. Thanks to ad hocism, this basic rule of deployment has not been observed and very often the BSF has been used in internal security for which it has not been trained. A classic example of this syndrome was at Bijbehara in the Valley when the BSF was called upon to control a violent mob and so opened fire indiscriminately. All paramilitary border security forces like the Indo Tibetan Border Force need to be placed under one head. This rationalisation needs to be examined in greater detail. In the East, for instance, all internal security duties should be vested in the Assam Rifles instead of the present system of having a plethora of security agencies involved. This would allow the regular army to watch our main detractors from across the border. The number of Assam Rifles battalions could be increased after a careful assessment, and all internal security duties in that troubled region be placed under the DG Assam Rifles. Similar rationalisation in the deployment and use of the CRPF and the CISF should be examined so that paramilitary forces are deployed and commanded for the purpose that they have been raised. There is little doubt that in J & K the responsibility of counter-terrorist operations should be vested in the Rashtriya Rifles. The rationalisation and employment of the BSF was discussed with that very eminent erstwhile DG BSF, K F Rustamji, and he supports this recommendation fully. This vexing question of rationalisation must be examined by the NSC for better utilisation of security forces that would result in the reduction of the alleged human rights violations.

Our major security problems are China and Pakistan. We should avoid falling into the trap of becoming Pakistan-centric as such an attitude is fraught with problems. This major confrontational issue must be viewed as short term and long term. There can be little doubt the our short-term security problem is Pakistan enhanced by the situation in Afghanistan. There is bound to be increased cross-border terrorism that Musharraf euphemistically describes as a freedom struggle. With Pakistan insisting that the Kashmir problem is its *raison d'etre* so far as Indo-Pakistan relations go, low intensity conflict will continue, perhaps on an increased scale. The stage may will be reached where India is driven up the wall and compelled to cross the border to remove and eliminate this debilitating problem. We should be prepared for such an eventuality and invoke the induction of suitable force multipliers.

As of now, Musharraf is trying desperately hard to justify his total commitment to his pro-US stand in Afghanistan even to the extent of jeopardising his own survival in Pakistan. It is in our ultimate interest to have a stable Pakistan on our borders and therefore it is essential to remind ourselves constantly whether toppling Musharraf is in our overall strategic interests or to work towards his political survival, in the current scenario. Is it not better to deal with the devil you know than some obscure mullah who, using the tool of religious fundamentalism, seizes power in this sensitive state with its nuclear capability? Cool, hard strategic long-term thinking should determine our course. Hastily conceived knee-jerk reactions must be shunned. This is one of the major problems that our National Security Council need to be on the *qui vive* along our international borders.

If Kashmir has joined the Indian Union legally, and the Chinese continue to not only occupy but also construct roads in Aksai Chin, the question of settling this alleged dispute along the LOC or bargaining on the issue is out of the question. Be that as it may, in the foreseeable future, Pakistan and Kashmir will continue to be our immediate problems.

Our major long-term strategic problem will be China and its historic contention that it is the middle kingdom, and in that context its driving desire to be the dominant power in Asia. China claims possession of many areas along our border as its own, especially in NEFA. Have we considered the historical fact that the old China of antiquity was the area south of the Great Wall? Chinese globalistic aims are manifest in certain hard facts as its occupation of Tibet that was never a part of historical China culturally or politically, its occupation of Aksai Chin ceded to it by Pakistan although part of Ladakh, its challenge to areas delineated by the McMahon Line, the trans-Himalayan road accesses at Kunjerab, Kodari, Natu La, Bum La in Nepal, and the old Ledo Road leading into the Brahmaputra Valley and NE India. There constant warnings being received from the Chief Minister of Arunachal Pradesh of road building activities. Such activities will be used by China to support its claims to these areas.

Why is China extending the Lanchow-Gormo rail link to Lhasa with plans to extend it to Shigatse, and then on to Sinkiang when the Chinese Premier is on record as saying: "This (railway project) is a political decision (and) we will make this project succeed at all costs even if there is a commercial loss." The eminent and well-known journal *Scientific American* reported recently that China is planning to tunnel the north side of the Himalayas to construct a massive water channel using nuclear power, to divert the waters of the Tsangpo into the Gobi desert and the implication of such action on the waters in the Brahmaputra. On the flip side of the same coin is another report that China will release the flood waters of this river into the Brahmaputra causing flooding. India loses on both counts. When this issue was raised with the nine member Chinese delegation of academics including two serving officers, Major

General Fan Zhenjiang, Professor Teaching Division Strategic Studies, National Defence University, PLA and Colonel (now Brigadier) Fu Cheng II, Professor, Senior Colonel, Department of Foreign Military Studies, Academy of Military Science, PLA, their response was that it was CIA inspired. The very strong and immediate denial of any such move indicated the degree of sensitivity of the Chinese to this issue. Equally, the role of China in assisting Pakistan with nuclear and missile technology and perhaps also to Iran and Libya, was also brushed aside and India was assured that any military aid to Pakistan would never be used against us. We need to monitor such unfriendly activities on our borders particularly in Tibet with which we have a long common border.

Equally, in relation to what was discussed at the SAARC meeting in Dhaka, we need to use all our diplomatic skills to monitor and develop friendly ties with Myanmar and Bangladesh to counter the unusual Chinese interest in these two border states. Equally we need to monitor carefully Chinese expansionist plans in the South China Seas and possible encroachment into the Bay of Bengal and Indian Ocean based on its decision to build a blue water navy. Its involvement in the Coco Islands is on record and if any clarifications are needed, I am sure Admiral Bhagwat, who was our Naval Chief then, will be only too happy to comment on this strategic issue. To further strengthen this interest, and if you have not already done so, you would do well to read three semi-fiction works by professional China watchers: Humphrey Hawksley, BBCs Asia Specialist's *Dragon Fire* and *Dragon Strikes*, and Patrick Robertson's *The Shank Mutiny*. In this context I recall a conversation I had with the late General B.C. Joshi, Army Chief who visited China while in service. He said that as a result of his visit he believed that the Sleeping Dragon would slumber peacefully until the year 2005, building a strong economic base and modernising its armed forces, and having done so, it would begin flexing its muscles and demanding the return of territories that it thinks are historically its own. Compare this date to that mentioned in the three books, and that is 2007.

Now that China has been given the privilege to conduct the 2008 Olympic games, we have enough leeway to prepare ourselves economically, in matters of defence and at the diplomatic level. Our diplomacy must be directed at developing better relations with the SAARC and ASEAN countries, and the maritime nation in the Far East, Japan. More than that, based on the 1962 incident, the occupation of Tibet and the cozy relation that China has with Pakistan, we must watch the situation not aggressively but with abundant caution. It is being said that China will fight to the last Pakistani and the Pakistanis to the last Kashmiri.

In the current Afghan scenario we have done well in establishing a liaison office in Kabul and extending medical aid. We should now ensure that at the diplomatic level our involvement in restoring this war-ravaged country to a stable one by being involved in its rehabilitation is maintained. On no account should we permit the Afghan question to be linked with Kashmir, whichever way one views it, bearing in mind the Indo-Pakistan standoff. A stable Afghanistan is equally essential to our security interests so that Taliban and al Qaeda terrorists do not find their way into J & K. This calls for pragmatic diplomacy.

It is a matter of deep concern that in critical areas such as defence and external affairs we resort to the same minister wearing two hats. When the September 11 episode occurred, the Foreign Minister was given charge of defence as well. Surely some other answer could have been found. Likewise, it is beyond imagination why the most important post of head of the National Security Council should be given to bureaucrat Brajesh Mishra who also heads the PMO's Office and handles foreign affairs, thereby wearing three important hats, on the specious plea "that he has the Prime Ministers ears". This situation should be avoided and the National Security Council be headed by one who has no other responsibilities. This cavalier attitude indicates the government's sidelining the NSC. In view of the current situation, it needs to be remedied immediately. In the same context, the National Security Council needs to be revamped and its members drawn from all those organisations dealing in national security. This Council needs to add two more exclusivist cells, if not already in position, handling intelligence and terrorism. The Council should solicit views of experts in matters of defence, including terrorism. The tendency to accord defence matters the veil of secrecy and treat it as a sacred cow must now be placed on the back burner.

Which leads one to the long delayed appointment of a Chief of Defence Staff to enable single window clearance on defence matters. The delay in doing so and resorting to ad hocism by appointing a Lieutenant General as *pro tem* CDS must end. The advantages of having a full-fledged CDS cannot be overstressed. When, for instance, will the proposed command and control responsibility for nuclear war be set up? The proposal to delegate this important function to the CDS appears to rest solely with the Prime Minister with the CDS being the implementing authority.

Perhaps the wisest step the government has taken is the establishment of the Tri Service Andamans Command. By so doing we shall ensure that we shall not tolerate any unfriendly activities in the Bay of Bengal and the southern Indian Ocean. The very presence of such a force will send the right message to ASEAN countries. There will be initial teething problems but these can be overcome given the will to do so. Disasters affect national security. Therefore, it is for consideration why the government does not establish a Disaster Relief Ministry, under perhaps a Minister of State to coordinate and attend to all matters related to disasters, man-made and natural, including nuclear war. Such single point control cannot be overemphasized. It will need to network with sub-organisations deployed right across India so that relief methods are implemented speedily and efficiently. To expect the overburdened Home Ministry to so respond is begging the issue. This Ministry should have elements from Home, Defence,

Railways, Health, Civil Supplies, Transport, Civil Aviation et al, all fine-tuned into a responsible group.

Now that terrorism in all its *avatars* has taken top billing in national security, there is an urgent need to setup a special cell or body to deal exclusively with terrorism in all its manifestations. Such a body will inevitably include RAW, IB, other security agencies, Home, MEA, Defence et al. The key to success will inevitably be the acquisition of timely intelligence and quick reaction. Each state of the union will need to replicate a similar but smaller group given state-of-the-art secure communication links. One central head responsible for producing the desired results will go a long way to tackle this pernicious problem in our multicultural society.

Arising from what has been said on the terrorism threat is the vital and urgent need for an efficient intelligence system to collect, collate, interpret and disseminate information affecting our nation's security. We need to recall the disastrous after effects of lack of intelligence at Kargil and the attack on the Srinagar Assembly. The urge to go high-tech must be weighed against the importance of human intelligence, i.e., Elint versus Humint. In this context we need to learn the effectiveness of Humint from Israel's Mossad based on the effectiveness of their field operatives.

Finally, in this infotech age the importance of the media in the field of national security cannot be overemphasized sufficiently enough. The media, both electronic and print, can play a most effective role in reporting events objectively and allowing moderate voices to be heard.

35

Alternative Strategy for Equality, Universal Primary Education in Remote and Isolated Areas of India

*Hemlata Talesra**

Universalisation of elementary education has been the goal of the education policy ever since the independence of India, starting with the constitutional directive of providing "free and compulsory education to all till they attain the age of 14 years within 10 years of the commencement of the Constitution" (Article 45). The commitment has been reiterated several times. The National Policy on Education[1] gives unqualified priority to universalisation of elementary education through emphasis not only on the provision of minimum infrastructure but also ensuring universal enrolment and universal retention of children up to 14 years of age and also a substantial improvement in quality. The policy target is that all children who have attained the age of 11 years will have five years of schooling or its equivalent through formal or non-formal stream and likewise it will also be ensured that free and compulsory education to all children up to 14 years of age is provided by 1995.[2] The policy also lays emphasis on removal of disparities

**Retd. Professor and Head, Department of Educational Planning, Management and Administration, Vidya Bhawan G. S. Institute of Advanced Studies in Education, Udaipur (Rajasthan).*

and equalisation of educational opportunities by attending to specific needs of those who have been denied opportunity so far.

The Programme of Action (POA)[3] states that the existing gap in educational infrastructure in remote and inaccessible areas, islands, hills and desert regions will be identified and plans to remove backlogs will be prepared.

The policy goal of universal elementary education will be attainable only to the extent disadvantaged groups and areas are able to utilise the educational facilities. Experience has shown that mere provision of facilities does not ensure its utilisation. For this, there is a need to understand the special problems of these areas and groups and then plan education keeping in view their special problems. Realising this reality, the policy has suggested decentralised and micro-level planning.

This paper makes an attempt to analyse the specific problems of remote and isolated areas of India, strategies adopted in different parts of India to overcome some of the constraints, and suggests some alternative strategies which may be adopted to promote education in these areas.

The paper starts by highlighting the socio-economic and cultural specifics of these areas and analysing the factors which constrain educational developments. It examines some of the specific strategies adopted for promoting education of children in these areas, and finally spells out alternate strategies which would promote educational development of the areas.

REMOTE AREAS : SOME UNIQUE CHARACTERISTICS

Remote areas are usually regions of extreme climatic conditions and difficult terrain. These include mountains, deserts, forest areas or scattered islands. The areas are characterised by weak interaction not only with the outside world but even intersettlement contacts are poor because of poor means of transport and communication.[4]

The areas are sparely populated and manpower is limited. Not only is density low but the distribution of population is highly uneven and clustered in a few villages. A large number of habitations have very small population with houses scattered over a wide area.

Economically, these are underdeveloped areas with low agricultural potential. Though some of the areas abound in natural resources, the same have not been exploited fully. Economies are at a very low level of inter-sectoral or intrasectoral diversification. The primary sector has preponderance. Here also diversification is low. Agriculture is mostly dependent on irrigation but the mode of irrigation is primitive. In a large number of areas shifting cultivation or '*jhum*' cultivation is in vogue. A large number of people living in the interiors are still at the pre-production stage.

Electricity and other infrastructure are weak in these areas. Transport and communication lines so important for development are also very scanty. Roads are also few and do not connect all the settlements.

People living in these areas maintain their distinct cultural identify and traditional outlook. They have their dialects and sometimes their own language. They have their own social customs. They want to retain their distant identity and culture. The areas are self-contained and the people highly contented due to fatalistic and deterministic attitude towards life. They are not vocal and suffer from the 'culture of silence.'

EDUCATIONAL CONSTRAINTS

A major educational problem in these areas is the task of providing schools within walking distance for all the children. Small size of habitations, scattered population even within the habitation and long inter-settlement distances preclude the opening of schools within habitation or within easy walking distance. Even the relaxation of national norms does not help in a situation where physical distances measured in kilometres are compounded with other ecological constraints. In certain areas there is the added problem of mobile population groups who keep on moving from one area to another in search of food. Opening of small schools is not only financially but even academically non-viable.

Besides the provision of schools, even basic educational equipments like blackboards, chalk, charts, maps, books and furniture are in short supply in schools located in these areas. Even whatever is provided does not reach the schools in time. Though provision of physical infrastructure is not a guarantee for quality, yet a basic minimum is considered essential for ensuring good teaching and learning situation.

A major constraint which affects the educational development in these areas is the non-availability of adequate number of qualified teachers. Outsiders are not willing to work in these areas and local teachers are not available with the requisite qualifications. As a result, many posts remain vacant perpetually and even those that are filled, the teachers appointed do not have the requisite qualifications and training to work in these areas. A large number of schools are single-teacher schools. Teacher absenteeism and non-functioning of schools is characteristic in these areas.

The educational supervision also poses a problem. Regular supervision of schools is difficult because of long distances at which schools are located and due to difficulty of terrain. The normal practice of assigning a number of schools to an inspector for supervision is non-viable for these areas.

Other major educational constraints in these areas are the curriculum, textbooks, and the medium of instruction. Due to the isolation for centuries these areas have their own distinct culture and language. The curriculum which reflects the majority culture is alien to them. The textbooks do not include examples from the local milieu. Hence these do not interest the children living in these areas. Even the methodology of teaching is not geared to their free cultural style. The disinterest caused by irrelevance of curriculum and drab textbooks is compounded by the medium of instruction alien to children living in these areas. The whole educational process, therefore, turns counter-productive to the development of the area. Similarly, school timings and vacation also are not suited to the lifestyle and ecology of the area.

POSITIVE FACTORS

While the constraints to educational development of these areas are many, there are certain positive factors which are expected to help the planners and administrators in developing these areas fast. Firstly, the absolute size of the population living in these areas is small. Any intervention is likely to show very quick results.

Secondly, there is a political will to develop these areas first because most of the states follow welfare policies and aim at giving equality of opportunity. Secondly, most of these areas are on the border and no national government today can ignore them. Hence, special attention is being paid towards overall development including economic and educational infrastructure.

Thirdly, people living in these areas are simple and hard working. For the mere subsistence they have to work hard. Being cut off from the modern developed urban culture, they are simple folks.

Fourthly, most of the people living in these areas are still in pre-industrial society and they have an egalitarian outlook. Hence group or sex differentials are not too sharp amongst them.

Lastly, most of these areas still have the tradition of community involvement. If properly guided they can prove to be of great asset for their own betterment. There are also certain traditional institutions in these areas which can be utilised for promoting education.

Specific Strategies used for promoting Education in Remote Areas

A number of strategies have been used in India and other countries to meet the needs of children living in remote and isolated areas. These refer to reorganisation of schools, deployment of teachers, use of methods and materials, participation of community, shortened school day or the like. Some of the specific strategies are describe below:

1. *Opening of schools in relaxation of existing norms:* In many countries the norms for opening schools in remote and inaccessible areas are quite liberal as compared to general norms. In India, the national norms of 1.5 km. of walking distance for opening of primary schools section is relaxed in the case of hilly and remote areas or in the areas where there is concentration of tribes.
2. *Opening of ashram/residential schools:* Such schools are most common in India. They intend to serve the needs of tribal areas where habitations are so small that schools become not only financially unfeasible but also academically non-viable. These schools serve the needs of several habitations. The are located in the natural environment of tribes. The teachers are specially chosen for these schools and live with the children in residence. All facilities, i.e., board, lodge, books and equipment are provided free of cost to children. Pedagogy is supposed to emphasise dignity of labour and respect for cultural life and tradition of tribes. The experiment is only partially successful since the schools failed to translate the philosophy into practice.[5]
3. *Mosque schools:* In remote areas of Pakistan, mosque schools enrol children in classes I and II. The schools make use of mosque structures. Mosque leaders and local literate persons teach in these schools. At the beginning of class II, children go to the nearest primary schools. In India also in certain regions Maktab structures are being

used for universalisation of elementary education and modern education in science and mathematics.[6] Similarly, in areas where Buddhism is predominant '*gompas*' (Buddhist monasteries) are utilised for promoting education of children.[7]

4. *Mobile schools:* For nomadic population groups, mobile schools have been established in certain countries. Here the teacher is attached to the group and moves with it. He/she gives lessons where and when appropriate. Such teachers are also known as parapetic teachers. In India such schools are known as 'tent' schools. In Thailand the mobile school concept is a little different. There a group of teachers proceed to slum areas and select a place as 'temporary' school. Teachers go from house to house recruiting pupils. Incentives are provided to children in the form of learning material and clothes. In this model, schools goes to the pupil, while in the tent school concept, the school moves with the pupil.
5. *Alternate intake school:* This concept is relevant for scattered school population. The school has two-grade intake every alternate year. One teacher is responsible for two classes. Hence in a six grade school only three teachers are required. The method reduces cost and is suitable for the areas where population is scattered and very few children are available for each grade. The system is in vogue in Thailand.
6. *Non-graded schools:* Here children are not grouped by age and they proceed at their own pace. Children who enter primary school late may rapidly complete their units, and not be forced to go through all five grades. The non-graded concept is based on continuous evaluation. End term exams are therefore not necessary. There are no pass and fail in the system, hence children do not drop out because of failure situation. Many states in India have adopted the system and thus have increased retention rates.

7. *Learning post schools*: This strategy is adopted in among the school system in Indonesia.[8] It is based on use of available village structure for schools and local people as instructors. Focus is on use of self-instructional materials. A primary school serves as the focus for the scheme and learning posts are established around it. The flexible nature of the scheme makes it attractive for poor children who can interrupt their studies. They are encouraged to drop in' at Learning Postage and take up their studies from where they left. Meher UPE Project in Bangladesh[9] is also based on this approach of use of community structure and local persons as teachers. The project is in existence since 1976.

The strategies outlined above have certain communality. Common to all the strategies is a flexible approach," "a more efficient use of facilities, teachers and time." 'Consideration of Child's need' is the common feature. Therefore, if the child cannot go to school, take the school to the child. Basic to all the strategies in a non-formal approach.

There are diversities with regard to teachers, cost and community involvement. In certain approaches the cost is borne by government while in others it is shared by the community.

All the strategies made useful contribution to UPE, especially in reaching education to disadvantaged areas. These need to be supported. A lot has already been achieved over the past three decades. However, education has yet to reach the most disadvantaged. To reach the rock bottom and also ensure retention and performance some alternative strategies have been suggested for the country.[10]

In concrete terms the following strategies may be adopted to achieve the goals:

Provision of Schooling Facilities

As it is not economically feasible nor academically viable to open schools in areas where there are very few children in the relevant age group, opening of ashram schools at a central place may seem to be a viable alternative. In India, such schools are available in a number of states especially for the Scheduled Tribes and Scheduled Castes.

For mobile population, peripatetic teachers and tent schools may be the only solution. In some of the hilly states this is already in operation.

Teachers' Training and Orientation

Considering that the areas are remote and underdeveloped it may not always be possible to recruit fully qualified and capable teachers for schools located in these areas. The outsiders are not willing to go to these areas. Sometimes even if they go they are not welcomed as in the case of Ledakh and Lakshadweep. Hence, for some time less capable local people will continue to be recruited as teachers for primary and middle schools. To enable these teachers to perform efficiently, it will be necessary to provide them frequent in-service training.

Teachers' training programmes will need to be developed not only to overcome the deficiency in qualification and training but with a view to orient them regarding (i) the cultural traits and life pattern of communities with whom they will be interacting; (ii) teaching learning processes of disadvantaged groups; (iii) skill of preparing low-cost educational aids from local materials; and (iv) new curricula and techniques of teaching. In upgrading the skills of teachers in certain critical areas the open-learning system can play an important role.

Reorienting Curriculum, Content and Medium of Instruction

The problem of indifference to education on the part of children and parents, and the high rate of non-enrolment and dropouts are attributed generally to non-relevance of curricula to socio-cultural milieu and requirement of disadvantaged areas. A more important reason for low performance is the pedagogy which is urban-based and alien to the ecology of the place.

One common curriculum cannot meet the needs of different cultural and linguistic groups. Therefore, there is a need to have differentiated curricula with the framework of national goals and objectives of the education. Major ingredients of curricula should be drawn from local environments and social cultural milieu. More importantly, curriculum transaction must be based on local cultural and environmental factors. Teachers should be familiar with the local dialects. Transition from local to regional/national language should be smooth.

Provision of Teaching-learning Materials

On the basis of a review of about 70 studies, the world Bank has come to the conclusion that amongst the factors which affect most the quality and quantity of education, the most important are textbooks, equipment and qualification of teachers. Provision of textbooks and basic equipment to schools in these areas poses a problem because of difficult accessibility of terrain and poor means of transport and communication. In India, under 'Operation Blackboard' priority is being given to provide basic infrastructural facilities to schools in disadvantaged areas. Efforts need to be made to ensure that at least textbooks and learning material reach the pupils in time.

Administration and Supervision

The isolation of teachers is emerging as an important factor affecting teachers' motivation and morale. The remoteness of some of the areas and difficulty of transportation make the task of supervision difficult. Innovative methods will have to be developed for supervision of schools and for providing guidance to teachers. Supervision by community leaders to some extent will need to be initiated. Some alternate ways to communicate with teachers will also need to be looked into.

IMPLEMENTATION STRATEGIES

For effective implementation of programme of development in the remote areas, a decentralised approach and community participation in planning and management of education are considered useful. Diversity of local conditions necessitate a variety of strategies for achieving the goal. Hence, micro-level planning is considered useful.

Micro-planning helps focusing attention on non-participatory groups, helps in adoption of relevant and concrete measures for increasing enrolment, reducing dropout. Finally, monitoring and evaluation are better accomplished. People's participation contributed to ensuring the involvement of community; creating awareness and interest of all in education; ensuring that benefits of development reach the silent groups of the society; and finally for generating resources for education. People's participation also ensures regular functioning of school and accountability of teachers in areas where outside supervision poses problem because of difficulty of terrain. People's participation, to be real, needs to be enlisted right from planning, to implementation and finally monitoring the evaluation stage. There is now enough evidence to show that even poor and illiterate people can be involved in planning, implementation and evaluation of programmes meant to benefit them. The results have been found to be encouraging, especially as there has been marked improvement in utilisation of available infrastructure.

REFERENCES

1. *National Policy on Education, 1986*, New Delhi, Ministry of Human Resource Development, Government of India, p.11.

2. Ibid., p.12
3. *Programme of Action*, New Delhi, Ministry of Human Resource Development, Government of India, September 1986.
4. Singh, Harjit, 'Problems of Education in Trans Himalayas', in *Man and Nature*, December 1979.
5. Manglagiri A., Nanda, B., *Primary Education in Koraput: Problems, Policies & Possibilities*, New Delhi, NIEPA, 1998, (Mimeographed).
6. NIEPA, *Action Research Project on Universalisation of Elementary Education* (ARISE), NIEPA, New Delhi.
7. UNESCO, 1984, *Towards Universal Primary Education in Asia and the Pacific Country Studies,* Indonesia APIED, Bangkok, pp. 40-42.
8. UNESCO, 1984, *Towards Universal Primary Education in Asia and the Pacific Country Studies,* Bangladesh APIED, Bangkok, pp. 40-42.
9. Recommendations are based on the deliberations of the UNESCO-sponsored, 'National Seminar on Universal Primary Education for Disadvantage', organised by NIEPA, 1988.
10. Heyneman, Stephen P. and Others, *Text Books and Achievement: What we know, worked,* Bank Staff Working Paper No.298, 1978.

36

A Study of Democratic Values in Educated Tribal and Non-Tribal Youth of South Gujarat

*A. V. Parmar**

INTRODUCTION

This phenomenon of penetration of democratic and educational institutions and practices of rider society into the tribals religion has been adequently documented in several studies. On this theme, the literature is quite expansive. Besides, there are census monographs and ethnological descriptions of individual tribals. These literatures cover aspects of socio-economic, political and cultural life of the tribals. These tribals studies tell us what is happening to the tribals living in villages and in urban areas. But we have very few studies which can throw light on the values of the tribals and non-tribals.

The present study, therefore, was planned to study the democratic values of tribals and non-tribals of South Gujarat. The study deals with a single tribals and non-tribals community. The main objectives of the study were: (1) to examine the difference between tribals and non-tribals students (independent variable) in values, their personality characteristics in democratic values (dependent variables) and

**Principal, M. D. Shah Commerce & B. D. Patel Arts College, Mahuda Gujarat.*

(2) to study the extent of variance in the dependent variables explained by demographic variable like urban-rural background and sex.

VALUES

The various definitions attributed to the concept of the values can be briefly stated as follows:

> As Chattopadhya 1961 asserts, "The values are part of our culture and they are always in the process of evolution." Lee, while analysing valuation by philosophers and linguists has defined value as a conception, Implicitly or explicitly of an individual or characteristic of available modes, means and ends of action. The term value refers to two sorts of meaning. It may refer to the standard or principals of worth. It may also refer to the worthy things themselves, the valuables.

HYPOTHESES

This study attempts at studying the personality characteristics in democratic values of tribals and non-tribals students of South Gujarat region. The study further seeks to examine the relevance of levels of sex and background. Specifically the following main hypotheses have been formulated and examined in the present research:

1) There will be significant differences in the democratic values and characteristics of the tribals and non-tribals subjects.
2) Male subjects will differ significantly from female subjects in their democratic values, characteristics and values.
3) There will be significant differences in the democratic values characteristics and values of subjects coming from urban and rural backgrounds.

SAMPLE

In order to test the above mentioned hypotheses of the present-study a suitable sample was taken. The total sample consisted of 600 having equal number of tribals and non-tribals subjects. The sample was drawn from colleges of South Gujarat. The total number of colleges was 10 of which five were from urban areas and five were from rural areas. The sample of tribals consisted to 150 boys and 150 girls. Similarly, the sample of non-tribals consisted of 150 boys and 150 girls. The urban population was defined as those students who were studying in urban colleges and had their permanent address of town or was living in the town for most part of the year. The rural population was defined as those students who were studying in a college situated in the village or was living in the village for most part of the year.

TOOLS

In the present study a personal value questionnaire developed by Dr. C. P. Sherry and R. P. Varma was used to measure values of respondents. The format of PVQ is that of forced choice type with multiple choice items. A question consisted of two parts: (i) a Stem and (ii) 3 items. In the stem of the question a criterion situation for seeking the value preferences was depicted. The items depicted the values for which the respondent had to express his comparative preference under the stimulus of the criterion situation.

The PVQ was given three try-outs. The final draft contains 40 questions. Each values has an equal number of items and there are 12 items for each value. The instructions for filling out the questionnaire are given in the manual.

RELIABILITY

Two indices of reliability of the PVQ were found out. Firstly, its reliability was determined by Hoyt's method using analysis of variance which method is as efficient as Kuder Richardson's but less cumbersome. Secondly two test-retest reliabilities were determined, one after an interval of 11 months and the other of three months.

Reliability coefficients obtained after a time gap of three month are fairly high. Analysis of variance method of determining reliability yielded reliability coefficient ranging from 47 for economic value to 70 for the democratic value. These indices of reliability of the different scales of the values of PVQ are also satisfactory.

VALIDITY

The validity of PVQ was obtained by finding out the hierarchy of democratic value of the sample of 20 students in two ways. First, they were administered PVQ and the hierarchy of ten values was determined. Then they were asked to rank the ten values. The ten values were functionally defined in terms of the contents of PVQ. The two hierarchies were correlated and rank order coefficient of co-relation of 64 was found. Thus it may be said that PVQ is a fairly valid tool to determine the hierarchy of democratic values of a group.

STATISTICAL PROCEDURE

The obtained scores of personality variable and values were subjected to analysis by using the technique of analysis of variance. A $2 \times 2 \times 2$ factorial design with two levels of race, two levels of sex and two levels of background was used to analyse scores of the respondents. This made it possible to study the main as well as interaction effects. The application of test (Analysis of Variance) in this case, tests only the overall difference among the groups of the variables under study, but does not indicate the significant difference between any two specific sub-groups in the pairs of combination formed by different levels of variables interacting with one another. In order to test the significance of difference between such subgroups, the 't' ratios were calculated.

ANOVA Table—F' (Democratic Value)

Source of Variance	*df*	*Sum of squares*	*Mean squares*	*'F'*
Race	1	202.38	220.38	34.00 *
Sex	1	52.79	52.79	8.15 *
Background	1	49.89	49.89	7.70 *
Race X Sex	1	36.31	36.31	5.60 *
Race X background	1	11.35	11.35	2.06 NS
Sex X Background	1	33.85	33.85	5.52 **
Race X Sex X Background	1	26.31	26.31	3.59 NS
Within	592	840.81	6.48	

Table 36.1 (A) 't' values

Significant of difference between means on democratic value: Main group wise

Sr. No.	*Main group*	*Mean*	*SD*	*'t' Values*
1.	Tribals	13.81	6.14	3.28 *
	Non-tribals	12.30	5.10	
2.	Male	13.67	9.05	2.11**
	Female	12.45	4.66	
3.	Urban	13.70	7.15	2.15**
	Rural	12.40	4.28	

Democratic value is defined in terms of charity, kindness, love and sympathy for the people, efforts to serve God through the service of mankind, sacrificing personal comforts and gains to relieve the needy and the afflicted of their misery. The results of the analysis of variance on this value are shown in Table 36.1.

Table 36.1 (B) 't' values

Significant of difference between means on democratic value: Tribals, Non tribals-sub groups—sexwise.

Sr. No.	Sub-groups	Mean	SD	't' values
1.	Tribals male	12.60	5.18	1.02 NS
	Tribals female	12.01	5.40	
2.	Non-tribals male	14.74	6.00	2.84 *
	Non-tribals female	12.89	5.41	
3.	Tribals male	12.60	5.18	3.14 *
	Non-tribals male	14.74	7.75	
4.	Tribals female	12.01	4.80	1.62 NS
	Non-tribals female	12.89	5.26	

Table 36.1 (C) 't' Values

Significant of difference between means on democratic value: Tribals—Non tribals Sub groups—background wise

Sr. No.	Sub-groups	Mean	SD	't' Values
1.	Tribals urban	12.84	5.37	0.67 NS
	Tribals rural	12.19	5.14	
2.	Non-tribals urban	14.91	5.69	3.49 *
	Non-tribals rural	12.92	4.80	
3.	Tribals urban	12.84	5.82	4.22 *
	Non-tribals urban	14.91	5.01	
4.	Tribals rural	11.19	5.49	0.96 *
	Non-tribals rural	12.72	4.88	

The 'F' ratio of 34.00 in the case of race is significant beyond 01 level of confidence. The mean scores of tribals and non-tribals students are 13.81 and 12.30, respectively. These two means are found to be statistically significant (Table 36.1 (A); 't' = 3.28). Thus, tribals students obtain significantly higher mean score than non-tribals students on democratic value of PVQ.

The main effect of sex variable is also found to be a significant 'F' ratio. The mean score of female student's (12.45) is higher than the mean score of male students (13.67). These two mean values are also found to be significantly different (Table 1 (A); 't' = 2.11). Thus, female students are attached more importantly to democratic value than the male students.

Table 36.1 (D) 't' Values

Significant of difference between means on democratic value: Sex and back groundwise.

Sr. No.	*Sub-groups*	*Mean*	*SD*	*'t' Values*
1.	Urban male	14.69	6.12	3.41 *
	Urban female	12.64	4.81	
2.	Rural male	12.65	5.39	1.05 NS
	Rural female	12.26	4.92	
3.	Urban male	14.69	6.12	3.23 *
	Rural male	12.65	5.39	
4.	Urban female	12.64	4.80	0.69 NS
	Rural female	12.26	5.10	

The main effect of background is insignificant. This indicates that considering both the levels of background as one independent variable, it does not cast any influence on democratic value. The mean scores of urban and rural students are more or less the same and they do not differ significantly.

However, these main effects, significant or insignificant, have to be understood with caution and reconsidered in the light of some interaction of these variables.

The first interaction of race X sex is found to be insignificant 'F' ratio. This shows that means of tribals and non-tribals students of male group are not significantly differing from the difference shown between the means of tribals and non-tribal students of the female group.

This interaction effect includes the comparison of four groups. The mean score of tribal male students is 12.60 and the mean score of tribal female students is 12.01. These two mean values are statistically insignificant. On the other hand, the mean score of non-tribal male is 14.74 and the mean score of non-tribal female is 12.89. These two means are significantly different (Table (B); 't' = 2.84). It indicates that non-tribal females attach more importance to democratic value than non-tribal males.

Further, when keeping sex variable as constant factor, it is seen that the mean score of tribal male student's (12.60) is higher than the mean score of non-tribal female students (12.74). Both these mean values are found to be significantly different (Table 36.1 (B); 't' = 3.14). In the case of female students, the mean score of tribal female students is 12.01 and the mean score of non-tribal female students is 12.79. These two mean values are also found to be significantly different (Table 36.1 (B); 't' = 1.62).

The interaction of race X background is also found to be insignificant 'F' ratio. Thus, it indicates that means of tribal and non-tribal students of the urban group are not significantly differing from the difference shown between the means of tribal and non-tribal rural students. The mean scores of this interaction are recorded in Table 36.1 (C).

As it can be seen from the table, the mean score of urban students (12.84) is lower than the mean score of rural students (12.19) in the tribal group. Both the mean values differ significantly (Table 36.1 (C); 't' = 0.67). In the non-tribal group, the mean score of urban students (14.91) is higher than the mean score of rural students (12.92). These two mean values are also found to be significantly different (Table 36.1 (C); 't' = 3.49). Thus, urban students are higher on this value than rural students in non-tribal group.

Comparing urban students of tribal and non-tribal groups, it is found that the mean scores of urban tribal students and urban non-tribal students are 12.84 and 14.91, respectively. These two mean values are found significantly different.

The third interaction is between sex X background which has a significant 'F' ratio. This indicates that the means of male and female students of urban background are significantly different from the difference between the means of male and female students of rural background. This interaction includes the comparison of four groups.

As it can be seen from Table 1 (D), mean scores of urban male and female students are 14.69 and 12.64 respectively. These two mean scores differ significantly (Table 1 (D); 't'-3.41). In the case of rural background, the mean score of male students is 12.26. These two mean values are also found not to differ significantly (Table 1 (D); 't' = 1.05).

Similarly, the mean score of urban male students and rural male students are more or less the same. They do not differ significantly. In the case of urban female students and rural female students, the mean scores are 12.64 and 12.26, respectively. These mean scores do not differ significantly also.

The interaction of race X-sex X background is insignificant. Thus, it does not cast a significant influence on the democratic value of PVQ. In other words, each variable, i.e., race, sex and background is independent of each other.

An IBM 360/44 computer was used for the analysis carried out in this study, However, a few analysis were carried out manually.

REFERENCES

Adroo, T. W., Frankel-Brunswik, *The Authoritarian Personality,* New York: Harper, 1950.

Dhapola, T. S., *The Kumoon Character—A Study of an Indian Socio-Cultural Group.*

Kluckkohn, C. et al, Values and Values, Orientation in the Theory of Action in T. Parson and E. A. Shils (eds) *Towards a General Theory of Action*, Cambridge, Flarward Uni. Press, 1952.

Kool V. K., *Measures of Author Inarianism and Hostility*, Himalaya Publishing House, Bombay, 1980.

Lee, Dorothy, Culture and the Experience of Value in Maslo, A. H. (ed.), *New Knowledge in Human Values*, New York : Harper & Row, 1959.

37

Reducing Stress through Creativity

*Anita Talesra**

Stress is an everyday fact of life. We cannot avoid it. It is any change that we must adopt to ranging from the negative extreme of actual physical danger to achieving some long desired success. The day-to-day living confronts even the most well managed life with a continuous stream of potentially stressful experiences. Sometimes stress is essential to life. Whether the stress we experience is the result of major life changes or the cumulative effect of minor everyday worries, it is how we respond to these experiences that determines the impact stress will have on our life. Stress researcher Richard Lazarus has argued that stress begins with our appraisal of a situation—how dangerous or difficult the situation is and what resources we have to help and cope with it.[1]

The ground work for the modern meaning of 'stress' was laid by Watter B. Connon, a physiologist at Harvard. He was the first to describe the "fight or fight response" as a series of biochemical changes that prepare us to deal with threats or danger. Hans Selye, the first major researcher on stress, was able to trace exactly what happens in our body during the fight or flight response. He found that any problem, imagined or real, can cause the cerebral cortex (the thinking part of the brain) to send an alarm to the hypothalamus, then stimulate the

**Joint Secretary, RCEAM, M. Sc., Ph.D., 12-A, Panchwati, Udaipur (Rajasthan).*

sympathetic nervous system to make a series of changes in our body.[2] Our heart rate, breathing rate, muscle tension, metabolism and blood pressure all increase. Our hands and feet get cold as blood is directed away from our extremities and digestive system into the larger muscles that can help us fight or run. We experience butterflies in our stomach. Our diaphragm and anus lock. Our pupils dilate to sharpen our vision and our hearing becomes more acute.

While all of this is going on, something else happens that can have long-term negative effects if left unchecked. Our adrenal glands start to secrete corticoids (adrenaline, epinephrine, and nor-epinephrine) which inhibit digestion, reproduction, growth and tissue repair and the responses of our immune and inflammatory systems. In our words, some very important functions that keep our body healthy begin to shut down.

The same mechanism that turned the stress response on can turn it off. This is called the relaxation response. Herbert Benson suggested that we can use our mind to change our physiology for better improving our health and perhaps reducing stress. He coined the term "the relaxation response".

CREATIVITY

Studies have proved that students with high creativity become more successful and reduce the stress. Psychologists are busy in searching for the creative persons because they have less stress and are more responsible for future scientific and technological developments. They are developing the ways by which the exuberant energy of the creative persons may be channellised in some creative tasks. At present it is the voice of developing countries like India to recognise the creative persons and to channellise their creative abilities in various creative fields. The results of this will reduce the stress and overcome the stressful experiences.

Creative behaviour in related to the operational aspect of human intellect. According to the *Encyclopedia of Psychology*, "Creative thinking is the type of thought which is illustrated in the production of a work of art or solving of a scientific problems."[3] Gilford defines creativity as "divergent thinking variable".[4] He states that the creative individual must be fluent, flexible and capable of elaborating and redefining problems, originality also been considered as a factor. These qualities reduce the stress among the individuals.

How can Creativity Reduce the Stress?

To answer this question, we selected the four mental processes which develop creativity and reduce the stress:

1. *Fluency:* Fluency is a readiness, a smoothness or ease with which thoughts come to mind, a quality of flowing, freely and abundantly. These qualities will close the door for a person who has stress. If a person obtained these qualities then he or she cannot move with stressful negative qualities.
2. *Flexibility:* Flexibility is the main quality of a creative person and the opposite quality for a stressful person. Flexibility removes the stress through adaptability, freedom from stiffness or rigidity, capacity for rapid and varied execution or delivery.
3. *Originality*: Originality means producing/proceedings directly or independently to the person. It is first-hand, off-beat, unconventional, divergent thinking or action. These qualities remove the stress.
4. *Elaboration:* Produce something with much labour or explain the things up to its maximum limits. Through this quality stress can easily be released.

The four man variables of creativity reduce the stress, but the important thing is to associate the person who has stress and engage him or her in the above creative activities.

Characteristics of Creutivity that help to Reduce Stress

The following are the characteristics of creativity useful for reducing stress:

1. *Divergence of thinking:* A creative person is a divergent thinker. He discovers or offers uncommon thoughts or ideal unexpected suggestions and unconventional views. According to Andrews,[5] "A creative person has a positive self-integrating force, a process of self-actualisation and expression, positive and divergation of thinking will reduce the stress."
2. *Unique expression:* Creative people express some novel idea, piece of art, some scientific principles, some material or abstract product that is unique. The quality of these types of unique expressions release the stress and associate the person to unique original expressions.
3. *Act of mind*: Creative persons have good quality presence of mind and act of mind. We can motivate them very easily, their perception, learning and thinking is good. According to Rogers, "The creative process is the emergence in action of a novel relational product growing out of the uniqueness of the individual on the one hand, and the materials, events, people or circumstances of his life, on the other. Rogers mentioned the three essential inner conditions in the creative process which remove the stress:

    A. *Openness to experience—extensionality*: Each stimulus is freely relayed to the person who has stress through the nervous system without being distorted by any process of defensiveness.

    B. An international locus of evaluation.

    C. The ability to toy with elements and concepts.

Creative Environment Removes Stress

A creative environment motivates a person to produce new ideas, patterns or relationships. Rogers mentions four environmental conditions that may foster creativity:

a. Accepting the individual as of unconditional worth.
b. Providing a climate free from external evaluation.
c. Understanding empathically.
d. Psychological freedom.

Different Theories of Creativity Provide the Basis for Reducing Stress

Different theories of creativity provide the basis of reducing stress and overcoming the problems. The person will resture and find the solution to the problems:

1. The psycho-analytical theory provides the way to control the ego and develop rational thinking process. This will overcome the stress. This theory provides a preconscious level of thinking which facilitates associations between ideas related to the immediate problem and other potentially useful ideas. To engage in preconscious thinking, one must allow oneself today to dream and fantasise.
2. The Gestalt theory describes productivity thinking as a process of successive restructuring of the problem. Through this, the structural features of problem itself set up the stresses and strains in the thinker. This model is more applicable to convergent problems with only one or a few right answers than to divergent problems with many problems solutions.
3. Associationist theories involve the common assumption that creativity results from novel or unusual associations. According to Medrick. "The forming of associative

elements into new combinations which either meet specified requirements or are in some way useful releasing the stress is based on the degree of creativity and relative remoteness, used to form the new combination." Creative people are likely to give some remote or uncommon responses which help them to release the stress.

4. Composite theories highlight two thinking processes, and help to develop independent ideas which will help to remove stress. According to this theory, when people direct all their efforts towards some goal, the problems occupying their conscious thoughts, which will spill imagines and dream. This theory develops personal characteristics, such as openness to experience on internal locus of evaluation and the ability to toy with elements, and concepts facilitate creativity. The perceptual openness allows an individual to approach an object repeatedly from various perspectives.
5. The cognitive theory believed that creativity is a cognitive mental ability combined with motivational factors. Gilford developed a model of structure of intellect (S. I. Model) in which creativity or divergent thinking is one of problem solving and release from stress.

To sum up one can say that creativity provides a framework and defines a path for our working. It actually enables us to work in a systematic and planned way, thus reducing stress.

Index